Liberal FAITH

Essays in Honor of

Philip Quinn

edited by

PAUL J. WEITHMAN

University of Notre Dame Press
Notre Dame, Indiana

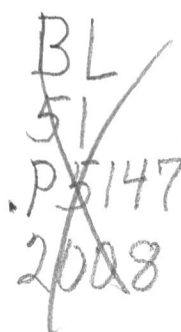

Copyright © 2008 by University of Notre Dame
Notre Dame, Indiana 46556
www.undpress.nd.edu
All Rights Reserved

Manufactured in the United States of America

Library of Congress Cataloging-in-Publication Data

Philip Quinn Memorial Conference (2005 : University of Notre Dame)
Liberal faith : essays in honor of Philip Quinn / edited by Paul J. Weithman.
    p. cm.
"This volume collects some of the papers from the Philip Quinn Memorial Conference held at the University of Notre Dame in December 2005"—Acknowledgments.
Includes bibliographical references and index.
ISBN-13: 978-0-268-04416-9 (cloth : alk. paper)
ISBN-10: 0-268-04416-3 (cloth : alk. paper)
1. Religion—Philosophy—Congresses. I. Quinn, Philip L. II. Weithman, Paul J., 1959– III. Title.
BL51.P5147   2008
210—dc22
                                              2008027218

∞ *The paper in this book meets the guidelines for permanence and durability of the Committee on Production Guidelines for Book Longevity of the Council on Library Resources.*

Contents

Acknowledgments   vii

Introduction
  Paul J. Weithman   1

PART 1 *Epistemology*

ONE
Self-Trust and the Diversity of Religions
  Linda Zagzebski   27

TWO
An Epistemology That Matters
  Richard Foley   43

PART 2 *Philosophy of Religion*

THREE
Presence and Omnipresence
  Eleonore Stump   59

FOUR
Self-Annihilation or Damnation? A Disputable Question in Christian Eschatology
Paul J. Griffiths   83

PART 3   *Political Philosophy*

FIVE
Moral Foundations of Liberal Democracy, Secular Reasons, and Liberal Neutrality toward the Good
Robert Audi   121

SIX
Egalitarianism without Equality?
Paul J. Weithman   145

SEVEN
Torture, Justification, and Human Rights: Toward an Absolute Proscription
Sumner B. Twiss   176

Afterword: A Eulogy for Phil Quinn
Paul J. Weithman   202

Contributors   207

Index   209

Acknowledgments

This volume collects some of the papers from the Philip Quinn Memorial Conference held at the University of Notre Dame in December 2005. The conference was made possible by the John A. O'Brien Chair of Philosophy at Notre Dame and by the university's College of Arts and Letters. The conference could not have been held without the organizational work of Angela Smith of the Notre Dame Philosophy Department and Harriet Baldwin, conference organizer for the College of Arts and Letters at Notre Dame. It is a pleasure to acknowledge their indispensability. I am also grateful to Alex Jech for his work on the index for this volume.

Some of the papers included in this volume have previously been published. They appear here by permission.

- Linda Zagzebski's "Self-Trust and the Diversity of Religions" was previously published in *Philosophic Exchange* 36 (2005–6): 62–76.
- Robert Audi's "Moral Foundations of Liberal Democracy, Secular Reasons, and Liberal Neutrality toward the Good" was published in the *Notre Dame Journal of Law, Ethics and Public Policy* 19 (2005): 101–23.
- Sumner B. Twiss's "Torture, Justification, and Human Rights: Toward an Absolute Proscription" also appeared in *Human Rights Quarterly* 29, no. 2 (May 2007): 346–67.
- Paul J. Weithman's "Eulogy for Philip Quinn," which appears here as an afterword, was previously published at *Proceedings and Addresses of the American Philosophical Association* 78, no. 5 (2005): 179–81.

Introduction

Paul J. Weithman

Philip Quinn was the John A. O'Brien Professor of Philosophy at the University of Notre Dame from 1985 until his death in November 2004. The present volume collects some of the papers presented at a memorial conference for Professor Quinn held at Notre Dame in December 2005. The papers in the collection are by some friends of Phil's whose work he regarded highly. The contributors also thought quite highly of Phil—as evidenced by the quality of papers they produced for the memorial conference. The conference papers brought together here have been supplemented by papers written by Robert Audi and myself, who were departmental colleagues of Phil's at the time of his death, and by Richard Foley. Foley, who is now dean of the Faculty of Arts and Science at New York University, was the chair of the Philosophy Department at Notre Dame who lured Phil away from Brown.

Commemorative volumes are not just supposed to recall those whom they commemorate. Those who contribute to a volume like this are supposed to honor Phil by putting their talents to work advancing discussion of a representative sample of the questions he cared about. Those who know Phil's work know that no one set of papers would be adequate to this task. Phil had so wide a range of philosophical interests, and his knowledge of philosophy was so broad, that it would be virtually impossible to identify any one set of questions and issues as representative of those that engaged his attention.

In the years after he left Brown for Notre Dame, Phil was most prominently associated with the philosophy of religion. In the last years of his career, he developed an interest in some questions within political philosophy—especially questions about human rights and about the place of religious argument in political life—the latter of which became the subject of his American Philosophical Association presidential address. Phil also retained a lively interest in the core areas of analytic philosophy, including epistemology, as Richard Foley notes in his acknowledgments. Questions in the philosophy of religion, philosophical theology, political philosophy, and epistemology are all taken up in the papers of this volume.

Phil's own positions on many of the religious and practical questions that interested him grew out of what I have referred to in the title of this volume as a "liberal faith." Liberal faith is more a sensibility than a set of creedal commitments. It takes its cue from liberal political thought, which began as a family of theories about how to cope, ethically and politically, with the religious pluralism of post-Reformation Europe. Adherents of liberal faith continue to recognize enduring pluralism as one of the salient features of the world in which they live and move and have their being. They instinctively favor certain characteristic responses to it. Thus Phil accepted the inevitability of religious and cultural pluralism in the modern world. He was acutely aware of the challenges it poses and the possibilities it opens in education, in religion, and in politics. In response to pluralism and disagreement, he invariably favored the liberal values of tolerance, autonomy, and free discussion.

The catholicity of Phil's intellectual interests, which included history, literature, and the visual arts as well as philosophy, reflected an abiding faith in liberal education. He believed that such an education, supplemented by cross-cultural studies, could liberate students from prejudice and parochialism. But he remained steadfastly committed to the kind of disciplined intellectual inquiry that philosophy exemplifies. He eschewed the academic fads that dismissed traditional philosophical methods or that questioned the value of rigorous argumentation.

Phil's religion was also that of a liberal. The rituals of his childhood faith had a vestigial hold on him that became apparent to his friends at the end of his life. Throughout his career, he seemed to hold liberal positions in ecclesiology and in matters of observance and dogma. Interestingly, the one Christian doctrine on which Phil did a good deal of serious work was the Atonement, which is not dogmatically defined.[1] Though his work in the philosophy of religion would have been identified as Christian, his was not an insular Christianity. He was deeply interested in comparative religious studies and in the problems posed by pluralism for religious faith. His interest in comparative religious studies is what led, I believe, to his deeper involvement with the American Academy of Religion in his last years.

Phil's was not the religious faith of the utopian Christian, who thinks that the Kingdom can someday be realized or approached here on earth. The fulfillment of such utopian yearnings would require a perfection of humankind that Phil would have thought it unrealistic to expect. That he would have thought it unrealistic is suggested by some of his most compelling work on religion and literature, which—as we shall see—bespeaks a preoccupation with the darker themes of human life. The most moving of these essays, on Shusako Endo's book *Silence*, laments God's reticence and distance in the face of terrible dilemmas that can arise within the Christian life. Another of Phil's essays on literature—one on Albert Camus's *The Fall*—showed that, far from hoping for a Christian utopia, Phil was troubled by the possibility that humanity would bring about a sort of hell on earth.

As he hints at the end of his essay on Camus, Phil did repose a certain faith in liberal political arrangements. But as he was not a utopian in religion, so he was not a utopian in politics either. He believed in the value of free political discussion, and he believed that religion had something to contribute to that discussion. But he also recognized that religion could be manipulated for political ends and that terrible things could be done in its name. He recognized the vulnerability of human beings to evil wrought by those in power. And he concluded that a regime of scrupulously observed human rights is necessary to protect the vulnerable. Liberal political arrangements that protect human rights, prize discussion, and eschew hierarchy—these arrangements are the best hope for governing and protecting human beings under conditions of pluralism. But the best we can realistically hope for, Phil thought, may be only a slight improvement over what we already have.

If a single commemorative volume cannot represent all of Phil's interests, a collection that touches on some of the epistemological, religious, and political questions that were of greatest interest to him in the last years of his working life seems an appropriate tribute. This volume gets its unity because Phil's interest in those questions grew naturally out of liberal faith as I have described it. In the remainder of this introduction, I shall try to display that unity by asking questions about and drawing connections among various of the essays that Phil's friends and colleagues have so generously contributed.

Epistemology

The first paper in this volume, Linda Zagzebski's "Self-Trust and the Diversity of Religions," opens by broaching the concerns raised by religious pluralism. "The diversity of religions," Zagzebski writes, "is widely regarded as one of the most serious problems for conscientious belief in a particular religion, both among ordinary people and among professional philosophers." The task Zagzebski takes on is that of spelling out this problem and addressing it.

Zagzebski contrasts her own formulation of the problem posed by religious diversity with what she calls the "Enlightenment worry." That worry takes root, she says, because disagreement over religious belief seems to be irresolvable. She observes immediately that irresolvable disagreement does not pose a serious problem for conscientious belief in a particular religion all by itself. The claim that religious disagreements are irresolvable would pose a problem, however, if it were conjoined with two other claims: the claim that at least some parties to religious disagreements are normal human beings and the claim that Zagzebski calls "epistemic egalitarianism." Epistemic egalitarianism is the thesis—which Zagzebski associates with Locke and which she says "govern[ed] much of Enlightenment philosophy"—that "all normal human beings are roughly equal in the capacity to get knowledge."

Zagzebski argues that what we find troubling about religious pluralism cannot be the Enlightenment worry because, to be troubled by that worry, we would have to be epistemic egalitarians. But, she says, epistemic egalitarianism is not a position most of us hold. Instead she thinks our conscientious belief in a particular religion is threatened by religious disagreements among admirable people and by the fact that we sometimes find ourselves in religious disagreement with those we admire. But, Zagzebski observes, we are right to worry about disagreement in these cases only if we ought to "trust" our emotion of admiration. She adds immediately that she thinks that we must and should trust it. She develops her view of trust in one's own emotions in dialogue with some work of Richard Foley's on self-trust.

In brief, Zagzebski thinks that the admirable is "something like the imitably attractive." She continues, "We feel a positive emotion toward the person we admire that would lead to imitating the person given the right practical conditions." To trust our emotion of admiration is "to have confidence that it is appropriate to feel the kind of attraction and desire to imitate that is intrinsic to admiration." Since Zagzebski thinks we must trust our emotion of admiration, we must—at least sometimes—think the attraction and desire to imitate is appropriate. It is appropriate, she thinks, even if we lack evidence that the person whom we admire is epistemically reliable.

Having argued that we must trust our emotion of admiration even in these cases, Zagzebski is in a position to recast the problem posed by religious diversity. Suppose I encounter someone with whom I disagree about religious questions but whom I greatly admire. I may admire how she has arrived at her religious beliefs or the way she holds her beliefs. If I must trust my admiration in these cases, then I must think it appropriate to want to imitate that person, even in the absence of evidence that she—or the ways she arrives at her beliefs—is epistemically reliable. But imitation of that person would require affirming her religious beliefs and practices instead of my own. If I also continue to trust "the aspects of myself from which I gain my beliefs and the traditions that support them," then I face "a genuine problem of religious diversity": trust in my own beliefs conflicts with my appropriate desire to imitate someone whose beliefs are different.

"The problem of [Zagzebski's paper]"—the problem posed by irresolvable religious disagreement—is not a conflict that arises because I have evidence for my own beliefs and evidence of the reliability of someone with whom I disagree. Rather, Zagzebski thinks, it arises because I trust my own beliefs and trust my emotion of admiration of the person with whom I disagree. This conflict is therefore, she says, "a conflict that arises within self-trust."

The claim that we sometimes cannot help admiring those of other faiths is bound to appeal to the person of liberal faith, who cherishes diversity as he appreciates its challenges. The conclusions Zagzebski draws from this claim obviously raise a number of questions. There are two it may be useful to discuss briefly.

First, while *a* "genuine problem of religious diversity" may arise because I disagree with someone whose ways of forming or holding beliefs I admire, it is by no means clear that this is the only or the primary problem religious diversity poses for conscientious belief. Many religious faiths are, in various ways, exclusivist: they make truth claims that are incompatible with claims made by other religions, including the claim to offer the sole route to salvation. Imagine an adherent of an exclusivist religion who sees in those of a different faith the decency or justice or benevolence that she thinks her own faith is supposed to inspire. Imagine that she does not in the least admire the way they have arrived at their religious beliefs. Nor does she admire—or desire to imitate—their religious rituals, their devotions, or their spirituality. But she may admire their behavior toward others. She may find it hard to believe that God would condemn such people. Then she faces a conflict between the admiration she has for those of the other faith and the trust she has in the exclusivist pretensions of her tradition. She may choose to resolve the tension by reaffirming her admiration for some of the qualities she sees in others while being more selective in her trust of her religious tradition. In particular, she may decide that she can no longer trust its exclusivist claims. The conflict to which I have drawn attention differs from the problem of religious diversity on which Zagzebski focuses. And so the first question raised by Zagzebski's conclusion is whether there is a single problem raised by religious diversity, which she has correctly identified.

The problem I have tried to point to is one that, like the one Zagzebski points to, "arises within self-trust." For the adherent of the exclusivist faith has some evidence that those with whom she disagrees about religion are epistemically reliable when it comes to interpersonal morality: they observe a code of interpersonal morality that she thinks is correct, even if they do so for what she thinks are the wrong reasons. This brings us to a second question raised by Zagzebski's paper, the question of what it means for a problem to arise *within* self-trust. One can usefully develop this question by turning to the second paper in this volume.

That paper, "An Epistemology That Matters," is by Richard Foley, on whose work Zagzebski drew in her opening essay. Like Zagzebski, Foley begins by criticizing an assumption of John Locke's. That assumption is not the one Zagzebski criticized, the assumption of epistemic egalitarianism. It is, rather, the assumption that there is a necessary connection between someone's being justified in believing a claim and her "meeting the higher standard of knowing that a claim is true." Foley proposes that "epistemologists should resist the temptation to assume any kind of necessary tie between justified belief and knowledge." The temptation Foley wants epistemologists to resist is one to which much of traditional epistemology has acceded, since knowledge has traditionally been defined as justified true belief. Foley therefore proposes to "reorient" the discipline of epistemology.

An epistemology thus reoriented promises to be, as Foley suggests, "an epistemology that matters." One of the things to which it will matter is our everyday evaluation of people's beliefs. Everyday evaluations, Foley notes, more often turn on whether people "have been appropriately careful and responsible in regulating their opinions" than on whether they have met a standard for knowledge. Everyday evaluations therefore presuppose a standard of belief assessment that bears no necessary connection to knowledge. Foley suggests that the standard our everyday evaluations presuppose is that of justification as he understands it.

As we shall see, Foley thinks that justification is a species of rationality. Severing the connection between justified belief and knowledge severs the connection between rational belief and knowledge. To ask whether a belief is rationally held can therefore be quite different from asking whether the belief is held in such a way that, if it is true, it would constitute knowledge. Once that distinction is drawn, philosophers are free to propose an account of rational belief that treats the rationality of believing in the same way as the rationality of acting, deciding, or adopting strategies and plans. Thus a reoriented epistemology also matters, Foley thinks, to our ability to treat the rationality of believing as part of an account of the rationality of other actions.

Foley does not discuss problems in the philosophy of religion or problems posed by religious diversity. But once these problems are in view, as they are bound to be after Zagzebski's paper, we can see another way in which a reoriented epistemology may matter.

Suppose that we come upon or read about persons whose views about religion are arrived at very differently from our own. Perhaps they read sacred texts literally, ignoring hermeneutical strictures and techniques that we think are critically important. Or perhaps they attribute natural phenomena to divine beings who animate the physical world. Or perhaps they accept on faith various accounts of the history of the world that we think have been disproven by science. Or perhaps they think God speaks directly to them in private revelations.

Our encounters with such people or our acquaintance with them raises the question of what to say about how their beliefs are held. We may not admire the way such people arrive at their religious beliefs, at least as Zagzebski defines *admire*. Our reasons for not admiring them may make us very reluctant to say that their beliefs are held in such a way that, if they were true, they would constitute knowledge. On the other hand, we may be very reluctant to dismiss their beliefs as irrationally or unjustifiedly held. The dismissal may seem too harsh to be plausible to the person of liberal faith, especially if they are—as it were—just people who are doing their epistemic best by their own lights. Foley's proposal may seem to open just the evaluative space that needs to be available for handling such cases. For it may allow us to affirm that such people hold their religious views rationally and justifiedly, while allowing us to deny that they have arrived at their beliefs admirably or in ways that produce knowledge.

Of course, whether it does depends upon the conditions under which a belief is rationally or justifiedly held. Foley proposes what he calls a "template" for rationality that elucidates those conditions. He says: "An action A (or decision, plan, intention, etc.) is rational in sense X for S just in case it is *epistemically rational* for S to believe that A will do an acceptably good job of satisfying goals of kind X."

The template avoids circularity because the notion of epistemic rationality on the right side of the biconditional is, Foley says, to be explicated without reference to "any other notion of rationality or any of its close cognates." The template accommodates justified belief, Foley says, because "S justifiably believes P if it is epistemically rational for S to believe that her procedures with respect to P have been acceptable: that is, acceptable given the limitations on her time and capacities and given all of her goals."[2] If Foley's template is correct, then whether the religious believers I discussed a moment ago hold their beliefs rationally—in some sense of *rationally*—depends upon what goals they have and what goals it is rational for them to adopt. These questions raise difficulties that go beyond the scope of this introduction. Instead of pursuing them, I want to return to the implications of Foley's essay for Zagzebski's piece.

Trust in others is sensitive to and responsive to reasons. Someone's possession of the traits that make her trustworthy is a reason to trust her. Someone's duplicity and unreliability are reasons to distrust her. Trust in our own faculties and affections is also responsive to reasons. That someone's infatuations regularly lead him into unhappy relationships is a reason for him to distrust his romantic judgments. If he finds himself irresistibly drawn to someone else, he can ask whether it is rational for him to trust his infatuation with her. Similarly, a person who finds herself admiring another can ask herself whether it is rational for her to trust her admiration. She may find that she must trust her own admiration, at least in some cases, just as Zagzebski says. But this finding does not imply that she cannot ask about the rationality of her admiration for others. It may show instead that she simply cannot escape the conclusion that her admiration is rational.

Since Foley's template for rationality is supposed to be generally applicable, it must apply to the rationality of admiration. If that template is right, and if it is in some way rational for me to trust my admiration of someone of a different faith, then it is epistemically rational for me to believe that trusting my own admiration of that person would acceptably satisfy some of my goals.[3] If it is also in some way rational for me to trust my own religious tradition, then—again assuming Foley's template is right—it is epistemically rational for me to believe that trusting my own tradition would acceptably advance some of my goals.

So if Foley's template is right, then the problem that Zagzebski thinks is posed by religious disagreement with those we admire seems ultimately to be a problem about what it is epistemically rational for me to believe about what acceptably advances some of my goals. I can and should reflect upon what goals it would be rational for me to have. If I face a conflict posed by religious diversity, I could resolve the conflict by rationally changing my goals.

To see this, let us return to the example I provided earlier, that of a conflict that arises when the adherent of an exclusivist religion encounters someone of a different faith whose justice toward others she admires. I said that she could resolve the conflict she faces by rationally changing what she trusts her own tradition to do. She might continue to trust it to provide familiar spiritual comforts while no longer trusting it to provide exclusive access to the means of salvation. This resolution of the conflict is achieved by a refinement of her goals. She still trusts her tradition and trusts her admiration of others. She resolves the conflict by deciding that it is acceptable for her admiration of others to track their justice and decency; she decides that she wants her trust in religious traditions to track something other than the credence she gives to their exclusivist claims.

The question of what goals may rationally be adopted in the face of conflicts may be questions *about* self-trust. Perhaps the Foley template can be used to show that, as Zagzebski suggests, they also arise *within* self-trust. For it may be that we cannot but trust ourselves about some of the goals we should pursue. Perhaps, for example, some people cannot but trust their inclinations to admire those who are just toward others, and to modify their trust in exclusivist religions accordingly.

These questions are too large to be pursued here. Their great interest suggests that the conversation between Foley and Zagzebski, evident in Zagzebski's paper, is bound to continue.

Philosophy of Religion

The next two papers in the volume are in the philosophy of religion. As we shall see, they touch on concerns that animated the two papers Phil wrote in philosophy and literature that I referred to earlier: the papers on Endo and Camus.

Eleonore Stump's "Presence and Omnipresence" explores the claim that love includes a desire for union with the beloved. What, Stump asks, is the desire for union with the beloved a desire for? In particular, she asks, what is it that adult human beings who are friends but not lovers desire when they desire union with one another? The answer to this question, Stump thinks, "sheds light on the general nature of the union desired in love, and it also highlights a neglected side of the standard divine attribute of omnipresence."

In Stump's view, "Union between friends requires mutual closeness and personal presence." The kind of presence that is required is what Stump calls "significant personal presence." Such presence, she argues here, requires "direct and unmediated causal and cognitive contact," second-person experience of the other, and shared attention.

Moreover, significant presence requires closeness to the person to whom one is significantly present. Stump discusses several conditions of closeness, of which I shall mention just two. First, A is close to B only if A shares his thoughts and feelings with B. Furthermore, B has to receive A's revelations. She has to understand what A is revealing to her. "If she is willing enough but uncomprehending, she will not be close to him." Second, closeness requires "psychic integration and wholeheartedness." If someone has desires with which he does not identify, or that he wishes he did not have, he is "alienated from himself." "A person alienated from himself," Stump says "cannot have someone else close to him." "Even God cannot be close to a human person alienated from himself."

As is hinted by the last remark, Stump thinks her analysis of union between friends applies to the union between persons and God: "On the account of presence and omnipresence I have given here, the only thing decisive for the kind of personal presence, significant or minimal, that an omnipresent God has to a human person is thus the state and condition of the human person himself." From this claim, Stump draws a strong conclusion: "Whether omnipresent God is present to Jerome with significant personal presence is dependent not on God but on Jerome." She reiterates this conclusion at the end of her paper: "If Paula wants God to be significantly present to her, the establishment of the relationship she wants depends only on her, on her single-mindedly and wholeheartedly wanting that relationship. . . . If she does, then the presence that the omnipresent God has to her will be significant personal presence." And since significant personal presence entails the other condition on union—closeness—then it follows that if someone wholeheartedly loves God and wholeheartedly wants union with him, she can have it.

Stump's claim that significant personal presence requires causal and cognitive contact that is "direct and unmediated" raises a number of fascinating questions about how God can be present to us through religious texts, which might seem to make God present in a significant way but through the medium of a holy book. It also raises questions about how God can be made present through representations of himself and representations of holy persons, such as icons. If Stump's account of significant personal presence is correct, and if God is significantly present through icons, then this has implications for the vexed question of how icons represent.[4] For they would have to represent without mediating.

This is, I think, an implication that would have intrigued Phil, for he was a voracious consumer of art books and had an extensive knowledge of painting. But what is most interesting and challenging about Stump's paper is its bearing on some work of Phil's, which can be brought out by reading it in conjunction with his paper on the novel *Silence* by Shusaku Endo.[5]

The first half of Phil's paper on *Silence* is a synopsis of the novel that I shall not recapitulate here. In brief, the novel tells of Sebastian Rodriguez, a Jesuit who undertakes a clandestine mission to the persecuted Catholics of seventeenth-century Japan. I mention just three pivotal points in the novel as Phil retells it.

First, Rodriguez is deeply troubled by what he takes to be God's silence in the face of terrible torture and death visited on the persecuted. As Phil recounts a critical episode in the novel: "'Why have you abandoned us so completely?' Rodriguez prays in a weak voice. 'Have you just remained silent like the darkness that surrounds me? Why? At least tell me why.'" But the sea remains cold, and the darkness stays stubbornly silent.[6]

Second, when Rodriguez himself is betrayed and captured, he is faced with a terrible dilemma in which—as Phil tells it—he is forced to choose between love of God and love of neighbor. For Rodriguez is told that if he will trample on a bronze representation of the face of Christ, then some of the persecuted prisoners will be released from torture. At that point, Phil says, "Rodriguez fights a battle with Christianity in his own heart."[7] He does not want to trample on the face of Christ, but he wants to relieve the sufferings of the persecuted Christians. He is therefore deeply divided. Yet at just this point God seems to Rodriguez finally to break his silence. Again in the words of Phil's essay: "And then the Christ in bronze speaks to him. 'Trample! Trample! I more than anyone know the pain in your foot. Trample! It was to be trampled on by men that I was born into this world. It was to share men's pain that I carried my cross!'"[8]

Finally, Phil says that when the moment of Rodriguez's trial has passed, the priest realizes "he has come to love Christ in a new way. And, more important, everything he had been through had been necessary to bring him to this new love. Moreover, it seems that he is not self-deceived on this point, for his new love bears good fruit. He is able to love his neighbor in a new way too."[9] A couple of pages later, Phil says of Rodriguez:

Because his new love is a suffering love just as Christ's love for him is a suffering love, he is in some ways closer to Christ than he has ever been before. . . . Astonishingly, Rodriguez is even able to affirm that his whole life, including his dilemma and its tragic consequences, was necessary to bring him to this new love. And since his deepest desire had always been to draw close to Christ in love, his life's most important thread is not cut off at the point of his tragic dilemma. . . . His life's project continues beyond that point, transformed in ways he could not have anticipated.[10]

How does Phil's treatment of these three pivotal points bear on Stump's account of union with God?

Consider first Rodriguez's frustration with the silence of God. Much later in his life, as Rodriguez recalls the trial that changed his life forever, he seems to hear Christ saying, "I was not silent. I suffered beside you."[11] Thus Christ asserts that he was intimately present to Rodriguez and to the persecuted Christians, sharing their suffering. Yet Rodriguez did not recognize his presence at the time or understand why God allowed the suffering to continue. Because Rodriguez did not then understand God's intentions and desires, it follows from Stump's account that he was not close to God. Further, since significant personal presence requires closeness, it follows that Rodriguez was not significantly personally present to God and that God was not significantly personally present to him. But we may wonder whether this is so or whether an account of closeness and presence that implies it can be correct. For we may think that God can be present to us in significant ways, perhaps even sustaining us, at times when we are tried most severely, when his intentions are hidden from us and when we do not know why we must endure what life subjects us to.

Stump also insists that God cannot be close—hence significantly personally present—to someone who is alienated from himself, who lacks psychic integration and has a divided will. Even if the division is momentary, she may think, it poses an obstacle to closeness and presence that is not removed so long as the division lasts. Yet it is at the moment in his life when Rodriguez is most deeply divided, the moment when "he fights a battle with Christianity in his own heart," that Christ seems to speak to him at last. Indeed, it is at that moment that Christ satisfies the rest of Stump's conditions on significant personal presence. For Christ has direct and unmediated contact with Rodriguez, addresses him in the second person, shares attention with him, and reveals his deepest thoughts to him. The example seems to drive home the point that Christ can make himself present to us when we are most troubled and in doubt.

Stump may grant that God's presence to Rodriguez in these instances was significant and personal but deny that it tells against her account. For, she may say, what she is interested in is the kind of presence that is desired by someone who loves God and wants union with God. Neither of these cases exemplifies that kind of presence, even if the presence they exemplify is in some ways significant and personal.

But now consider Phil's claim that Rodriguez's deepest desire had always been to draw close to Christ in love. Rodriguez, it seems, had always desired union with Christ above all else. Yet if Phil is right, he could achieve it only after facing the most tragic dilemma of his life and reconciling himself with the action he took when he faced it. The reconciliation brought about a change in Rodriguez that he needed to make before he could be united with Christ in the way that he had always wanted. This reading of the novel may bear out Stump's point that a person's union with God depends upon "the state and condition of the person himself." It does, however, call into question Stump's claim that if someone "wants God to be significantly present to her, the establishment of the relationship she wants depends only on her, on her single-mindedly and wholeheartedly wanting that relationship." For Rodriguez single-mindedly wanted union with Christ all his life. But for much of his life he was not ready for it. Moreover, nothing he would or could have chosen for himself could have effected the changes in his "state and condition" that had to take place before he could be united with Christ in suffering love.

The story of Rodriguez, we may think, illustrates important truths. Attaining union with God is a project that unfolds over the course of a life. Since God knows our hearts and minds even if we do not choose to reveal them to him, he knows us better than we know ourselves. He guides us in that project, helping us to make use of events that seem the most formidable obstacles to union with him. Thus Phil might point out that the execution of the project depends, not just upon our wanting it single-mindedly and wholeheartedly, but also upon God's providential care for each of us.

Perhaps Stump would agree with these claims. Certainly the questions I have raised about her paper by drawing on Phil's essay are not intended to show that Stump's account of presence is wrong, for the paper in this volume provides just a glimpse of the deeper and more extensive work she has done on presence and closeness. Rather, those questions are meant to show the continuing interest of some of Phil's writings and to continue a philosophical conversation to which Phil himself can no longer contribute. For her part, Stump has carried on that conversation, elaborating and ramifying her account of presence in some forthcoming work—work that Phil's essay on Endo suggests he would greatly have appreciated.[12]

The project that Stump considers, the project of attaining union with God, is at odds with another project in which all of us are engaged—what Paul Griffiths in his paper calls "the project of sin." That, according to Griffiths, is the project of extricating ourselves from participation in the God who created and sustains us. What of those who succeed in this project? What of those who do not want union with God but instead will single-mindedly to be separated from God?

The most developed answer in the Christian tradition is that after death and the Last Judgment they will suffer eternal damnation. In his "Self-Annihilation or Damnation?" Griffiths explores the possibility that success at the project of sin could instead result in the annihilation of the sinner. If self-annihilation is possible, then, Griffiths thinks, it is possible that the soul is not immortal. Since the immortality of the soul seems so central to the tradition, Griffiths tries to defend the compatibility of self-annihilation with orthodoxy.

The subtitle of Griffiths's paper is "A Disputable Question in Christian Eschatology." As an exercise in eschatological thinking, I believe the paper would have been of considerable interest to Phil. For some of Phil's own work in the philosophy of religion concerned questions raised by the doctrine of the Atonement, according to which Christ's suffering and death reconciled fallen humanity to God. Questions about the Atonement, like the question explored by Griffiths, are eschatological. In Phil's hands, it became clear that they, too, are disputable—and deeply puzzling—questions in Christian eschatology.[13]

But Phil would have been interested in Griffiths's paper for another reason as well. At the beginning of his paper, Griffiths writes: "Depicting what happens when we die is always at least an extrapolation from what we take ourselves to be while alive; it is also among the more important tools we have for focusing and elaborating our self-understanding and for meditating discursively and visually upon what we take ourselves to be. Disputes in eschatology are always also disputes in anthropology." So we should expect that when we explore neglected possibilities in Christian eschatology we will expand the possibilities of Christian thought about what human beings are. But are anthropologies developed in response to Christian concerns—especially to Christian eschatological concerns—detachable from distinctively Christian commitments? Can newly elaborated Christian anthropologies also enrich secular thought about what human beings are? Can the eschatologies that go along with those anthropologies tell us something new about what the future may hold in this world? Or are the presuppositions of any Christian anthropology so firmly at odds with secular views of the human person that any Christian anthropology, whether traditional or novel, is bound to seem utterly alien to nonbelievers?

We should hope that the alienation is not complete. For believers and nonbelievers, Christians and non-Christians, cohabit contemporary societies. The political arrangements of those societies have to be premised on some assumptions about what human beings are like, what sorts of well-being politics should aim at, and what threats to human well-being most urgently need to be averted. So if contemporary societies are to be regulated by arrangements that all can support, there will have to be some agreement on those assumptions and hence some overlap on the anthropological questions that are relevant to politics. Is such an overlap possible? This is, in effect, a question Phil took up in another of his papers on philosophy and literature—this one on Camus's novel *The Fall*.[14]

According to the dominant tradition in Christian anthropology, human beings are driven to engage in what Griffiths calls "the project of sin" by their pride. It is pride that drives us to try to emancipate ourselves from participation in and subjection to God. According to the dominant tradition in Christian eschatology, the fate of those of us who succeed in the project is hell. In Camus's novel, the pride is that of the narrator, the "judge-penitent," who describes his own descent into hell. In Camus's portrayal of hell, the damned person is painfully aware of his own guilt. He is damned because awareness of guilt does not lead—as it does in the case of Rodriguez—to repentance or to pity for others who have fallen. Rather, the wills of the damned are "everlastingly fixed on evil."[15] Their awareness of their own guilt makes them merciless rather than pitiful toward one another.

But the hell Camus describes is not torment in another world that awaits some after death. It is instead the hell that our world might become. The hellishness of the world does not depend upon any specifically Christian assumptions, such as the assumption that distance from God is itself a torment. Nor does the possibility that our world might become such a hell depend upon any such assumptions. That possibility *is* predicated on certain assumptions about the vice of pride and its consequences for our collective life. But those assumptions are not distinctively Christian. For the pride Camus describes is what Phil, following Judith Shklar, calls an "ordinary vice": a vice of the sort Shklar—and Phil—thought liberals like themselves should be most concerned with, one directed against other human beings rather than God.[16]

At the conclusion of his essay, Phil writes, "I consider pride an ordinary vice. So it seems to me that the hellish world Jean-Baptiste Clamence prophesies is not just a figment of an existentialist's overheated imagination, but a real possibility for a post-Christian culture. The popularity of nihilism in our century leads me to believe that there is some positive probability . . . that such a world lies in our future."[17] Thus the question *The Fall* forces upon us, according to Phil, is how a pluralistic world can avert the future Camus depicts. It poses that question so powerfully and insistently precisely because it reaches to the depths of collective memory, deploying the conceptual resources of traditional Christian anthropology and eschatology in ways that chill even those who reject traditional Christian doctrines.

Griffiths's essay explores a nontraditional but Christian anthropology and eschatology. Reading it in conjunction with Phil's piece on Camus raises a number of very interesting questions. How might the consequences of nihilism be depicted using the conceptual resources of the nontraditional frames of thought Griffiths urges us to consider? In particular, how might they be represented by an artist who takes seriously the alternative Griffiths explores? Would the artistic representations of those consequences chill and horrify in the way that Camus's novel does? Griffiths's quotation of Philip Larkin's poetry gives just some indication of the answers. But a good deal remains to be said about how a nontraditional Christian eschatology could help us understand the deadening possibilities of a "post-Christian" future.

Political Philosophy

Phil's own hope for averting the possibility lay in what he called in his essay "secular faith." This is not, he hastens to add, faith in the possibility of some earthly utopia: "I am instead thinking of the modest beliefs that human pride can be humbled, or at least kept in check, without divine chastisement and that acknowledging guilt in ourselves need not render us merciless toward others. If a post-Christian culture can mobilize such resources as these, it may well prove strong enough to resist the seductions of the false prophets of nihilism."[18]

I once argued that pride is an ordinary vice and that liberal political culture and political arrangements can keep it in check.[19] I believe Phil agreed. If Phil and I were right, then the secular faith he confesses here is the political manifestation of that underlying and unifying sensibility that I called his "liberal faith." And if Phil is making a veiled profession of faith in liberal political arrangements at the close of his essay on Camus, then—given the interesting connections between that essay and Griffiths's essay on eschatology—it is natural to move from Griffiths's piece to the third set of essays in this volume, those on liberal political theory. Though Phil was best known for his work in the philosophy of religion and, earlier, the philosophy of science, the papers on political philosophy are those that engage his interests and his work most obviously and are therefore those that call for the briefest introductions.

It is possible that liberal democracy is justified simply on the grounds that liberal democratic institutions are the best check on the ordinary vices. This is a line of argument pursued by Judith Shklar in her later work.[20] But a long tradition of political thought has, of course, sought more ambitious arguments in favor of liberal democracy. Robert Audi's contribution to this volume falls squarely within that tradition. The bulk of Audi's essay "present[s] one plausible way in which liberal democracy can be morally grounded."

Audi's attempt to provide an intuitionist grounding of liberal democracy is bold and provocative. What most interested Phil about this work, I believe, were the corollaries that Audi draws from his foundational work.

Liberalism began as a response to the religious wars that racked Europe in the early modern period. Questions about how liberal regimes should accommodate religious institutions and citizens remain pressing. Equally pressing are questions about what demands religious institutions and citizens can legitimately make of liberal institutions. Audi argues for what he calls "appropriate neutrality" of government toward religion. He also argues that there is a sort of "appropriate religious neutrality" that applies to citizens. Citizens, he says, are prima facie obligated to obey what he calls the *principle of secular rationale*: "In liberal democracies, citizens have a prima facie obligation not to advocate or support any law or public policy that restricts human conduct, unless they have, and are willing to offer, adequate secular reason for this adequacy or support."

By defending the principle of secular rationale, Audi enters a lively debate in contemporary political philosophy, one that concerns the appropriate grounds for political action and advocacy. This is a debate to which Phil also contributed, using the occasion of his APA presidential address to do so.[21] In that address, Phil criticizes the stronger *principle of secular motivation* that Audi defends in other writings.[22] He also criticizes the principle of secular rationale on the grounds that it is unfair to religious believers.

In brief, Phil's argument is that the principle is most plausibly defended on the ground that "in a religiously pluralistic society religious reasons cannot justify laws or policies that restrict conduct in terms of considerations all citizens can share or cannot reasonably reject." But, he points out, "if the fact that religious reasons cannot be shared by all in a religiously pluralistic society suffices to warrant any exclusion of religious reasons for advocating or supporting restrictive laws or policies, then much else ought in fairness also to be excluded on the same grounds."[23] Since Audi does not defend comparable exclusions on those secular reasons that "are no better off than . . . religious reasons in terms of being shared or not being reasonably rejected," Phil concludes that Audi's principle is unfair.

Audi may think that reliance on religious reasons that others cannot accept differs in some morally significant way from reliance on secular reasons that others cannot accept. Some of his remarks suggest he thinks reliance on religious reasons is especially likely to prove dangerously divisive.[24] Phil attempted to rebut this argument as well.[25] Since Audi continues to defend the principle of secular rationale, it would be interesting to know whether Phil thought that Audi's later writings contain adequate responses to his criticisms.

As Phil notes in his presidential address, John Rawls defended principles of public reasoning that seem to evade these criticisms. His strictures apply to what he called "comprehensive doctrines" of all kinds—both religious, such as Christianity, and secular, such as Kantianism and utilitarianism. Rawls allowed that citizens may appeal to their comprehensive doctrines in public debate at any time, provided they are willing to supply public reasons to support whatever policy their appeal to comprehensive doctrine is said to support.[26] Phil goes on to criticize Rawls's view as well and to defend instead what he calls an "inclusivist ideal" of political discourse.[27] The closing sentences of his presidential address are a nice summary of the political side of his own liberal faith.

> If we look away from the debates about liberal theory in the academy, we will notice that, in the rough and tumble of American politics, liberalism has recently suffered serious reverses. If they are to overcome these setbacks, liberals need new allies. They might find some in America's religious communities if their ideals were more inclusive. Thus it may be important for the future of American liberalism that something like the inclusivist ideal should prevail in practice, even if it remains disputed in the theory, of liberalism for our time and place. I hope it will prevail.[28]

The last two papers in the volume are by authors who share some of Phil's hopes for liberalism. The one immediately following Audi's is my own "Egalitarianism without Equality?" It asks, not about the moral grounds of liberal democracy, but about the moral grounds for the egalitarian distributions to which some liberals—especially Rawlsian liberals—are committed.

If one believes in human equality, it is natural to think that this claim has some fundamental importance in justifying political arrangements. In particular, it is natural to think that it has some fundamental importance in justifying the distribution of basic, socially generated benefits. In a very provocative essay, T. M. Scanlon challenged this view, arguing that the value of equality, as such, is *not* of fundamental importance in political philosophy.[29]

I argue that, while Scanlon may be correct about what is and is not important in the theory of domestic justice, the correct account of justice across borders does require a fundamental appeal to human equality. If I am right about that—and of course I leave it to the reader to determine whether I am—then the conclusion may have implications for Rawls's account of public reason. For fundamental appeals to human equality may require fundamental appeals to comprehensive doctrines. If they do, then the account of public reason that Rawls put forward for deliberation about domestic justice may hold only in some qualified form for deliberation about justice across borders.

This is not a question I take up in the paper, but it is—I think—a question that would have interested Phil; surely the interest would have been a natural outgrowth of the interests he pursued in his presidential address. Perhaps Phil was so taken with "Egalitarianism without Equality?" because it touched on this interest. Be that as it may, I was pleased that he liked the paper, and I am even more pleased to return the favor by including it in a volume that is a tribute to him.

The last paper in the volume is by Sumner Twiss. Twiss is also concerned with the moral foundations of certain liberal commitments. In his case, the concern is not with egalitarianism but with human rights and an absolute proscription on torture. This is the paper in the volume that bears most explicitly on Phil's work, for Twiss explicitly considers a paper of Phil's: "Relativism about Torture: Religious and Secular Responses."[30]

In that paper, Phil pointed out that the prima facie wrongness of torture is part of our society's common morality. But, according to Twiss, he also acknowledged that "there might be certain hard cases where some in our society might view torture as justifiable." He also expressed skepticism that the claim that torture is always wrong "is part of a common morality of humanity as a whole." And he argued that that claim cannot be "justified to [all] members of any other societies" by any one argument, since any argument that purports to support an absolute prohibition will rest on one or more premises that can be reasonably contested. How, then, to gain acceptance for the absolute prohibition Phil favored?

Phil thought that artistic and other representations of the evils of torture might go some way toward cultivating a shared, pretheoretical abhorrence of any use of torture. And he thought that arguing piecemeal—offering different arguments to different groups and societies—might build consensus on some specific moral judgments about the categorical wrongness of torture.

Twiss boldly takes up the challenge issued in Phil's paper, attempting to show that an absolute proscription on torture can be grounded without reliance on "essentially contestable premises that undermine its ability to be convincing *now* to all people of goodwill, whatever their social or cultural location." The "now," which Twiss emphasizes in his own paper, is essential. For Twiss believes that the decades since adoption of the UN's Declaration of Human Rights have deepened our understanding of torture and its consequences for victims, perpetrators, and communities. Twiss's argument for an absolute prohibition can be "more firmly grounded than [Phil] may have thought" on these consequentialist grounds, conjoined with "full comprehension of the nature of torture" that is now available.

Philosophers will find the consequentialist strands of Twiss's paper the most vexing. They will be tempted to concoct counterexamples in which torture does not have the bad consequences on which Twiss's argument relies—for example, "ticking bomb" scenarios in which, immediately after the torture, both torturer and tortured are given drugs that blot the incident from their memories—or in which the gains from torture seem to outweigh those consequences. Anticipating such responses, the "epilogue" of Twiss's paper is an extended argument against the use of unrealistic counterexamples "to inform our moral intuitions about bedrock proscriptions." As with Twiss's paper, so with Audi's, readers will wonder what Phil would have made of this response to his earlier work. Unfortunately, because of Phil's death at age sixty-four, it is impossible for us to find out.

The papers collected in this volume all touch, in many and diverse ways, on the philosophical work of Philip Quinn, and they all raise many questions that would have interested him deeply. I have tried to show some of the directions in which further discussion of those questions might be carried. That these papers raise questions that can be the subjects of much further discussion is itself a tribute to the authors, as the volume is their tribute to Phil. For commemorative volumes should not honor by standing like monuments of polished stone, revisited with quiet reverence but untouched by the passage of time. Rather, they should confer honor by keeping alive the ideas and arguments of those whom they commemorate, inviting further engagement with their ideas and interests. I hope I have brought out just how completely the contributors to this volume have succeeded in their attempt to confer such honor on Phil. The continued vitality of one's ideas is not, I think, the only form of life after death in which Phil believed. But I think it is one that would have had its own special appeal to a philosopher of liberal faith.

Notes

1. Philip L. Quinn, "Christian Atonement and Kantian Justification," 3 (1986): 440.
2. Note that where the template had the biconditional formulation "just in case," this instance is in the form of a conditional.
3. Relying on the biconditional formulation.
4. The English-language literature on icons with which I am familiar is fascinating for its treatment of historical and religious questions but generally lacking in sophisticated philosophical discussion of representation. An exception is some recent unpublished work on icons by Nicholas Wolterstorff.
5. Philip L. Quinn, "Tragic Dilemmas, Suffering Love, and Christian Life," *Journal of Religious Ethics* 17 (1989): 151–83.
6. Ibid., p. 158.
7. Ibid., p. 166
8. Ibid., p. 165.
9. Ibid., p. 176.
10. Ibid., p. 180.
11. Ibid., p. 166.
12. Eleonore Stump, *Wandering in Darkness: Narrative and the Problem of Suffering* (New York: Oxford University Press, forthcoming), esp. ch. 7.
13. See, for example, Quinn, "Christian Atonement."
14. Philip Quinn, "Hell in Amsterdam: Reflections on Camus's *The Fall*," *Midwest Studies in Philosophy* 16 (1999): 89–103.
15. Ibid., p. 102.
16. Judith Shklar, *Ordinary Vices* (Cambridge, MA: Harvard University Press, 1984).
17. Quinn, "Hell in Amsterdam," p. 103.
18. Ibid.
19. Paul J. Weithman, "Toward an Augustinian Liberalism," *Faith and Philosophy* 8 (1991): 461–80.
20. Judith Shklar, "The Liberalism of Fear," in *Liberalism and the Moral Life*, ed. Nancy L. Rosenblum (Cambridge, MA: Harvard University Press, 1989), pp. 21–38.
21. Philip Quinn, "Political Liberalisms and Their Exclusions of the Religious," *Proceedings and Addresses of the American Philosophical Association* 69 (1995): 35–56, reprinted in *Religion and Contemporary Liberalism*, ed. Paul J. Weithman (Notre Dame: University of Notre Dame Press, 1997), pp. 138–61. Page references will be given to the reprinted version.
22. Ibid., 139–42; for the principle of secular motivation, see Robert Audi, "The Separation of Church and State and the Obligations of Citizenship," *Philosophy and Public Affairs* 18 (1989): 278.

23. Quinn, "Political Liberalisms," p. 144.
24. See the closing remarks of Audi, "Separation."
25. Quinn, "Political Liberalisms," pp. 143–44.
26. For exposition and defense, see John Rawls, "Idea of Public Reason Revisited," in *Law of Peoples* (Cambridge, MA: Harvard University Press, 1999), pp. 129–80.
27. Quinn, "Political Liberalisms," esp. pp. 152–53.
28. Ibid., p. 160.
29. T. M. Scanlon, "The Diversity of Objections to Inequality," in *The Difficulty of Toleration: Essays in Political Philosophy* (New York: Cambridge University Press, 2003), pp. 187–218.
30. The essay appears in *Religion and Morality*, ed. D. Z. Phillips (New York: Palgrave Macmillan, 1996), pp. 151–70.

Part One

Epistemology

One

Self-Trust and the Diversity of Religions
Linda Zagzebski

The Problem of Religious Disagreement

The diversity of religions is widely regarded as one of the most serious problems for conscientious belief in a particular religion, both among ordinary people and among professional philosophers. The problem is not unique to religious belief because people have the same reaction to any instance of irresolvable disagreement. I think it is illuminating that this is not just a philosopher's puzzle. If the philosophically untutored think of it, that probably means there is something in ordinary beliefs and experiences that generates the problem. But since few, if any, people worried about it for millennia, those beliefs and experiences are probably modern in origin.

I think that there are two modern sources of the perception that diversity is a threat. One is a principle about human nature that I think we should reject, but the other is a kind of experience that I think we ought to take very seriously. I will argue that we should trust the experiences that generate the problem because of self-trust, and I think that the way out of the problem requires us to look more deeply at what self-trust commits us to.

At some time in the distant past, people probably began to realize that some of their most cherished beliefs conflicted with the beliefs of other groups of people, but for many centuries nobody saw this as a problem for their own beliefs. They simply responded by saying, "We are right, and they disagree with us, so they are wrong, and that's the end of that." Some people still take that line. (And there are people who wouldn't dream of taking that line about religion who don't hesitate to take that line about other things, such as politics.)

However, we are past the time when we can take this line in good faith. Ever since the much-maligned Enlightenment, the perception of the world in the West has changed irreversibly. People gave up the idea that each of us can treat our own point of view as epistemically privileged just because it is our own. The story of why we did that is interesting because I think it combines an important advance in human sensibilities with at least one philosophical mistake. An important assumption governing much of Enlightenment philosophy is intellectual egalitarianism, a position endorsed by John Locke.[1] The idea is that all normal human beings are roughly equal in the capacity to get knowledge. Aside from the fact that some have acquired greater expertise or have greater access to information in some fields, there are no epistemic elites. Given this assumption, I am not being epistemically honest if I treat my own viewpoint as privileged. Locke combined his egalitarianism with optimism about the human ability to get knowledge, but there is a pessimistic interpretation that also comes from the Enlightenment. We could think of subjective points of view as equally bad ways to get the truth. All of them are limited and distorted, so it does no good to replace your own perspective with someone else's, equally limited and distorted. Notoriously, the Enlightenment enshrined the perspective of the impartial observer, a being without culture or history or personal preferences. But we also know that many disagreements in belief cannot be resolved from such a perspective. If a conflict in belief can be resolved neither from the impartial perspective nor from the point of view of the disputants, and if I accept epistemic egalitarianism, I have to admit that my belief is no more likely to be true than the belief of my opponent. A conscientious believer finds this bothersome. Let me call this the Enlightenment worry: *Irresolvable disagreement over a belief threatens the conscientiousness of the belief.*

The Enlightenment worry is unstable for at least two reasons. One is that conscientiousness in belief has two aspects, only one of which is expressed in the worry over irresolvable disagreement. If we think disagreement threatens the conscientiousness of our beliefs, it is because we think that disagreement makes our own beliefs less likely to be true, and we might think we can escape the perceived threat to the truth of our belief if we withhold belief—neither believe nor disbelieve. But if we do that, we violate another demand of conscientiousness. A conscientious believer not only wants the beliefs she has to be true, she also wants to acquire beliefs in the domains she cares about as conscientiously as she can. To deny ourselves beliefs in important domains denies us important elements of a desirable life. People who do not have beliefs in important domains, who turn away from ultimate questions, tend to be shallow people. So one source of the instability of the Enlightenment worry is that it reflects one of the demands of conscientious belief but not the other.

There is another problem with the Enlightenment worry. The truth is, most of us are not epistemic egalitarians, and we would be hard pressed to defend egalitarianism if we wanted to. In particular, I don't think many of us worry about disagreements with people whom we do not admire. If you believe acts of terrorism or genocide are wrong (by whatever definition you want), I doubt that you think the conscientiousness of your belief is threatened when you find out there are people who disagree, even though you are not likely to resolve the conflict by talking it over with them. If you think that it is a bad idea to devote your life primarily to acquiring money and fame, I doubt that it will bother you to find out that there are people who think the contrary. Nor should it. What really bothers us, I think, is that we recognize admirable people among those who believe differently than we do about certain things and we observe that the beliefs of different exemplars conflict with each other. The exemplars I have in mind are people who have a sense of the importance of certain domains of life and the beliefs needed to sustain those domains, and who are epistemically admirable in the way they believe as well as in the way they act.[2]

This version of the disagreement worry is also modern because sympathetic contact between people of different cultures has occurred on a large scale only in the last few hundred years. That experience, I think, is much more important than the Enlightenment principles that allegedly threaten the conscientiousness of our beliefs. When we have direct and sympathetic contact with people of another culture, it is almost impossible not to notice that many of them are as admirable as the most admirable people in our own culture. So my position is that it is not irresolvable disagreement per se that causes a problem. What really worries us is irresolvable disagreement among people whom we admire and between people we admire and ourselves.

This form of the problem would not be threatening unless we ought to trust our emotion of admiration, and I think that we not only ought to but have no choice but to do so. But to explain that, let me turn to some observations about self-trust.

Self-Trust

Richard Foley argues in his book *Intellectual Trust in Oneself and Others* that any normal, nonskeptical life will have to include a significant degree of self-trust in our intellectual faculties, procedures, and opinions.[3] The reason is that any defense of our most fundamental faculties and opinions will make use of those same faculties and opinions, so there are no non-question-begging guarantees of our own reliability. For example, we test our memory by perception, we test one perception by another perception, we test much of what we believe by consulting other people, so we use beliefs about them to test other beliefs, and so on. There is no way to get out of the circle of our faculties and opinions to test the reliability of the opinions and faculties in the circle.

Foley prefaces his observation about the need for self-trust with the claim that there is no answer to the radical skeptic and that the project of classical foundationalism has failed. The proper reaction to that, he says, is to accept it and to acknowledge the consequence that intellectual inquiry always involves a substantial element of trust in our own faculties and the opinions they generate. But I think we need not accept Foley's contention that there is no answer to the radical skeptic to agree with his view on the need for self-trust. There are many kinds and degrees of skepticism. No matter what you think of global skepticism, we are still left with concerns about the reliability of our faculties and the trustworthiness of our beliefs, and Foley's point about the lack of noncircular tests for our reliability seems to me to be justified independently of his views on global skepticism.

Foley gives an interesting argument that self-trust logically commits us to trust in others. He begins by defining three positions with respect to epistemic trust, each of which has an ethical analogue (85–89).[4] The first is *epistemic universalism*. According to the epistemic universalist, *the fact that someone else has a belief gives me some reason to believe it*. That reason may be outweighed by other reasons; nonetheless, the fact that another person has a certain belief is a mark in favor of its credibility. The ethical analogue is the position that the interests and goals of other persons always count morally for me. Again, they can be outweighed by some other value, but they should always count in my deliberations.

What Foley calls egoists and egotists reject universalism. The *epistemic egoist* maintains that *the fact that someone else has a belief can be a reason for me to believe it, but only if I have evidence that the person is reliable, that is, I have evidence that her beliefs will further my desire for the truth*. So I may believe what another person believes on her say-so, but only because I have information that her beliefs are reliably calibrated with truth in the domain in which she is making the claim.

This view also has an ethical analogue. The ethical egoist says, *I may care about the interests of others, but only when I adopt their interests as my own interests*. The egoist insists that I am under no obligation to care about somebody else's interests and that I am not irrational if I do not. But sometimes I take an interest in their interests. Similarly, the epistemic egoist says that I am not irrational if I pay no attention to what another person believes, but sometimes I see for myself that what she believes serves my interest in getting the truth because I see for myself that she is reliable. So notice that for both kinds of egoist I have no reason to pay attention to what others say or to their interests unless I see that what they say serves my interests; I see (or decide) that their interests are my interests.

The most extreme position identified by Foley is *epistemic egotism* (86). Epistemic egotists maintain that *it is never rational to grant credibility to the opinions of others simply because it is their opinion*. The only legitimate way for someone else to influence my beliefs is through Socratic demonstration. Anyone who wants to convince me of her belief must demonstrate to me that, given what I already believe, her opinion is one I ought to adopt, but it is never reasonable for me to believe what she believes on her say-so.

This is the analogue of ethical egotism, the view that I should not adopt the interests of others as my interests just because they are their interests. If I act in the interest of others, that is because my interests and theirs happen to coincide, but the mere fact that something is in their interests ought to play no part in my deliberations. Similarly, the epistemic egotist says that I might believe what somebody else believes, but the fact that she believes it ought to play no part in my reasons for believing it.

Now Foley argues that self-trust makes both epistemic egoism and epistemic egotism incoherent. Because of the social construction of belief, if we have basic trust in our own opinions and intellectual faculties, we cannot coherently withhold trust from others because insofar as the opinions of others have shaped our own opinions, we would not be reliable unless they are. And this trust is not limited to people who preceded us historically. If our contemporaries were shaped by many of the same conditions that shaped us, then on pain of inconsistency, if I trust myself, I should trust them.

But Foley does not stop there. He argues that even though we tend to be fascinated with differences between people and we like to exaggerate them, there are many more commonalities than differences in human faculties and environment. In fact, the similarities extend to people all over the world at all times. So the fact that some person somewhere at some time has a certain belief gives me *some* reason to believe it myself, given that I have trust in myself and I am relevantly similar to them. Self-trust therefore commits me to universalism (103), but notice that Foley assumes epistemic egalitarianism to get the conclusion. Self-trust, together with epistemic egalitarianism, requires me to accept epistemic universalism. The conclusion is that given that I have reason to believe that someone else believes P, I have at least a weak reason to believe P myself. I do not need to know anything special about the reliability of the person (105). Self-trust commits me to trust others unless I have reason to think they are unreliable. I need special reason not to trust them. I do not need special reason to trust them.

Now suppose that I have a belief that conflicts with the belief of another. Foley argues that my belief defeats the belief of the other person because by my lights the other person has been unreliable (108). Since it is trust in myself that creates in me a presumption of trust in another, then unless I have evidence that the other person is more reliable than I am (e.g., the other person is a medical specialist and I am not), my trust in that other is defeated by my trust in myself. Notice first that the

Self-Trust and the Diversity of Religions 33

fact that someone else has a belief that conflicts with one of mine is not evidence that the other person is unreliable. After all, it is only a single case. But more importantly, notice that Foley's treatment of the conflict case makes him an epistemic egoist in such cases, although he does not say that in his book. In order to trust the other person, I need evidence that he is more reliable than I am, but I do not need evidence that I am more reliable than he is in order to trust myself. That is epistemic egoism. Yet according to his own argument, I would not be reliable unless the other was.[5]

Foley says nothing about religion in his book, but we can easily apply his points to religious belief. The *religious epistemic egoist* would be a person who accepts no religious belief on the word of another. He expects a demonstration of the existence of God that uses premises he accepts himself, and he will accept the beliefs of a particular religion only if the same conditions can be satisfied for each doctrine of the religion. It is very unlikely that these conditions can be satisfied by any religion. Theism might satisfy these conditions for some people and atheism for others, whereas still others will be convinced neither by arguments for atheism nor by arguments for theism and will become agnostic. Either religious epistemic egotism puts the agnostic in the position of caring very much about a domain about which he does not have conscientiously acquired beliefs, thereby violating one of the demands of conscientiousness I mentioned earlier, or perhaps more likely, it leads him to cease to care. I suspect that many contemporary atheists and agnostics satisfy this definition of a religious epistemic egotist.

The less extreme *religious epistemic egoist* will accept religious beliefs on the word of another provided that there is good evidence of the reliability of the source. John Locke is an epistemic egoist about belief in Christianity. Locke defines revelation as a communication from God, and faith as the acceptance of beliefs in the word of God.[6] He says we have good evidence that the Gospels are a communication from God, given the miracles performed by Jesus. We have reason to believe the miracles occurred in the same way that we have reason to believe testimony about other historical occurrences. Miracles are evidence that the source of the teachings of Jesus is divine and hence is reliable.

For the egoist, belief in particular Christian teachings does not require demonstration of the content of the revelation, as it does for the egotist. But reason judges whether something *is* a revelation—that is, whether it is reliable. And Locke allows that it can be rational to believe a revelation even when the content is improbable. He says that improbable content is to be expected, since revelation is about matters above the limit of our faculties to attain on our own, such as the revelation that the angels rebelled against God.

I think Foley is correct that epistemic egotism and epistemic egoism are not coherent positions, given that we have self-trust, and his argument applies to religious epistemic egotism and egoism. I think this is an interesting consequence because both positions are so common. But given Foley's egalitarianism, the only option left is universalism, so the position to which we are committed by self-trust, according to Foley's argument, is religious epistemic universalism. The *religious epistemic universalist* would grant prima facie credence to the religious beliefs of all other persons.

I find Foley's approach to self-trust generally helpful, but unfortunately I don't think it is helpful in giving the conscientious believer guidance in cases of conflict. For people who already have religious beliefs (or antireligious beliefs), self-trust means that my own belief trumps the belief of others, assuming I am being careful. I assume they are unreliable because they disagree with me, and as I've said, this view reduces to epistemic egotism. Furthermore, I think it is too much like the "I'm right so they must be wrong" view that I've said we can no longer support.

What about cases in which a person is agnostic in religious matters? In that case Foley's position also is not very helpful because the agnostic can't choose between conflicting religious beliefs without evidence of the relative reliability of one group over another—atheists, deists, Christians, Buddhists, et cetera—in order to adjudicate the conflict, and she's not likely to get that. So Foley's approach is not helpful whether or not a person already has religious beliefs. Still, I think a closer look at self-trust reveals something interesting about both the source of the worry over religious diversity and the way a person who trusts herself ought to proceed.

Emotional Self-Trust and Conflict

In my judgment Foley is right that any nonskeptical intellectual life must include a substantial amount of self-trust in whatever aspects of ourselves produce or support our beliefs. What those aspects are depends upon the nature of the self, and what you think that is is one of the things you need to trust. Foley limits the aspects of the self that are relevant to epistemic self-trust to cognitive and perceptual faculties and a set of beliefs one already has, but I think they must include more than that. Foley does not mention emotions, but I think we must trust our emotions for the same reason we must trust our perceptual faculties, memory, and beliefs. Emotion dispositions can be reliable or unreliable, and particular emotions may fit or not fit their objects. But we can't tell whether our emotion dispositions are reliable without using those same dispositions in conjunction with our other faculties. How can we tell whether our disposition to pity is reliably directed at the pitiful, whether our disposition to disgust is reliably directed toward the disgusting, whether we reliably fear the fearsome or admire the admirable, without appealing to further emotions? We trust what we think we see when we take a hard look in good environmental conditions, and if others agree we take that as confirmation. Similarly, we trust what we feel when we feel admiration or pity or revulsion, and we take the agreement of others as confirmation. So the grounds for trusting our emotions are parallel to the grounds for trusting our perceptions and memory.

Emotions are the ground of many beliefs that lead to action, so trust in those beliefs depends upon trusting an emotion. Fear of a situation grounds the belief that I ought to escape. Compassion for a person grounds the belief that we ought to give her aid. Respect for a person grounds the belief that we should not treat her in certain ways, and so on. So the self-trust we need in order to act requires trust in beliefs that depend upon trust in emotions. If epistemic self-trust includes trust in the beliefs that ground action, then epistemic self-trust requires emotional self-trust. It follows that to live a normal, nonskeptical life we need to trust our emotions as well as our faculties, procedures, and beliefs. Our emotions are therefore within the set of faculties, procedures, and beliefs whose reliability we need to depend upon but whose reliability we cannot test in a noncircular way.

Foley says that we need to trust the beliefs we have that we acquired at some time in the distant past that we can't remember. And he concludes from that that we must trust the people from whom we acquired those beliefs. But more follows from that observation as well. Many beliefs are not just passed along from one person to the next like a virus.

Beliefs are embedded in traditions from which we both acquire and learn how to interpret the beliefs, so trusting those beliefs commits me to trusting the traditions from which I acquired them. If I am a little slice of history, trusting myself commits me to trusting the longer span of history of which I am a part. So one modification I want to make to Foley's line of reasoning about self-trust is to extend it in two ways. In addition to trusting our faculties, procedures, and beliefs, we need emotional self-trust, and we need trust in traditions and historical institutions from which we acquire our beliefs and learn how to interpret our experience.

To trust an emotion means to have confidence that the emotion is appropriate for the circumstances. In my theory of emotion *an emotion is an affective state whose intentional object is seen as falling under a distinctive thick affective concept,* so pity is feeling pity for someone seen as pitiful, love is loving someone seen as lovable, contempt is feeling contempt for someone seen as contemptible, reverence is revering what is seen as sacred, admiration is admiring someone seen as admirable.[7] The admirable cannot be understood apart from the feeling that is a component of the emotion of admiration, but we can say something about the admirable. I think it is something like the imitably attractive. We feel a positive emotion toward the person we admire that would lead to imitating the person given the right practical conditions. To trust the emotion of admiration, then, means to have confidence that it is appropriate to feel the kind of attraction and desire to imitate that is intrinsic to admiration.

Notice, however, that even though self-trust is a crucial part of any nonskeptical life, we do not trust ourselves equally all the time, and this applies both to our beliefs and to our emotions. Suppose that I give up in adulthood a belief I had as a child. I think the later belief is better than the earlier one. Similarly, if I have a different emotion in a certain situation in adulthood than I had as a child, I think the later emotion is more appropriate. I believe that my older self is more trustworthy than my younger self, and I believe *that* primarily because I trust my older self more than my younger self. There are defenses for this attitude, but the defenses also require self-trust. For example, we might think that other things being equal, greater experience is more trustworthy than less experience, but that also is not something for which we have a noncircular defense.

I also trust some of my current beliefs more than others. I trust the beliefs I have when carefully reflecting, considering open-mindedly contrary views, treating opponents fairly, and not indulging in strong emotional reactions that tend to distort beliefs into extremes. So I trust beliefs arising from my intellectual virtues and not those arising from vices. It is probably true that I have a better track record of getting the truth when my beliefs are formed in the virtuous ways I've mentioned rather than in vicious ways, but there is still no noncircular way for me to tell that the virtuously formed beliefs are the reliable ones. That is because my final decision about what the truth is in some cases is determined by what I believe when I'm being as virtuous as I can.[8]

I trust some of my emotions more than others for the same reason I trust some of my beliefs more than others. I trust the ones that are stable, do not change upon reflection, and do not arise from vices. Again, there is no noncircular way to tell that the virtuously formed and stable emotions are the trustworthy ones, since I need emotions to tell whether a previous emotion was trustworthy.

But if there are no noncircular grounds for trusting some of my beliefs and emotions more than others, why do I trust myself more in some circumstances than in others? The answer, I think, is that I admire myself more when I am behaving in an intellectually virtuous way than when I am not. Self-admiration is not an emotion we are comfortable with, and I hesitate to use the term because of its connotations of vanity and conceit,[9] but I think it is fairly obvious that if we are capable of admiring and not admiring others, we are capable of admiring and not admiring ourselves. We trust ourselves more in some of our beliefs than in others because we admire the way we came to believe some of our beliefs more than others. Again I want to make it clear that I do not treat my intellectual virtues as evidence that I am admirable and have grounds for trusting myself. Being trustworthy is not something I infer about myself in a noncircular way, nor is being admirable.

Now if I am consistent, I admire the way some people form some of their beliefs more than I admire the way I form some of my beliefs, so consistency requires me to trust the beliefs of others formed in these ways more than my own when my own are not admirable. So self-trust commits me to trusting more than myself those who are more admirable than myself, who have the traits I trust in myself in a greater degree than I have myself.

This means we must reject intellectual egalitarianism. We know that there are people who are generally more virtuous than others in epistemic behavior. So my trust is not universal, and its nonuniversality is based on the way I treat trust in myself. And this explains why I do not trust those who are not admirable. I do not trust the beliefs of terrorists about terrorism, not because I have evidence of their unreliability, but because I don't admire them. The difference between those we trust intellectually and those we do not cannot be explained by the fact that we have evidence of the reliability of the admirable and the unreliability of the nonadmirable. So the position I am endorsing is not a form of epistemic egoism.

I think, then, that Foley is right that epistemic egotism and egoism are incompatible with self-trust, but epistemic egalitarianism, which Foley uses to support epistemic universalism, must be rejected. So I differ from Foley's position in two further respects. First, I think that self-trust leads to trusting the people I admire more than the people I do not admire and that the difference does not rest upon the fact that I have evidence of the greater reliability of the former. Second, I maintain that self-trust commits me to trusting some other people more than myself. I am forced to these conclusions by trusting my own emotion of admiration.

Now let us return to conflict in beliefs. Suppose that I trust my emotion of admiration of some person more than I trust a given belief I have. Maybe I do not admire the way I formed my own belief as much as I admire the way the other person formed hers. And suppose the other person's belief conflicts with mine, and I am not aware of another person I admire just as much whose belief agrees with mine. Self-trust would lead me to trust the admired person's belief more than my own. If I am able to imitate the admired person by adopting her belief without changing anything else about myself that I trust even more than I trust my admiration for her, then self-trust should lead me to change my belief. For example, suppose that I hastily form a belief about a recently published book without reading it and then become aware of a contrary opinion about the book by an acquaintance whose intellectual judgment I admire and who has clearly made a more careful study of the book than I have. If I am not aware of anyone else I admire just as much whose opinion agrees with mine, and if I can change my belief without changing anything else about myself that I trust more than I trust the judgment of my acquaintance, then I probably should change my belief.

This seems to me the right thing to do for beliefs that are not deeply embedded in the self. I think, then, that Foley is mistaken in saying that self-trust will always lead me to decide a conflict between my belief and the belief of another in favor of my own.

But even if I trust my admiration for another person more than I trust my belief, it does not always follow that I should change it. Whether I should change a belief is determined not simply by how much I trust the belief itself but by how much I trust the other aspects of myself that I would have to change if I changed the belief. Foley emphasizes the social construction of belief, but as I've pointed out, that commits me to trusting much more than the individual persons from whom I learned the belief. To trust myself commits me to trusting the traditions that shape me and the institutions on which I depend. Religious beliefs are usually connected with an entire network of other beliefs as well as religious emotions, experiences, communal loyalties, and connections with many other admirable people, all of which I trust. Admiration is an emotion that leads me to imitate the admirable person in suitable circumstances, but often the circumstances are not suitable. So I can admire the belief system of a Hindu without the inclination to adopt that system for myself.

Suppose, however, that I trust my admiration for the Hindu more than I trust the aspects of myself I would have to change if I imitated the Hindu by adopting her religion. I still might not imitate her because it might not be possible. Just as I can admire an Olympic swimmer without the slightest inclination to imitate her, I can admire a devout Hindu without the inclination to imitate, and the reason is the same in both cases: I can't do it. But some people can. It *is* possible to convert to another religion, and I would not accept any position on religious diversity that rules out conversion for the conscientious believer.

If I convert to Hinduism, there is a sense in which I can imitate the devout Hindu and a sense in which I cannot because what one converts to is never what one sees when one admires an exemplar from a radically different culture. When I see an admirable person with a very different belief system, I see an alternate self. I don't mean that *that* person is an alternate self. Rather, I mean that I know that if I had met that person at an early age, I might have imitated her because then I might have trusted her more than I trusted my conflicting beliefs. If so, I would be a very different person today. And even now becoming an alternate self is still an option through conversion. So respect for admirable others in other religions includes recognition of an alternate self. This forever changes the way I relate to them. But I only get one life. I might respect the self I could have been, but it does not follow that I should now try to become that self. I *might* trust my alternate Hindu self more than my present self, in which case I should convert, but given the nature of self-trust, we would expect conversion on that scale to be rare, and I am arguing that that is perfectly compatible with conscientiousness.

In a situation in which a choice whether to convert is made, some element of self-trust becomes the bottom line—that to which we refer in adjudicating between those elements of ourselves that pull us one way and those that pull in another direction. Lee Yearley gives a brief but moving account of this process in himself while contemplating an enormous Buddha and imagining what it would be like to become a Buddhist. Yearley writes: "I could imagine attempting to incarnate the excellences I saw in the Sokkurum Buddha that morning in Korea. I admired them, they tempted me, and I believe I could have chosen them and remained myself. But I did not want to choose them, and I hoped that those about whom I most care would not choose them."[10]

Notice Yearley does not say he didn't want to become a Buddhist because he thinks his Christian beliefs are true and Buddhist beliefs are false. Presumably, he *did* think that, but that is not sufficient to explain why he would not become a Buddhist. As long as it was possible for him to change his beliefs, given his admiration for another religion, imitation of that religion was possible. And Yearley might have been conscientious if he did become a Buddhist on that morning in Korea. If his admiration for Buddhism had been strong enough and he had trusted it more than the other aspects of himself he would have had to change if he became a Buddhist, I think he would have been a conscientious believer. But he didn't change, and his reason seems to me not only to show a high degree of self-knowledge but also to give us a hint about how self-trust often operates. He genuinely admires Buddhism, but he does not like the self he would become if he converted to Buddhism, nor does he want those he loves the most to adopt such a self. He does not try to find some *reason* to reject Buddhism in either its doctrines or its way of life. I am assuming that he has already thought through the reasons and still admires Buddhism. The bottom line is that he doesn't *like* himself as a Buddhist. He trusts that emotion, and not only do I think that he can be conscientious in doing so, but I've tried to show that he has few other options. Whatever he does, there will be some element of the self to which he defers in a situation of this kind.

The problem of this paper is therefore a conflict that arises within self-trust. I trust my admiration of others and my other emotions, and I trust the aspects of myself from which I gain my beliefs and the traditions that support them. I think this conflict produces a genuine problem of religious diversity. In contrast, the problem that arises from an assumption of intellectual egalitarianism seems to me to be much less threatening because I have less reason to trust egalitarianism than to trust my emotions. So I am not much taken with the well-known argument that says, "Other people are as well placed to get the truth as we are. There is an irresolvable conflict between their beliefs and ours. Hence, we have no more reason to think our beliefs are true than that their beliefs are true." This is what I called the Enlightenment worry. What I do take seriously is the admiration I have for alternate ways of life and the beliefs that go with them. I may have full confidence in my beliefs, emotions, and their sources in the traditions that shape me, and I am conscientious in doing so. But as long as I trust my emotion of admiration and admiration includes the urge to imitate, conversion is also compatible with conscientiousness, and the diversity of religions will put some people in the position of making a choice, a position that puts those aspects of themselves they trust the most in the forefront of their consciousness.

Admiration may not require me to change my beliefs, but it adds something to the dialogue between people with conflicting religious beliefs that did not exist in the premodern era. What it adds, I think, is the feeling that I *would* imitate them if I had grown up with a different social construction of the self. That prevents me from taking the line "We're right, so they're wrong, and that's the end of that." Of course, we think we're right, but there's more to be said. Respect for others comes from trusting that we *are* right in the admiration we have for many people who have very different beliefs, and *that* logically requires us to think of them as like the self we could have been if we had been raised in a different way.

Admiration is a tricky emotion. On the one hand, it is of central importance to the moral life because most of what we learn is by imitation, and admiration is the emotion we use to distinguish those who are worthy of imitation from those who are not. But admiration raises the problem of the boundaries of the self. We would not want to imitate every admirable person in every way they are admirable, even if it were possible, which it isn't. There is a domain of the self that does not respond by imitation even when the admiration is genuine. Many of our central beliefs are in that domain. The problem of conflict between our own beliefs and the beliefs of those we admire reflects the complexity of admiration. We *are* inclined to imitate the admirable beliefs of others, but we are also right to know the difference between being as admirable as *we* can be and trying to become another person.

Notes

1. John Locke, *An Essay Concerning Human Understanding*. See Nicholas Wolterstorff, *John Locke and the Ethics of Belief* (Cambridge: Cambridge University Press, 1996), for a recent interpretation of Locke's epistemology.

2. I have argued elsewhere that the ability to sense the important affects the ethics of belief and blurs the lines between moral and intellectual exemplars. See "Epistemic Value and the Primacy of What We Care About," *Philosophical Papers* 33 (November 2004): 353–77.

3. Richard Foley, *Intellectual Trust in Oneself and Others* (Cambridge University Press, 2001), 99. All further citations to this work are made parenthetically in the text.

4. The ethical analogues play no role in either Foley's argument or mine, but I mention them because they are interesting.

5. Foley has said in conversation that he has changed his mind about the conflict situation.

6. *Essay Concerning Human Understanding*, bk. 4, ch. 19, "Faith and Reason." See also Locke's *Discourse of Miracles*.

7. For a fuller account of this theory of emotion, see my "Emotion and Moral Judgment," *Philosophy and Phenomenological Research* 66 (2003): 104–24, and *Divine Motivation Theory* (Cambridge: Cambridge University Press, 2004), ch. 2.

8. I am not suggesting that truth is *defined* as what I believe when I am being as careful as I can.

9. An alternate is *self-approval*, but that term does not capture the aspect of a tendency to imitate, which I think is included in admiration. We want to imitate our better selves as well as admirable others.

10. Lee Yearley, "Conflicts among Ideals of Human Flourishing," in *Prospects for a Common Morality*, ed. Gene Outka and John P. Reeder Jr. (Princeton: Princeton University Press, 1993), p. 247.

Two

An Epistemology That Matters

Richard Foley

The two most fundamental questions for an epistemology are, what is involved in having good reasons to believe a claim, and what is involved in meeting the higher standard of knowing that a claim is true? The theory of justified belief tries to answer the former, whereas the theory of knowledge addresses the latter.

The history of epistemology, however, can in large part be read as a history of trying to establish that there is a necessary connection between the answers to these two questions. A traditional view is that justified beliefs are ones arrived at using an appropriate methodology and that use of an appropriate methodology produces knowledge. Descartes, for example, argued that one is justified in believing that which one clearly and distinctly understands, and that if one restricts oneself to such beliefs, one can be assured of knowledge. Locke had an only slightly less optimistic position. He asserted that one is justified in relying on one's reason and the evidence of one's senses, and that provided one's opinions conform to one's reason and sensory evidence, most of one's beliefs will be instances of knowledge.

Neither Descartes nor Locke, however, could find a way of keeping justified belief and knowledge cemented to one another without invoking God. Descartes maintained that God would not permit us to be deceived about what we clearly understand, while for Locke the general reliability of our cognitive faculties is assured because they were created by God.

Contemporary epistemologists are reluctant to use theological assumptions to solve epistemological problems, but they are also reluctant to abandon the view that justification and knowledge are inextricably connected. So semantic stipulation has replaced theology as a way to ensure the connection. Knowledge is said by definition to involve justified belief.

On this view, the direction of the link is reversed from that sought by Descartes and other classical foundationalists. Having justified beliefs does not guarantee knowledge. The idea, rather, is that knowing P implies that one's belief P is justified, because knowledge by definition is a matter of having a true belief that is also justified.

My proposal, by contrast, is that at least at the beginning of the enterprise epistemologists should resist the temptation to assume any kind of necessary tie between justified belief and knowledge. The initial presupposition should rather be that the theories of justified belief and knowledge are distinct—separate and equal, as it were. It may well turn out that as the two theories are independently developed interesting connections between the concepts of justified belief and knowledge will emerge, but it should not be simply assumed from the start there is a simple, necessary link between them.

Relaxing the tie, moreover, is liberating. If knowledge is assumed to imply justified belief, the theory of knowledge is pressured either to pretend that people can always provide adequate intellectual justifications of what they know or to invent some kind of duly externalized notion of justified belief because the definition of knowledge is thought to require this.

The theory of justified belief is likewise liberated. If it is stipulated that the properties that make a belief justified must also be properties that turn true belief into a good candidate for knowledge, the concept of justified belief is placed in the service of the theory of knowledge and is thereby distanced from the everyday assessments we actually make of each other's opinions, which tend to focus on whether individuals have been appropriately careful and responsible in regulating their opinions rather than on whether they have satisfied the prerequisites of knowledge.

The presupposition that there is a necessary tie between knowledge and justified belief also does damage to the theory of rational belief. The concepts of rational and justified belief ought to be close cousins, but if justified belief is closely linked with knowledge, then rational belief will be linked with it as well. But the more closely rational belief is coupled with the prerequisites of knowledge, the more it tends to be separated from our ways of understanding the rationality of actions, decisions, strategies, plans, and the like, the result being that the rationality of beliefs is treated as if it were an entirely separate category from the rationality of other phenomena.

These are all regrettable outcomes. It ought to be possible to develop an approach to issues of justified and rational belief that makes these concepts relevant to the kinds of assessments of each other's opinions we make in our everyday lives and that also views them as not fundamentally different in kind from the concepts of rational actions, decisions, plans, strategies, and so on. In what follows, I will be outlining just such an approach, one that sets aside the presupposition that knowledge and justified belief are necessarily connected and in so doing reorients epistemology in new and beneficial ways.

A way into this approach is through the concept of rationality, understood as a goal-oriented notion. Whether the question is the rationality of actions, beliefs, decisions, intentions, plans, or strategies, what is at issue is the effective pursuit of goals.

Actual effectiveness is not, however, a necessary condition of rationality. What is rational can turn out badly. After all, in some situations no one might have been reasonably expected to foresee that the seemingly best option was likely to have unwelcome consequences. Considerations such as these suggest a general template of rationality: an action A (or decision, plan, intention, strategy, belief, etc.) is rational for a subject S if it is rational for S to believe that A would acceptably satisfy her goals.

An obvious drawback of this suggestion is that it makes reference to rational belief, thus leaving us within the circle of notions we wish to understand and, hence, without an adequate philosophical account of rationality. I will return to this drawback shortly. I need first to clarify a couple of other matters.

The first is that it is possible for an action to acceptably satisfy one's goals even if, of the available options, it is not the one that does the single most effective job of satisfying these goals. Something less than optimal may be good enough. As I am employing the concepts, reasonableness admits of degrees whereas rationality does not. In particular, reasonableness varies with the strengths of one's reasons, while the rational is that which is sufficiently reasonable. Thus, in some situations, more than one option meets the standard of being rational, even if some of these options are somewhat more reasonable than others.

To conclude that an action would acceptably satisfy one's goals is to make a judgment about its estimated desirability, which is a function of its probable effectiveness in promoting various goals and the relative importance of these goals.[1] Contextual factors are also relevant, however. The fewer alternatives there are with greater estimated desirabilities, the more likely it is that the action in question is rational, and if these alternatives are only marginally superior or are not readily accessible, it is all the more likely that the action is rational. It is rational because it is good enough, given the context.

A second clarification is that in assessing the effectiveness of an action (decision, plan, intention, strategy, belief, etc.), different kinds of goals can be taken into account. For example, if it is rational for S to believe that doing A would effectively promote her economic well-being, then A is rational at least in an economic sense. A can be rational in this economic sense, however, even if it is not rational all things considered because it does not do an acceptably good job in promoting the full range of S's goals, noneconomic as well as economic. There are, in other words, different kinds of rationality corresponding to different kinds of goals, and this suggests a further refinement of the general template of rationality: an action A (or decision, plan, intention, strategy, etc.) is rational in sense X for S if it is rational for S to believe that A will do an acceptably good job of satisfying her goals of type X.

Being clear about the kinds of goals, and hence the kinds of rationality, at issue is of particular importance when the questions concern the rationality of beliefs. When assessing someone's beliefs, we are typically not interested in the total constellation of his or her goals. Our interest, rather, is usually only in those that are distinctly intellectual. For example, when considering what it is rational for S to believe about some matter P, we as a rule would regard it as irrelevant that were S to believe P, it would make her feel more secure, which we can assume might be one of her goals. More notoriously, in assessing whether it might be rational for S to believe in God, we would be unlikely to join Pascal in regarding as relevant the possibility that S might increase her chances of salvation by having such a belief.

But why is this? Why do we ordinarily treat the potential practical benefits of belief as irrelevant in assessing what it is rational for someone to believe? On the face of it, this seems puzzling. What a person believes, like what she does or decides or intends, can have important consequences. Why shouldn't such consequences be taken into account in our assessments about what it is rational for her to believe? Yet our intellectual practice seems to dismiss these consequences as irrelevant.

I will return to this puzzle later and suggest an answer to it, but first, another distinction. In evaluating the rationality of beliefs, epistemologists have traditionally been concerned with not just any intellectual goal but rather a very specific one, that of now having beliefs that are both accurate and comprehensive.

There are interesting issues about how to balance appropriately the value of accuracy versus that of comprehensiveness, but I am going to pass over these issues in order to focus on another. Namely, the relevant goal is not to have accurate and comprehensive beliefs at some future time but rather to have such beliefs now. To understand the significance of characterizing the goal in this way, imagine that S's prospects for having accurate and comprehensive beliefs in a year's time would be enhanced by believing something for which S now lacks adequate evidence.

For example, suppose P is a more favorable assessment of S's intellectual talents than the evidence warrants, but suppose also that S's believing P would make her intellectually more confident, which would make her a more dedicated inquirer, which in turn would enhance her long-term prospects of having an accurate and comprehensive belief system. Despite these long-term intellectual benefits, there is an important sense of rational belief, indeed the very sense that traditionally has been of the most interest to epistemologists, in which it is not rational for S to believe P. One way of marking this distinction is to say that it is not rational for S in a purely epistemic sense to believe P, where this purely epistemic sense is to be understood in terms of the present-tense goal of now having accurate and comprehensive beliefs.

Foundationalists, coherentists, reliabilists, and others have different views about how best to explicate this notion of epistemically rational belief, but I am not going to try to adjudicate among these various views because what matters for purposes here is not their differences but rather something that they have in common. In particular, each account attempts to explicate the concept of epistemically rational belief without reference to any other concept of rationality. Foundationalists, for example, understand epistemic rationality in terms of basic beliefs and a set of deductive and probabilistic support relations by which other beliefs are supported by those that are basic. Moreover, foundationalists would view it a defect if they had to make use of some other notion of rationality (or a related notion, such as reasonability) in characterizing basicality or these support relations. Coherentists, on the other hand, try to explicate epistemic rationality in terms of a set of deductive and probabilistic relations among beliefs and a set of properties such as simplicity, conservativeness, and explanatory power, but they too would regard it as a flaw if their explication smuggled in a reference to a concept of rationality or a related concept. The same is true of other accounts of epistemically rational belief.

This point is of great importance for the general theory of rationality because it provides the theory with a potential escape route from circularity. In particular, the general template of rationality can be expressed using the concept of epistemically rational belief: an action A (decision, plan, intention, etc.) is rational in sense X for S just in case it is *epistemically rational* for S to believe that A will do an acceptably good job of satisfying goals of kind X.

Because accounts of epistemically rationally belief do not make use of any other notion of rationality or any of its close cognates, the template is now theoretically respectable. It makes no noneliminable reference to a concept of rationality. In effect, the concept of epistemically rational belief serves as a theoretical anchor for other concepts of rationality.

Of particular interest for epistemology is that epistemically rational belief potentially provides a theoretical anchor even for other concepts of rational belief. Let me explain.

According to the template, an action A (decision, plan, strategy, etc.) is rational in sense X if it is epistemically rational for S to believe that A will do an acceptably good job of satisfying goals of kind X. Recall that "X" can refer to all of S's goals or only a subset of them. This creates a risk of confusion. If, for instance, only economic goals are taken into consideration, it may be rational (in an economic sense) for S to do A, but if all of S's goals, both economic and noneconomic, are taken into consideration, it might not be not rational (all things considered) for S to do A.

These same possibilities for confusion arise when the issue is the rationality of beliefs. S's beliefs can be assessed in terms how well they promote the purely epistemic goal of now having accurate and comprehensive beliefs, but there is nothing in principle wrong with assessing them in terms of how well they promote the total constellation of S's goals. If it is epistemically rational for S to believe that believing P would effectively promote her overall constellation of goals, then it is rational for her to believe P, all things considered.

There are two kinds of rational belief being referred to here. The first is epistemically rational belief, which is defined in terms of the purely epistemic goal. The second is a notion of rational belief that is defined in terms of epistemically rational belief and S's total constellation of goals. With this distinction in hand, we can reformulate the puzzle I raised earlier in terms of the following question: Why do we so rarely evaluate beliefs in terms of this second notion?

Part of the solution is that our discussions and debates concerning what it is rational to believe usually take place in a context of trying to convince someone, perhaps even ourselves, to believe something. But insofar as our aim is to persuade, introducing nonepistemic goals is ordinarily ineffective.

Suppose that one of your goals is to be promoted but that you are skeptical about your chances. I am trying, however, to get you to believe that you are in fact going to be promoted. Even if I point out to you that you have strong pragmatic reasons to believe this claim (perhaps your nervousness about the promotion is adversely affecting your job performance, thus making the promotion less likely), this will ordinarily not be enough to convince you. By contrast, if I marshal evidence and information in support of the claim, belief often does follow.

Thus, insofar as we are interested in persuading someone to believe something, there is a straightforward explanation as to why we ordinarily are not concerned with pragmatic reasons for belief. Namely, it is normally pointless to cite them because they are not the kind of reasons that generate belief.

Similarly, in our own deliberations, we ordinarily do not consider what pragmatic reasons we might have for believing this rather than that, and the explanation is the same as in the third-person case. Deliberations concerning our pragmatic reasons for belief are ordinarily inefficacious and hence pointless. Hence, our practice is to ignore them.

There is a second and complementary explanation for why in general we do not deliberate about the pragmatic reasons we have for believing something. It is ordinarily redundant to do so, because ordinarily our overriding pragmatic reason is to develop and maintain an accurate and comprehensive overall stock of beliefs.

We are all constantly faced with the need to make an enormous number of decisions, and we usually do not know in advance the information we will need to make the full range of these decisions well. This might not be terribly important if, when faced with decisions, we had the opportunity to gather information and then deliberate in terms of it about which alternative is best, but ordinarily we do not. Most decisions have to be made without the luxury of extensive evidence gathering, consultations, or deliberations. We are instead forced to draw upon our existing stock of beliefs, and if that stock is either small or inaccurate, we increase the likelihood of making unfortunate decisions.

So ordinarily the beliefs that are likely to do the best overall job of promoting the total constellation of our goals are those that are both comprehensive and accurate. Only by having such beliefs are we likely to be able to fashion effective strategies for achieving our various goals. But then, since epistemically rational beliefs are by definition beliefs that are rational for us insofar as our goal is to have accurate and comprehensive beliefs, it is ordinarily rational, all things considered (that is, when all of our goals are taken into account), to believe those propositions that are epistemically rational for us. Thus, for all practical purposes, taking this phrase literally, we can usually safely ignore pragmatic reasons in our deliberations about what to believe.

To be sure, there are conceivable situations in which our epistemic reasons and our overall reasons for belief might be pulled apart. Pascal famously argued that belief in God is such an example, but it is not difficult to concoct nontheistic examples as well. If you are aware that a madman will kill your children unless you come to believe, and not merely act as if you believe, that the earth is flat, it is presumably rational for you to try to find a way, difficult as it may be, of getting yourself to believe this proposition.

In the vast majority of cases, however, the pragmatic benefits of belief are not nearly so powerful. So although what it is rational to believe, all things considered, in principle can be at odds with what it is epistemically rational to believe, in practice this is rare.

Nevertheless, pragmatic considerations do deeply influence what it is rational for one to believe—only they do so indirectly. In particular, the amount of time and effort it is reasonable to devote to acquiring accurate and comprehensive beliefs about an issue is largely determined by pragmatic considerations. In purchasing a laptop, for example, I will want to sort through information about various makes and models, but I need to decide how thoroughly to do so. Should I merely visit a computer store and rely on the salesperson, or should I in addition ask friends who are more expert than I, or should I study recent reviews in the literature, or all of the above? Similarly, if I am interested in how safe some prescription medicine is, I need to decide how much time to spend investigating the issue. Should I be content with the advice of my physician, or should I seek out a specialist, or should I go to the trouble of looking up articles in the relevant medical journals? And if it turns out that to understand these articles I need to brush up on my chemistry, should I do that?

The reasonable answer to such questions is a function of how important the issue is and how likely it is that additional effort on my part will improve my reliability. So it is not unusual for pragmatic considerations to influence what it is rational for us to believe, but they do so indirectly by determining the direction and extent of our intellectual endeavors. Within the confines of these endeavors, however, we regard it as irrelevant whether believing the claim in question would be useful. We are concerned only with its truth or likely truth.

Keeping these points in mind, consider again the concept of epistemic rationality. All of us have an enormous variety of ends, many of them overlapping but a number of them also in tension with one another. Epistemic rationality is concerned with only one of these ends, that of now having accurate and comprehensive beliefs. It is thus an idealized concept. No one is a purely intellectual being. On the other hand, its idealized character has advantages, one of the most important of which is that it makes the concept suitable to serve as a theoretical anchor for other concepts that are less idealized and hence potentially more relevant to our everyday intellectual concerns.

The complication is that the most straightforward way of introducing a derivative concept of rational belief is too crude to be of much relevance. According to the general template of rationality, it is rational, all things considered, for S to believe P if it is epistemically rational for her to believe that the overall effects of believing P are sufficiently beneficial. But it is rare, for the reasons already cited, for nonintellectual considerations to enter directly into our assessments of what we ourselves or others have reasons to believe. So if the concept of epistemic rationality is to anchor a derivative concept that is relevant for our everyday intellectual assessments of each other's beliefs, it has to do so in a subtler, more indirect way.

An initial step toward such an anchoring is to note that our everyday evaluations of each other's beliefs are reason-saturated. We tend to be interested in whether, in forming her beliefs about a topic, S has been *reasonably* thorough in gathering evidence and then *reasonably* thorough in sorting through and deliberating about this evidence. The standards of reasonability at work in these assessments are realistic ones. They reflect the fact that we all have nonintellectual interests, goals, and needs that constrain the amount of time and effort it is appropriate to devote to investigating an issue. Only a concept that is sensitive to such questions of resource allocation is capable of capturing the spirit of these everyday evaluations. I will be arguing that justified belief is just such a concept, only as I understand it, the concept is closely associated with responsible believing rather than with what is required to turn true belief into knowledge.

Justifiably believing a proposition is a matter of its being rational, all things considered, for one to have acquired (and subsequently retained) the belief. More precisely, again using the general template of rationality, S justifiably believes P if it is epistemically rational for S to believe that her procedures with respect to P have been acceptable: that is, acceptable given the limitations on her time and capacities and given all of her goals.

Justified belief, so understood, is sensitive to the fact that having accurate and comprehensive beliefs about some topics is not especially important and thus that it would be inappropriate to spend significant time and effort gathering information and thinking about them. About other topics, by contrast, it is terribly important to have accurate and comprehensive beliefs, and accordingly it is also appropriate to devote considerable time and effort in investigating and thinking about them.

The standards of justified belief thus vary with the importance of the issue. High importance translates into demanding standards; low importance into less demanding standards.

Accordingly, S can have justified beliefs about some topics even if she has spent little or no time gathering evidence or deliberating about them. Indeed, she can have justified beliefs even if she is in the possession of information that, had she reflected upon it, would have convinced her that what she believes is incorrect. This is one of the ways in which justified belief and epistemically rational belief can diverge. Even if S has evidence that makes it epistemically irrational to believe P, she may justifiably believe P because, given the unimportance of the topic, it would have been inappropriate for her to have taken the time and effort to sift through and think about this evidence.

The core intuition here is that having justified beliefs requires one to be responsible, but being responsible does not necessarily require one to go to extraordinary lengths in trying to discover the truth about an issue. More exactly, it does not require this unless the issue itself is extraordinarily important. When weighty issues are stake, it takes more to be a responsible believer, and hence the standards of justified belief are correspondingly higher. Indeed, they can be more stringent than those of epistemically rational belief. If, for example, having inaccurate opinions about some matter would put people's lives at risk, one should conduct especially thorough investigations before settling on an opinion. If one fails to do so, the resulting beliefs will not be justified, but they might still be epistemically rational. This is possible because epistemically rational belief does not require certainty, even moral certainty, whereas moral certainty sometimes is required for being a responsible believer.

The intellectual standards one must meet in order to have justified beliefs vary not only with the importance of the topic but also with one's social role. If it is S's job but not R's to keep safety equipment in good working order, the intellectual demands upon S are more stringent than those upon R. R's belief that the equipment is in good working order might be justified even if he has done little investigation of the matter. He need not have tested the equipment, for example. A cursory look might suffice for R, but this won't do for S. It would be irresponsible for her not to conduct tests of the equipment, and thus the standards of justified belief are higher for her.

One's social role can be relevant even when the issue at hand is primarily of theoretical interest. If S is an accountant and R is a geologist, S's justifiably believing in continental drift is likely to be a very different matter from R's justifiably believing this. S's familiarity with the issue may derive exclusively from popular science writing, and this kind of information may well be sufficient for her belief to be responsible. No more can be reasonably expected. On the other hand, much more is reasonably expected of the authorities themselves. They are part of a community of inquirers with special intellectual responsibilities. Thus, to have responsible beliefs about continental drift, they presumably need to have a working knowledge of the larger theory of plate tectonics and the fossil evidence for the theory.

In these and other ways, nonepistemic ends help determine what one justifiably believes, but not in the way Pascal envisioned. The idea is not they give one good reasons to believe a proposition for which one lacks adequate evidence. Rather, they define the extent of evidence gathering and processing that it is reasonable to engage in. They thus shape what it is justified for one to believe in an indirect rather than a direct way. They impose constraints on inquiry, but subject to these constraints the aim is to determine which beliefs are true, not which ones are useful.

One of the major virtues of this approach to epistemology is that epistemically rational belief and justified belief both become parts of a philosophically respectable, general theory of rationality. At the heart of the theory is a template: an action A (decision, plan, strategy, or whatever) is rational in sense X for S if it is epistemically rational for S to believe that A will do an acceptably good job of satisfying her goals of type X. This template is altogether general. It can be used to distinguish different kinds of rationality, for example, economic rationality and rationality-all-things-considered, and it can be used to understand the rationality of different kinds of phenomena, for example, the rationality of decisions as well the rationality of strategies and plans.

Even epistemically rational belief can be represented by the template. Inserting the purely epistemic goal into the template for "goals of type X" results in the following: Believing P is rational in an epistemic sense if it is epistemically rational for S to believe that believing P would acceptably contribute to the epistemic goal of S's now having accurate and comprehensive beliefs. This instantiation of the template is tautological, but for the sake of the generality of schema, this is just what is called for. It ensures that every belief that satisfies the requirements of epistemically rational belief will also be an instance of the general schema, where the relevant goal is that of now having accurate and comprehensive beliefs.

So the template is altogether general, and because the concept of epistemically rational belief, which the template uses as an anchor, is explicated without reference to any other concept of rationality, it is also philosophically respectable. As such, it can be used to understand various, derivative concepts, and among the most important of these, I have been arguing, is a concept of justified belief that is closely aligned with responsible believing. Understanding justified belief in this way has the additional advantage of making the concept of justified belief closely analogous with the concepts of justified behavior, decisions, plans, and so on.

The result is a cluster of overlapping concepts that are both theoretically respectable and capable of giving expression to the everyday concerns we have in evaluating our own and each other's beliefs. These concerns tend to focus not on whether we have met all the prerequisites of knowledge but rather on whether we are reasonably careful, reasonably cautious, and reasonably thorough in our opinions, where the standards of reasonability can vary from one situation to another and from one belief to another. This is the beginning of an epistemology that matters.[2]

Notes

I first began to develop the ideas of this essay while participating in an epistemology working group that met regularly during the 1980s at the University of Notre Dame. Phil Quinn was a core member of the group along with Mike DePaul, Marian David, Aron Edidin, and Al Plantinga. The meetings of that group were paradigms of philosophical discussions, and Phil was one of the principal reasons why.

1. The expression *estimated desirability* is Richard Jeffrey's; see *The Logic of Decision*, 2nd ed. (Chicago: University of Chicago Press, 1983).

2. This paper reworks the arguments in Richard Foley, "The Foundational Role of Epistemology in a General Theory of Rationality," in *Virtue Epistemology*, ed. L. Zagzebski and A. Fairweather (Oxford: Oxford University Press, 2001).

Part Two

Philosophy of Religion

Three

Presence and Omnipresence

Eleonore Stump

Thomas Aquinas, who has a rich, sophisticated account of love, thinks that love consists in two desires: the desire for the good of the beloved and the desire for union with the beloved.[1] In the contemporary literature on love, there is considerable discussion of the connection between love and the first of these desires, for the good of the beloved. In this paper, I want to reflect on the second of the desires of love, the desire for union with the beloved, and I want to consider what the nature of such union is. Union, of course, comes in different sorts, depending on the sort of love at issue. For ease of exposition, in this paper I am going to examine union in the love between friends, and I am going to restrict the kind of friendship at issue to that between normally functioning adult human beings who are not lovers or members of the same immediate family. What is it for someone to desire union with a person he loves in this way? It is not equivalent to a desire to be in the beloved's company. Others have pointed out that one can love a person but not want to be in that person's company.[2] And it is clear that being in a person's company is not equivalent to being united to that person. It is possible to be in the company of a person from whom one is entirely alienated, and it is also possible to be united with someone without being in the company of that person. But if being united to a person isn't a matter of being in that person's company, then what is it?

In my view, union between friends requires mutual closeness and personal presence. In what follows, I will argue that, to understand the nature of the union desired in love, we need to understand what it is for one person to be present to another and what the relation is between such personal presence, on the one hand, and closeness between persons, on the other. As I hope to show, this way of thinking about union between friends sheds light on the general nature of the union desired in love, and it also highlights a neglected side of the standard divine attribute of omnipresence.

Closeness and Presence

I want to begin by considering the connection between one person's being present to or with another person and her being close to that person. Can one person be present to or with another without being close to that person? Is being close to a person just one way of being present to or with that person? That is, is *being present* a genus within which *being close* is a species? Or is it the other way around? Is it the case that when there is a deep enough degree of mutual closeness between two people, it is then possible for each of them to be truly present to the other? Is *being close* a genus within which *being present* is a species?

The right answer to all these questions is "yes," in my view. The notion of one person's being present to or with another is ambiguous. Sometimes it is a genus within which closeness is a species, and sometimes it is a species that is within the genus of closeness. This ambiguity in the notion of being present holds also when the presence of God is at issue. So Augustine, for example, talks in one place about God's being present to everyone everywhere always;[3] in another place, however, he describes the overwhelming but sadly ephemeral presence of God that he perceived in a powerful religious experience.[4] When *being present* is a genus such that personal closeness is one of its species, I will call the relation "minimal personal presence" or "minimal being present." When *being present* is a species within the genus of personal closeness, for want of a better term I will call presence in this stronger sense "significant personal presence" or "significant being present."

Minimal personal presence is at issue when we say things such as

(i) "Some of those present were already asleep."
(ii) "Her family was present with her while she was comatose in the last hours of her life."
(iii) "The doctor himself was present and available to her only in the early morning."

Being present in these cases need not signify much or any closeness among the persons involved. Instead, presentness in these cases is being understood as a generic connection between persons, which can vary from minimal to great, depending on what else is true of the connection.

It should be said that there are gradations even within *minimal* personal presence. We sometimes indicate these gradations by differences in the prepositions needed to express the relation. When the relation can be expressed without any preposition at all, as in (i) above, the kind of presentness at issue is often only a matter of one person's being physically in a space picked out by reference to someone else. More is generally needed when the relation is expressed appropriately by adding the preposition *with*, as in (ii). In that case, the person said to be present is typically conscious, although the person he is present with does not need to be. Finally, when the relation requires the preposition *to* for its proper expression, as in (iii), all the persons standing in the relation are generally functioning as persons, as distinct from being comatose or otherwise unconscious. The first two cases, (i) and (ii), are the limiting cases of being present in the minimal sense. In what follows, I will leave these limiting cases largely to one side.

Significant personal presence, on the other hand, is a species within the genus of closeness between persons, and formulations indicating this sort of presence are generally expressed with the preposition *to*. So, for example, we say such things as

(iv) "She was distracted all through dinner and was never really present to me."
(v) "He was more present to his children after he lost his fortune than before."
(vi) "In mystical visions, Christ was present to Francis of Assisi."

Here we are thinking of presence in a different way from that in the preceding examples. In (iv), (v), and (vi), *being present* is a particularly significant or powerful way of being close to a person. On this sense of *being present*, being close to another person is necessary for being present to her but not sufficient for it. So, as I am using the phrase here, minimal personal presence is a prerequisite for closeness; and when the closeness between persons is great enough or deep enough, they will be able to be present to each other in the stronger sense of *being present*.

An Insufficient Account of Presence

With this much understanding of the relationship between presence and closeness, we can turn to their role in union. Across all the relationships of love, some variety of mutual closeness, which stems from and also makes possible presence between persons, is evidently necessary for the union desired in love. Since personal presence is the more foundational relation of the two, in what follows I will begin by considering it, in both its minimal and its stronger sense, and then go on to discuss the nature of closeness between persons.

In earlier work, in an attempt to take account of the doctrine that God is present to human persons, Norman Kretzmann and I tried to capture the relation of being present in terms of one person's having direct and unmediated causal contact with and cognitive access to another.[5] By "direct and unmediated" in this context, I mean only that the cognitive access or the causal connection does not have as an intermediate step the agency of another person; I do not mean that there is no intermediary of any sort. In this sense of "direct and unmediated," if I am wearing my glasses when I see a person, I still have direct and unmediated cognitive access to him; and if I am on the phone with him when I cause him grief by telling him that his mother has died, I am still exercising direct and unmediated causality on him.[6]

I now think, however, that the attempt to capture personal presence in terms of direct and unmediated cognitive and causal contact misses something even in the minimal sense of personal presence. Consider, for example, Homer's depiction of Zeus. Wherever in physical reality he is, Homer's Zeus has direct and unmediated causal connection with the Trojans and also direct and unmediated cognitive access to them. That is, he is able to know directly and immediately what is happening to the Trojans in the fighting with the Greeks, say, and he can affect the way the fighting goes just by willing it. But Zeus can continue to have such cognitive and causal contact with the Trojans even when he is (as Homer sometimes says) having dinner with the Ethiopians, for instance. While Zeus is among the Ethiopians, however, he is not present but rather absent from the scene of the Greek and Trojan war.

Direct and unmediated causal and cognitive contact is even more inadequate for the stronger sense of presence. If one person Paula is blind and falls over another person Jerome when he is unconscious in her path, she may cause him to be moved by falling over him; and she may know by touch that it is a human person she has fallen over. Paula will thus have direct and unmediated causal and cognitive connection with him; but she is not present to Jerome, in the stronger sense of personal presence, in consequence of falling over him while he is unconscious.

What must be added to the condition of direct and unmediated causal and cognitive contact, I now think, are two things, namely, second-person experience and shared attention. The first of these, second-person experience, is sufficient for the relation of being present to in its minimal sense; for the stronger sense, joint or shared attention is needed as well. I will discuss second-person experience first and then turn to joint attention.

Second-Person Experience

It is common in philosophy now to distinguish first-person from third-person points of view. Under one or another description, some philosophers have also called attention to the importance of a second-person point of view or experience.[7] For purposes of this paper, I will understand a second-person experience in this way. One person Paula has a second-person experience of another person Jerome only if (1) Paula is conscious of Jerome as a person;[8] (2) in being conscious of Jerome as a person, Paula has direct and unmediated cognitive access to Jerome and is in a position to have direct and unmediated causal contact with him; and (3) Jerome is conscious.[9]

Condition (1) can be met even if Paula does not have perception of Jerome. It is possible for one person to be consciously aware of another without seeing, hearing, smelling, touching, or tasting that other person. For example, if Paula and Jerome are engaged in an animated conversation with one another that they conduct by means of e-mail (or smoke signals), Paula has Jerome qua conscious person as an object of her consciousness, even if she does not perceive Jerome.[10]

It is hard to know how to make this element of condition (1) precise. It is possible for two persons to be engaged with one another in the relevant way even if neither of them has sensory perception of the other. On the other hand, Paula's just thinking of Jerome in Jerome's absence does not count as Paula's having a second-person experience of Jerome even if in thinking about Jerome Paula is conscious of Jerome as a conscious person. Second-person experience requires conscious contact with another person as a conscious person; contact of that sort does not need perception, but it does take more than an image or a memory of a person.

As for condition (2), I take Paula's interaction with Jerome to be mediated and indirect just in case Paula interacts with Jerome only in virtue of having direct and unmediated contact with a third person Julia. So condition (2) rules out cases of personal interaction that are mediated by one or more other people, but it does not rule out intermediaries that are machines or mechanical devices, such as glasses, telephones, and computers. If Paula's only contact with Jerome is by computer, but if the computer contact between them meets the other conditions for second-person experience, then Paula's computer contact with Jerome counts as a second-person experience.[11] On the other hand, Paula does not count as having a second-person experience of Jerome if her contact consists just in Julia's reporting to Paula something Jerome has said or done. In such a case, Jerome is conscious, and Paula is conscious of Jerome as a conscious person, in some sense; but this sort of consciousness of Jerome is insufficient to count as a second-person experience of Jerome because it is mediated by a third person.[12]

Finally, condition (3) requires that Jerome be conscious for Paula to have a second-person experience of him. It is not necessary, however, that Jerome be conscious of Paula. Paula would have a second-person experience of Jerome even if she were hidden from his view behind an arras watching while Jerome was quarreling with Julia.[13]

So a second-person experience, as I have described it here, is a matter of one person's being conscious of another person as a person when that other person is conscious and functioning, however minimally, as a person.[14]

A second-person experience is necessary for the relation of being present, in the minimal sense of being present, for all but the limiting cases of being present represented by (i) and (ii), which I am leaving to one side.[15] For example, if Paula were unconscious behind the arras, it would not be true that she was present with Jerome while he quarreled with Julia, except in the most minimal sense that her unconscious body was in the room. Similarly, if Paula were conscious of Jerome on that occasion only because Julia surreptitiously sent her an e-mail with information about him while Paula was in some other part of the house, it wouldn't be true that Paula was present with or to Jerome.

A second-person experience is also sufficient for being present in the minimal sense. If Paula was hidden and watching Jerome's quarrel with Julia, and Julia knew this about Paula, then Julia would have to concede that Paula was present if Jerome challenged her on this score. Paula's second-person experience of Jerome is sufficient for her counting as present on that occasion, in the minimal sense of presence. Clearly, however, a second-person experience is not sufficient for being present in the stronger sense represented by (iv), (v), and (vi). Paula is not present to Jerome in this sense if Paula is just secretly watching Jerome when he is not aware of her.

The same point applies, mutatis mutandis, even to God. It is one thing for God to be present always and everywhere to everyone with minimal personal presence, and another thing for God to be present to a person in the stronger sense of presence represented by (iv) through (vi).

In my view, we can see what has to be added to a second-person experience for significant personal presence by looking at the psychological and neurobiological literature on joint or shared attention. Joint or shared attention has been extensively investigated in children, and I will present it first in that connection before exploring its contribution to significant personal presence.

Joint Attention

The lamentable increase in the incidence of autism has prompted an outpouring of studies of the development of both autistic and normal children. One especially promising set of such studies has to do with the subject of joint or shared attention. The form of joint attention most extensively investigated is what researchers in the field call "triadic attentional engagement," that is, "the (conscious) joining of two people's attention upon a 'third' element or target."[16]

It is not easy to give an analysis of what is at issue in triadic attentional engagement. For example, one author says, "Joint attention . . . occurs when an individual (say, P1) is psychologically engaged with someone else's (P2's) psychological engagement with the world."[17] Another researcher says of two subjects engaged in joint attention directed towards some third object that "each subject is aware, in some sense, of the object *as* an object that is present to both subjects. There is, in this respect, a 'meeting of minds' between both subjects, such that the fact that both are attending to the same object is open or mutually manifest."[18] Peter Hobson says, "For an instance of infant social engagement to count as joint attention, it is not enough that the infant attends to some object or event that just happens to be at the focus of someone else's attention. Critically, the infant needs to be aware of the object or event *as* the focus of the other person's attention—and in addition, for full 'jointness,' he or she should share awareness of the sharing of the focus, something that often entails sharing an attitude towards the thing or event in question."[19] One philosopher attempting to explain joint attention says, "Just as the object [being attended to in cases of triadic shared attention] can be a constituent of your experience, so too it can be a constituent of your experience that the other person is, with you, attending to that object." On this account, "We can view joint attention as a primitive phenomenon of consciousness."[20]

Whatever the difficulty of finding a correct formulation and description of the phenomenon, the phenomenon itself is easy to recognize. To take just one example, somewhere in the period between nine and twelve months of age, most infants begin spontaneously to use a pointing gesture to call things to the attention of their caregivers and to share attention directed toward the object with the caregiver.[21] This pointing gesture "is intentionally addressed. . . . This is shown by gaze alternation between referent and addressee."[22] Autistic children show significant deficits in the triadic form of joint attention. In one study, it was found that "*not a single infant with autism* . . . during the first 2 years . . . [showed] referential use of eye contact, . . . and pointing at objects and following others' points."[23]

There is an even more fundamental form of joint attention than triadic attentional engagement, however, and that is what has come to be called "dyadic joint attention" or "dyadic shared attention." As researchers have demonstrated, triadic joint attention is a development of dyadic attention sharing, which begins much earlier in infancy, in mutual gaze and in gaze following: "[Gaze following] is the earliest joint attention behaviour to appear in normal development, emerging some months before the onset of other joint attention behaviours,"[24] and it involves "a dyadic component."[25]

In fact, by as early as two months of age, infants have some sophistication with regard to dyadic attention sharing. They can, for example, "respond to attention from others with ambivalence. The onset of mutual gaze is sometimes accompanied by the aversion of gaze or head or both. . . . [These reactions] are a response to mutual attention."[26] In fact, there is "a fairly substantial body of evidence demonstrating the very young infant's capacity both to discriminate and express human features. . . . Newborns are able to discriminate quite specific facial movements . . . and, moreover, are able to imitate these movements . . . and there is a close correspondence between the emotional expressions of mother and infant."[27]

It is hard to overemphasize the importance of dyadic attention sharing. As one researcher puts it, "this is the most direct sharing of attention and the most powerful experience of others' attention that one can have."[28]

Some researchers now propose that autism is fundamentally an impairment in the capacity for dyadic joint attention: "Early research findings focusing on the joint attention impairment [of autistic children] initially emphasized a specific impairment in triadic interactions rather than dyadic interactions. . . . Recently, however, the tide has begun to turn. Several studies show group differences in dyadic interaction between children with autism and those with other developmental delays. . . . The research shows that certain measures of dyadic interaction predict diagnosis of autism several years later."[29]

One puzzle with regard to autistic children and dyadic joint attention has to do with the nature of the autistic impairment. As one researcher puts it: "Why don't autistic children [share attention] . . . ? Our early research showed that it wasn't simply that they *can't* do it. In certain circumstances children with autism are actually very competent [at it]."[30] Why, then, don't autistic children engage in dyadic attention? Part of the answer has to do with the fact that there is voluntary control of attention. Autistic children are impaired as regards such control, but their difficulties are not across the board.[31] They appear almost exclusively in response to social stimuli: "The initial problem for a child with autism, therefore, may be that [autistic children] fail to benefit from face-to-face interaction. . . . In ongoing work we are investigating the link between early dyadic gaze patterns and triadic communicative gestures and language. . . . [Our] findings all indicate that very basic dyadic difficulties affect later triadic joint attention."[32] The same researcher sums up the recent findings by saying, "For individuals with autism, human stimuli may simply not be important early in development, and this may have serious implications for later development."[33]

These and many other studies make plain the importance of joint or shared attention, particularly dyadic joint attention. They do not give us a philosophical analysis of the concept of sharing attention, but they do give us some intuitive understanding of its nature and value for human life, even in infancy. In my view, *dyadic* shared attention also has a special role to play in significant personal presence.

Interim Summing Up

Obviously, joint attention can also occur among adults. For adults, joint attention will be partly a matter of mutual knowledge, of the sort that prompts philosophical worry about the possibility of unstoppable infinite regress: Paula is aware of Jerome's being aware of Paula's being aware of Jerome's being aware, and so on.[34] In dyadic shared attention, the object of awareness for Paula is simultaneously Jerome and their mutual awareness—Jerome's awareness of her awareness of his awareness and so on—and the object of awareness for Jerome is simultaneously Paula and their mutual awareness.

Focus on the nature of shared attention enables us to see that a second-person experience is an ingredient of shared attention. Consequently, it also helps us understand why a second-person experience is needed for minimal personal presence. Paula's second-person experience of Jerome is precisely her being aware of Jerome and attentive to him when he is in a position to share attention with her, whether or not he actually does so. Without this much connection to Jerome on Paula's part, Paula is not even minimally personally present to Jerome.

It is also the case, however, that, for adult human beings, full-fledged dyadic joint attention is required for significant, as distinct from minimal, personal presence. If Paula is in the same room as Jerome but is totally absorbed in her work and never looks up at him in the process, he will feel that she is not present to him on that occasion. What is missing is dyadic shared attention, expressed in one way or another.

Mutatis mutandis, the same point applies also to God. On this understanding of both minimal and significant personal presence, we can see why God's having direct and unmediated cognitive and causal connection with everything in creation is insufficient for his being present. For God to be present, it also needs to be the case that God is always and everywhere in a position to share attention with any creature able and willing to share attention with God.

Unlike infants, normally functioning adult human beings share attention as persons with developed minds and wills; and they can bring more or less of their minds and wills to the sharing of attention. And so, for adults, shared attention comes in degrees.[35] For shared attention to be maximally rich, there has to be a relation of mutual closeness between the persons sharing attention. The nature of close relationships is therefore what I want to turn to next.

It may help, however, if we first review the nexus of relations I have sketched so far. I claimed at the outset that two things are required for union between persons of the sort desired in love: personal presence and mutual closeness. I distinguished minimal personal presence from presence in a stronger sense, significant personal presence. I sketched the nature of a second-person experience, which includes direct and unmediated causal and cognitive contact between persons, and I explained that second-person experience is necessary for minimal personal presence.[36] I claimed that something more, namely, shared attention, is necessary in addition for significant personal presence. Since shared attention comes in degrees of richness, significant personal presence also comes in degrees. Maximally rich shared attention is necessary for the most significant sort of personal presence. Finally, I argued that minimal personal presence is necessary for mutual closeness; here I am also claiming that mutual closeness is necessary for the maximally rich shared attention requisite for the most significant sort of personal presence.

And so, on the view I am arguing for here, a complicated kind of personal engagement, based ultimately on direct awareness of persons and mutually shared attention among them, is necessary for union. (It may also be sufficient, but I am not making this stronger claim in this paper.) Given this nexus of connections, I can refine my original claim about union this way: the union desired in love requires mutual closeness and the most significant sort of personal presence.

Pointing to the foundational role of the awareness of persons and shared attention should not obscure the role of the will in effecting union. Especially with regard to the knowledge of persons, what one knows is at least partly a function of what one wants to know, and volition also plays a part in attention, as we indicate when we talk of turning our attention to something or paying attention to someone. Even for infants, joint attention has a volitional component. In the view of some psychologists studying joint attention in infants, "Selectively attending to something can be an intentional activity. . . . 'The meeting of minds' characteristic of joint attention is primarily a 'meeting of wills.'"[37] The role of the will is even more evident when it comes to mutual closeness, to which I now turn.

Closeness

I want to begin the examination of mutual closeness by starting with the more basic relation of one person's being close to another.[38] When each person in a relationship is close to the other, then they are mutually close to each other.[39]

We can start by acknowledging what is not sufficient for one person's being close to another. Propinquity alone will not produce such a relation, not even propinquity prolonged or often repeated. There can be mere propinquity but not closeness between a person and the old man who regularly sits by her in the lunchroom or the teenager who always gets on the subway when and where she does after work. Just adding conversation to propinquity will not produce closeness;[40] general benevolence plus conversation and propinquity is not enough either. The bright benevolence and lively conversation of a packed party is compatible with radical isolation on the part of those participating in it. As most people have experienced, it is possible to be more lonely and distant from others at a party than in the solitude of work in one's home or office.

And there is more to be garnered from this via negativa. The relation *being close to*, which holds only among persons as I am employing it here, is irreflexive (a person cannot be close to himself), asymmetric (a priest can be close to a family in crisis without its being the case that they are close to him), and intransitive (a mother can be close to her son and he can be close to his wife without its being the case that the mother-in-law is close to her daughter-in-law). So much seems relatively easy—at least on first pass, though there is one complication even here, to which I will return shortly.

But what can be said on the positive side? It is easy to see that there are some necessary conditions involving openness of mind. For example, Paula is close to Jerome only if Jerome shares his thoughts and feelings with Paula. Furthermore, not just any thoughts and feelings will do here. For Paula to be close to Jerome, Jerome has to share with Paula those thoughts and feelings of his that he cares about and that are particularly revelatory of him. Jerome would not be close to Paula if he shared with her a great many of his most trivial thoughts but nothing of what was important to him.[41]

It may seem as if I have things backwards here. That is, it may seem to some people that Paula is close to Jerome only if *Paula* reveals her mind to him, rather than the other way around. A little reflection, however, will show that my first formulation is correct. A priest is close to a family in his parish if one or more members of the family take him into their confidence. If the order of revelation were the other way around, if the priest shared his thoughts and feelings with one or more members of the family, we would say that the family was close to the priest. So Paula's closeness to Jerome requires self-revelation on the part of *Jerome*, not Paula.

Furthermore, Jerome's being actively engaged in self-revelation is requisite. If Paula is simply the sort of person who can see into others, so that she knows a great many things about Jerome without his telling them to her, she is not close to Jerome. Jerome's *choosing* to reveal his thoughts and feelings is necessary for Paula's closeness to him. In addition, for Paula to be close to Jerome, she has to receive his self-revelation, not only in the sense that she is willing to have him communicate his thoughts and feelings to her, but also in the sense that she can understand what he is revealing to her. If she is willing enough but uncomprehending, she will not be close to him.

Even here things get murky, though, because closeness manifestly comes in degrees, and it is not evident how much sharing of thoughts and feelings is necessary for any degree of closeness. It seems unlikely that precision is possible as regards this subject, however, and I will consequently leave concern for precision to one side.

Needs and Desires

There are obviously also other necessary conditions involving desires and states of will, and these are even harder to spell out. If Jerome revealed very many of his thoughts and feelings to Paula but what Paula thought or felt about what he was telling her did not matter to him, if her reactions to him were a matter of indifference to him, then, it seems evident, she would not be close to him. If Jerome revealed a great deal of himself to a slave whose life was entirely in his power, but if the slave's reactions to Jerome did not matter to Jerome, then Jerome would only be using the slave as a sort of sounding board. Most of us would consequently not see the slave as close to Jerome.

It is not clear how to frame this intuition as a positive claim.[42] I am inclined to think it has to be spelled out in terms of needs, but the notion of need in this context is itself not clear. When Augustine says to God, "You have made us for yourself, and our hearts are restless till they rest in you," he is evincing a need for the person of God; but what is needed is not needed in order to ward off a deficiency or remedy a defect in Augustine. It is true, of course, that a creature needs its creator to live. But the need Augustine is trying to call attention to in this line of his does not have to do with any inadequacy or deficit on Augustine's part. What sort of need is this?

Needs and desires are commonly associated, but they are nonetheless not correlative. It is possible to need something (e.g., a reform in one's smoking habits) without desiring it, and it is also possible to desire something without its being necessary for anything *other than the fulfillment of the desire itself*. If I have a great desire to hear Beethoven's *Christ on the Mount of Olives*, there may well be nothing for which my hearing that piece of music is needed, other than the fulfillment of my desire to hear it. There is no lack or shortcoming in me that is remedied by my hearing the music. I simply have a passion just then for hearing that particular piece of music. Nonetheless, if the desire is very powerful, then—looking for the CD and unable to find it—I might say truly, with exasperation, "I *need* to hear it." In this sense of *need*, then, what is at issue is only the fulfillment of the desire for the thing needed.

One person can need another in *this* sense, in my view;[43] and this is the sense of need Augustine is expressing in his memorable line. In this sense, even God can need his creatures.[44] Nothing about the traditional divine attributes rules out such need on God's part, since need of this sort implies no deficiency.[45]

Need so understood is required for closeness, in my view. Paula is close to Jerome only in case Jerome needs Paula in this sense. Furthermore, insofar as the fulfillment of Jerome's desire for Paula is at least in part in Paula's control rather than Jerome's, Jerome's having a need for Paula also makes Jerome vulnerable to Paula. And so Jerome's being vulnerable to Paula is necessary for Paula's being close to Jerome as well.

Someone might suppose that this last point cannot apply to God because the standard divine attributes rule out vulnerability in God. It is true that on the conception of God as simple, omnipotent, and impassible it looks as if nothing that matters to God is dependent on anything human beings do. But I think that such a conclusion would be hasty. In the first place, it is clear that God has allowed certain things to depend on human wills. That is why Aquinas, for example, has to distinguish between the antecedent and the consequent will of God. God's antecedent will is what God would have willed had things been up to him alone; God's consequent will is what God in fact does will, given what human beings choose. God's allowing human beings to affect what he wills is at least analogous to vulnerability insofar as God's consequent will diverges from his antecedent will. Furthermore, on the doctrine of the Incarnation, in love, for the sake of union with human beings, God assumes a human nature and thereby makes himself, in his human nature, vulnerable to the suffering other human beings choose to inflict on him.[46] So, mutatis mutandis, the kind of need at issue in closeness can be ascribed to God also.

In addition, it is clear that, for closeness, there have to be desires on Paula's part corresponding to those on Jerome's. That is, Paula has to be willing to have Jerome need her and be vulnerable to her. If Jerome needed her but Paula took great care to avoid Jerome, she would not be close to him.[47]

Internal Integration

Even if everything in the preceding account were spelled out correctly, however, we still would not have a complete account of what it is for one person to be close to another. At a minimum, we also have to say something about higher-order desires and acts of will.

It is possible for a person to be internally divided in will or in mind or in both. So, for example, Jerome's second-order desires might be in conflict with (at least some of) the first-order desires he has, and he might identify with his second-order desires. In that case, Jerome would be alienated from (some of) his own first-order desires.[48] It is also possible for there to be something analogous as regards the mind. It is possible for a person to be unclear, uncomprehending, or even mistaken about his own beliefs. A self-deceived person, for example, is someone who has invested considerable psychic energy in hiding from himself some of the beliefs, or the beliefs and desires, that he in fact has. He has a stake in not recognizing some of his beliefs and desires as his own, and he cares about seeing himself as other than he is. Such a person is divided within himself as regards his beliefs as well as his desires.

Because this is so, there needs to be some qualification of my original claim that the relation *being close to* is irreflexive. If Jerome is divided within himself as regards his mind or will, he is to this extent alienated from himself. In this condition, he is someone who has taken sides, as it were, in the civil war within himself. There are some parts of himself, we might say, from which he himself stands at a considerable distance. In this sense, then, he is not close to himself. And so my original claim has to be modified: it is possible to take the relation *being close to* as reflexive, in a certain sense. An internally divided person is someone who is, in some analogous or extended sense, not close to himself.

Or if that is too much to say, this much at any rate seems to be right. A person alienated from himself cannot have someone else close to him. Jerome cannot reveal his mind to Paula if Jerome has hidden a good part of his mind from himself. And if Jerome is alienated from his own desires as regards Paula—if he desires to have different desires from those he has regarding Paula because he thinks that his relationship to Paula is detrimental to his being what he wants and ought to be, for example—then Paula is not close to Jerome. Catullus's self-recriminating passion for his beloved Lesbia is a famous example of a relation that has such conflict between higher- and lower-order desires.[49] The resulting mix of attraction and repulsion, mingled with self-loathing, is not an example of one person's being close to another. As far as that goes, if Jerome desires not to have the desires he does with regard to Paula, then to that extent he does not so much as *desire* closeness with Paula.

Closeness therefore requires psychic integration and wholeheartedness. For Paula to be close to Jerome, Jerome has to be integrated in himself.

With the addition of these considerations regarding internal integration, we have a preliminary account of what it is required for one person to be close to another. For two people to be mutually close, each person in the relationship must meet these conditions with respect to the other. With this, we finally have the elements that are necessary for union.

Conclusion: Internal Integration, Closeness, Presence, Union, and Love

As I explained at the outset, on Aquinas's account, love consists in two desires: one for the good of the beloved and one for union with the beloved. In this paper, I have tried to explicate the nature of the union desired in love, on this account of love. I have claimed that two things are necessary for union among friends: the most significant personal presence and mutual closeness. Union comes in different sorts depending on the relationship at issue, but some things are common to union across the relationships of love holding among normally functioning adults. My focus in this paper has been on the relationship of friend (where *friend* is narrowly understood, so that it excludes lovers and family members); but the account I have given of union can be extended to other relationships of love as well, if it is relativized to the relationship in question, so that the degree of significant personal presence and the sort of closeness at issue are those that are appropriate for the relationship.

As I have tried to show, personal presence and closeness are interconnected in complicated ways. Minimal personal presence, understood as including second-person experience, is required for closeness; and mutual closeness is itself required for rich shared attention, which is in turn required for significant personal presence. My formulation of union as a matter of maximally significant personal presence and mutual closeness is therefore pleonastic, since the most significant personal presence entails all the rest of the items on the preceding list, including mutual closeness. There is nonetheless some heuristic value in the pleonastic formulation, because it keeps us from thinking of union itself as nothing more than an ephemeral thing. Significant personal presence *can* be momentary or episodic in human relationships, but it rests on mutual closeness, which is a matter of dispositions and shared history as well.

I have argued that a person's being integrated in himself is required for someone else's being close to him. This point holds for God as well; even God cannot be close to a human person alienated from himself. Consequently, God's being close to Jerome is in Jerome's control, not God's. Whether omnipresent God is present to Jerome with significant personal presence is dependent not on God but on Jerome. On the account of presence and omnipresence I have given here, the only thing decisive for the kind of personal presence, significant or minimal, that an omnipresent God has to a human person is thus the state and condition of the human person himself.

This point has an implication particularly worth noting. From Paula's perspective, if Jerome is not integrated within himself, then Paula's ability to be close to him or significantly present to him is limited or unavailing, no matter what she chooses to do. Although warding off closeness to Jerome is within Paula's control, effecting closeness to Jerome and being significantly present to him is not. But things are different when it comes to God. If Paula wants God to be significantly present to her, the establishment of the relationship she wants depends only on her, on her single-mindedly and wholeheartedly wanting that relationship. If she does not, then God will have only minimal personal presence with respect to her. But if she does, then the presence that omnipresent God has to her will be significant personal presence.

It is thus an implication of this way of thinking about presence and omnipresence that union with God is much more in our control than union with another human person is.

Notes

I am grateful to Jeff Brower, Frank Burch Brown, John Foley, John Kavanaugh, Scott MacDonald, Mike Murray, Mike Rea, and Theodore Vitali for helpful discussion of an earlier draft of this paper or its ideas.

1. For discussion of Aquinas's account of love, see my "Love, by All Accounts," Presidential Address, *Proceedings and Addresses of the American Philosophical Association* 80 (November 2006). For Aquinas's central claims about

love, see, for example, *Summa theologiae* II-II, q.25, a.3; I-II, q.26 a.4 and q.28 a.4; and I-II, q.26 a.2 ad 2, and q.28 a.1 s.c., q.66 a.6, and q.70 a.3.

2. David Velleman, "Love as a Moral Emotion," *Ethics* 109 (1999): 353.

3. *Confessions* 5.2.

4. Cf. *Confessions* 7.17. In a recent lecture, "The Presence of God" (work in progress), Scott MacDonald discussed Augustine's understanding in the *Confessions* of the presence of God and called attention to Augustine's puzzling over the point of invoking the presence of an omnipresent God.

5. Eleonore Stump and Norman Kretzmann, "Eternity, Awareness, and Action," *Faith and Philosophy* 9 (1992): 463–82.

6. For further discussion of the implications of this use of the phrase "direct and unmediated," see the section on second-person experience below.

7. See, for example, Stephen Darwall, "Fichte and the Second-Person Standpoint," *Internationales Jahrbuch des deutschen Idealismus* 3 (2005): 91–113; and Stephen Darwall, *The Second-Person Standpoint: Morality, Respect, and Accountability* (Cambridge, MA: Harvard University Press, 2006).

8. Condition (1) implies that Paula does not have a second-person experience of Jerome if Paula is dumped unconscious on top of Jerome; even if Jerome is conscious, it is necessary that Paula be conscious as well. Furthermore, if Paula is conscious but not conscious of Jerome—say, because Jerome is hiding and Paula doesn't know he is present—then Paula doesn't have a second-person experience of Jerome. In addition, the requirement that Paula be conscious of Jerome as a person rules out cases of the sort made familiar to us from the literature on agnosia, where the agnosia patient is conscious and one of the objects of his consciousness is another person, but because of his agnosia he does not recognize the other person as a person; he takes her instead to be, say, a hat on a hat stand. (This is the case made famous by Oliver Sacks in his eponymous *The Man Who Mistook His Wife for a Hat* [New York: Harper Perennial, 1985].) This requirement also rules out cases in which Paula has conscious awareness only of some subpersonal part (say, a brain) or subpersonal system (say, the circulatory system) of Jerome.

9. Insofar as consciousness comes in degrees, there is some vagueness in this condition. I mean to rule out only cases in which a person lacks sufficient consciousness to function as a person. Drowsiness is not ruled out; certain drugged states, such as the so-called twilight sleep, are. There are also gray areas here. I am inclined to say that a mother has second-person experience of her newborn infant but that a condition such as advanced Alzheimer's precludes second-person experience. My intuitions are not strong as regards such cases, however. I am grateful to Kathleen Brennan for calling my attention to the need to address this issue.

10. It may sound odd to say that Paula has direct and unmediated cognitive access and causal connection to Jerome if she is communicating with him by e-mail. But, as I am using "direct and unmediated," this conclusion is

correct. Her cognitive access to him is not mediated by the agency of another person; and she can cause him, for example, to laugh by what she writes without the intervention of any other person's causality.

11. Although Paula does not have sensory perception of Jerome in the process of e-mailing him (she does not see, hear, touch, taste, or smell Jerome in e-mail communication), that fact does not rule out e-mail contact from counting as second-person experience, provided only that it really is Jerome with whom Paula is in e-mail contact. If someone other than Jerome is e-mailing Paula in the persona of Jerome, then the e-mail communication doesn't count as Paula's having a second-person experience of Jerome. There are gray areas here, too. If it really is Jerome who is e-mailing Paula but Jerome is systematically deceiving Paula on all points about himself, it is considerably less clear whether the e-mail communication counts as a second-person experience of Jerome for Paula. I am grateful to John Kavanaugh for pointing out these complexities to me.

12. Here, too, there are complications. If Paula reads a letter sent to her by Jerome, Paula counts as having a second-person experience of Jerome on the conditions I have given. That remains the case even if Jerome dictated the letter to his secretary, since when Paula reads the letter, Paula does not have any personal interaction with the secretary. When she reads the letter, Paula is not conscious of the secretary; or even if she is, it is not the case that she is conscious of Jerome only in virtue of being conscious of Jerome's secretary. But if the same message from Jerome to Paula were delivered to Paula orally by Jerome's secretary, then Paula would not count as having a second-person experience of Jerome, on the conditions given here, because in that case Paula's consciousness of the secretary would mediate her consciousness of Jerome. This seems to me intuitively the right result.

On the other hand, however, suppose that Jerome's secretary delivers orally a message to Paula, who gives the secretary a response, which the secretary delivers to Jerome, who in turn gives the secretary a message to deliver to Paula, and so on. In such a case, is it still true to say that Paula does not have a second-person experience of Jerome because condition (2) is violated? It is not clear that the right answer is "yes."

And there are many other complicated cases here. Suppose that Paula does not know Jerome but finds a stack of highly revealing love letters written by Jerome to someone else. Does Paula's reading these letters constitute a second-person experience of Jerome? It is not clear that the answer to this question should be "no." I am grateful to Adam Peterson for calling my attention to this complication.

In all these cases, my intuitions are not clear. There may be boundary cases where adjudication regarding second-person experience could equally well go either way.

13. I am indebted to John Kavanaugh and Adam Peterson for helping me to see that there are complexities here too. If Jerome sends Paula an e-mail communication but then dies in the period between when he sent it and when Paula reads it, so that he is no longer conscious at the time Paula reads his message, does that communication count as Paula's having second-person experience of Jerome? And if it does, is the third of my conditions on second-person experience violated in such a case? I am inclined to say that Paula *does* have second-person experience in such a case but that the third condition is not violated. It is possible for the presentation of a conscious person Jerome to reach another person Paula after some delay, as the e-mail example makes clear. Nonetheless, the Jerome with whom Paula is in contact by this means is the Jerome who was conscious when he wrote the message, not the Jerome who is dead by the time of Paula's receipt of the message. Understood in this way, this example does not violate the third condition.

14. On this characterization, it is clear that a second-person experience is different from a first-person experience. In a first-person experience, I am directly and immediately conscious of a person as a person, but that person is only myself.

A second-person experience is also different from the sort of third-person experience a neurologist has of her subject. It is possible for the neurologist to function as a neurologist when she has only a brain of some dead person in front of her. Or, even if her subject is living and conscious as well, the neurologist can practice neurology just by interacting with some part of that subject, recording electrical potentials from the skull, for example. A neurologist can therefore do her work without being conscious of her subject as a person. (There are, of course, cases where a neurologist *is* conscious of her subject as a person. For example, there are cases where it is crucial for the neurologist to talk to her subject in order for her to carry out her neurological work, as when the neurologist is trying to determine whether stimulation of a particular area of the brain affects language function. In such cases, I am inclined to say that the neurologist uses a second-person experience of her patient in order to get information relevant to the third-person neurological account she is trying to construct.)

So a second-person experience is different in character from a first-person or a third-person experience because it is necessary for a second-person experience, as it is not for a first- or third-person experience, that you interact consciously and directly with another person who is conscious.

15. In the limiting cases of minimal personal presence, someone can count as minimally personally present who is not even conscious. And so the limiting cases of minimal personal presence can be thought of as defective versions of the species; something good and suitable to the species is missing. In the rest of this paper, I will omit the qualifying phrase "in all but the limiting cases," but it should be understood throughout.

16. Vasudevi Reddy, "Before the 'Third Element': Understanding Attention to Self," in *Joint Attention: Communication and Other Minds. Issues in Philosophy and Psychology*, ed. Naomi Eilan et al. (Oxford: Clarendon Press, 2005), p. 85.

17. R. Peter Hobson, "What Puts the Jointness into Joint Attention?" in Eilan et al., *Joint Attention*, p. 188.

18. Naomi Eilan, "Joint Attention, Communication, and Mind," in Eilan et al., *Joint Attention*, p. 5.

19. Hobson, "What Puts the Jointness," p. 185.

20. John Campbell, "Joint Attention and Common Knowledge," in Eilan et al., *Joint Attention*, p. 295.

21. Fabia Franco, "Infant Pointing: Harlequin, Servant of Two Masters," in Eilan et al., *Joint Attention*, p. 129.

22. Ibid.

23. Hobson, "What Puts the Jointness," p. 195.

24. Sue Leekam, "Why Do Children with Autism Have a Joint Attention Impairment?" in Eilan et al., *Joint Attention*, p. 210. See also Gerrit Loots, Isabel Devise, and Jasmina Sermijn, "The Interaction between Mothers and Their Visually Impaired Infants: An Intersubjective Developmental Perspective," *Journal of Visual Impairment and Blindness* 97 (2003): 407.

25. Ibid.

26. Reddy, "Before the 'Third Element,'" p. 97.

27. Lynne Murray and Colwyn Trevarthen, "Emotional Regulation of Interactions between Two-Month-Olds and Their Mothers," in *Social Perception in Infants*, ed. Tiffany Field and Nathan Fox (Norwood, NJ: Ablex, 1985), pp. 179, 193.

28. Reddy, "Before the 'Third Element,'" p. 85.

29. Leekam, "Why Do Children," p. 207.

30. Ibid., p. 212.

31. Cf. also Claire Hughes and James Russell, "Autistic Children's Difficulty with Mental Disengagement from an Object: Its Implications for Theories of Autism," *Developmental Psychology* 29 (1993): 498–510.

32. Leekam, "Why Do Children," p. 221.

33. Ibid., p. 220.

34. Because philosophers take knowledge to be a matter of knowledge *that*, a more common philosophical formulation of mutual knowledge would be in terms of knowing *that*: Paula knows that Jerome knows that Paula knows that Jerome knows, and so on. In the case of infants, of course, shared attention cannot be a matter of knowing *that* in this way. And the adult phenomenon that is, by extension, shared attention too is also, in my view, more a matter of awareness of a person than a matter of knowing *that*. So I have formulated the description of mutual knowledge in such a way that it applies to knowledge of persons as well as knowledge that something or other is the case. For an inter-

esting study of mutual knowledge in connection with joint attention, see Christopher Peacocke, "Joint Attention: Its Nature, Reflexivity, and Relation to Common Knowledge," in Eilan et al., *Joint Attention*, pp. 298–324.

35. Perhaps it does for infants as well. I do not mean to imply that it doesn't in virtue of claiming that it comes in degrees for adults.

36. With this qualification understood: in all but the limiting cases.

37. Johannes Roessler, "Joint Attention and the Problem of Other Minds," in Eilan et al., *Joint Attention*, p. 239. Roessler is here reporting work by Michael Thomasello. See also Joseph Call and Michael Tomasello, "What Chimpanzees Know about Seeing, Revisited: An Explanation of the Third Kind," in Eilan et al., *Joint Attention*, pp. 45–64.

38. In conversation and in correspondence, John Foley raised a series of difficult questions about my claims regarding closeness and need, and some of what follows in the text was worked out in conversation with him.

39. Aquinas himself speaks not of mutual closeness but of mutual indwelling, in the cognitive and appetitive parts of the soul. On his way of putting the general point, the lover is not satisfied with a superficial relationship to the beloved but seeks to gain so intimate a connection with the beloved that the lover enters into the very soul of the beloved (see *Summa theologiae* I-II, q.28 a.2). This is a wonderful way of putting the idea at issue here, but an exposition of Aquinas's way of putting the idea would take me too far afield in this paper. So I note it only and reluctantly leave to one side any further consideration of it. See also *Summa theologiae* I-II, q.28 a.3, where Aquinas explains the sense in which love leads to ecstasy, and I-II, q.28 a.5, where Aquinas explains that love melts the frozen or hardened heart so that the beloved is able to enter into it.

40. I accept the implication of these claims that copulation alone, even with the sort of conversation bad movies often associate with it, is not sufficient for closeness either. It does not follow from this that there can be no such thing as ephemeral union, provided that the notion of union is taken in a broad sense. It is obviously possible, for example, for there to be an intense and memorable sexual encounter between people who are in effect strangers to each other and who have no relationship with each other after that encounter. But in such a case there is no history of relationship, so that the persons involved do not get to know very much about each other or share very much with each other. In consequence, there is little if any closeness between them. The result is that there is very little or no union between them either. The memorability of the occasion is thus more a function of the sexual excitement of the encounter than of any union between them. We can talk about such an encounter as an ephemeral union, then, but only by extending the notion of union in this way.

41. I am grateful to Anja Jauernig for calling my attention to the need to make this point explicit.

82 *Eleonore Stump*

42. In an earlier version of this paper, I attempted to capture this intuition by claiming that Paula is close to Jerome only in case Jerome has needs and desires that depend on Paula for their fulfillment. John Foley has persuaded me that, as I originally explained it, this is at least misleading, if not actually false, because in the context *need* conjures up the notion of dependence, and dependence of a self-interested sort; but one person can be close to another without being dependent on or self-interested with regard to that other. Worse yet, Foley has made me see, it ought to be the case that just as God can be close to a human person, so a human person can be close to God; but if the relation *being close to* is defined in terms of needs in the way I originally suggested, then a human person could not be close to the God of traditional Christianity, who is not dependent on anything. I am grateful to Foley for calling my attention to these problems. My attempt to handle them is sketched out in what follows.

43. I am presupposing here that need, and also desire, can take as object a person rather than a proposition. In this respect, I am assimilating the need or desire for a person to knowledge of a person. For some idea of the countercultural nature of this approach to desire, see Timothy Schroeder, *The Three Faces of Desire* (Oxford: Oxford University Press, 2004).

44. Cf. the passage in Job where Job says to God, "You will call, and I will answer you. You will have a desire for the work of your hands" (Job 14:15).

45. Even unfulfilled desires of a certain sort can be attributable to God as traditionally understood. That very traditional theologian Thomas Aquinas accepts the biblical text "God will have all men to be saved" (1 Tim. 2:4) as describing an unfulfilled state of God's will (see, e.g., *De veritate* q.23 a.2).

46. I am grateful to John Foley for pointing out to me the need to address this issue.

47. We might wonder whether it does not also have to be the case that Paula's willingness has as at least part of its motivation her desire for Jerome's good; but, in my view, this desire is not necessary for closeness. That is because it is possible for Paula to manage to get close to Jerome in order to prey on Jerome. Exploitative relations, as well as loving relations, can include closeness. In a case where Paula is close to Jerome in order to exploit Jerome, it will not be true that Jerome is close to Paula, however. Furthermore, although in such a case Paula will be close to Jerome, Paula will not love Jerome just in virtue of failing to desire the good for Jerome.

48. See, for example, my "Persons: Identification and Freedom," *Philosophical Topics* 24 (1996): 183–214, for some introduction to the issues and the literature on them.

49. Odi et amo. Quare id faciam, fortasse requiris?
    Nescio, sed fieri sentio et excrucior.
                                    (Carmen 85)

Four

Self-Annihilation or Damnation?
A Disputable Question in Christian Eschatology

Paul J. Griffiths

By the fourth century, if not earlier, a picture of what happens to human beings at the death of the body had been largely agreed upon by Christians. It was a picture intimately linked with a particular anthropology, as all such inevitably are: depicting what happens when we die is always at least an extrapolation from what we take ourselves to be while alive; it is also among the more important tools we have for focusing and elaborating our self-understanding and for meditating discursively and visually upon what we take ourselves to be. Disputes in eschatology are always also disputes in anthropology.

What interests me in this essay is two facts about the Christian tradition. The first is that it had, by the fourth century, developed conceptual resources that could, if pressed only a little, easily yield the view that among the things we are capable of doing to ourselves is annihilation, taking ourselves quite out of existence, leaving nothing behind. These resources were of central importance to the tradition too. They weren't marginalia or the speculation of some insignificant figures. Some thinkers, notably Augustine, get quite close to explicitly affirming that we can take ourselves out of existence, and, given his anthropology, it would certainly have made good sense for him to say just this. But in fact he always draws back: although he canvasses the possibility explicitly on occasion, and more often implies it by saying things that seem quite naturally to lead to it, he never affirms it. When he does discuss the possibility it is always negatively; and when it is implied, or seems to be, the implication is never assented to. And in all this Augustine is entirely typical of Christian thinkers in late antiquity who discuss the postmortem questions. This is the second interesting fact that I'll explore in this essay: that a conclusion strongly suggested by some of the conceptual resources of a particular tradition is nevertheless resisted by the principal systematizers and transmitters of that tradition. When this happens, there is an internal tension. That's what I want to explore in the case of the question of self-annihilation: I want to understand why there is a tension of the sort I've briefly sketched and to suggest how it might be eased.

All this has something important to do with hell. Hell is, according to standard-issue Christian eschatology, a label for one of the only two postmortem destinies finally open to human beings, the other being heaven. If self-annihilation is or might be a possibility for Christian eschatological thought, then either hell's definition will have to be expanded to include it, or it will have to be added as a third eternal destiny alongside heaven and hell. In either case, if self-annihilation is permitted as a possibly Christian view, then it will also have to be said that Christians assert conditional immortality for human beings rather than inevitable immortality. For if annihilation is possible for some human beings (or for all), this just means that immortality is not inevitable for all. Conditional immortality is among the contraries of inevitable immortality, and while it is certainly true that the vast majority of Christians have asserted inevitable immortality, there have always been some Christian voices raised in support of conditional immortality, which is the view I intend to explore further in this essay.[1] To clarify the question, I begin with a conceptual analysis of self-annihilation.

Self-Annihilation

Conceptual Analysis

If something is annihilated, it is, as the word's etymology suggests, brought *ad nihilum*, to nothing. Whatever it was is now no more. Whatever was denoted by its personal proper name (if it had one) is now absent. A comprehensive list of the contents of the cosmos, postannihilation, will no longer yield whatever it is that has been annihilated, whereas that same list preannihilation would have yielded it. An annihilated thing will always leave traces or vestiges of itself: its having been brought to nothing does not mean there are no remains. It means only that it, whatever it was, is not among those remains. They do not conjointly constitute it. A thing's traces are not the thing, and when a once-present thing can now be found only in its traces, it has been annihilated.

This way of glossing annihilation depends upon a distinction between what something is and what its traces are. A similar though not quite identical distinction is the traditional one between a thing's essence and its accidents. I shall not defend these distinctions further here, and it is certainly possible reasonably to reject their coherence or usefulness (though I suspect that only philosophers do). I simply observe that the question about annihilation depends upon some such distinction. I can meaningfully ask whether you can annihilate yourself only if there is a distinction between you and what is not you, and this distinction in turn depends upon a distinction between you and your traces, for if there is no such distinction then all attempts to individuate one thing from another will be a matter of convention only.[2] And since I shall assume that I can meaningfully ask whether a particular thing has been annihilated or not, I shall also assume that there is such a distinction. Such an assumption does not carry in its train the thought that it is always or often easy to tell the difference between a thing and its traces; but it does carry with it the assumption that there is such a difference and that in some cases we can know what it is.

In the case of a human being, annihilation requires the removal of everything except its traces. Decisions about the boundary between a particular human being and its traces will depend upon decisions about the kind of thing a human being is, and no such decision is uncontroversial. If you're a physicalist where human beings are concerned, then you're likely to think that bringing a particular animate object to nothing is the same as bringing a particular human being to nothing. On this view, I can annihilate you just by killing you. If, by contrast, you think that every human being is, definitionally, a noncorporeal entity—a soul, a spirit, a mind, a collocation of causes, a congeries of emotions—then noting that a particular body has been brought to nothing will be irrelevant to the question of whether a particular human being has been brought to nothing. If you think that whatever is essential to or definitive of a particular human being is something that cannot, as a matter of principle, be brought to nothing, then you will also think that no matter what the appearances, no human being is ever annihilated. Christians, as we shall see, have generally found that last view attractive, though they usually hold neither of the first two.

Self-annihilation, to complete the conceptual analysis, is annihilation brought about by an action (or actions) of the thing annihilated. More precisely, you annihilate yourself when your own actions suffice to bring yourself to nothing, to take yourself out of existence. It seems fairly clear that inanimate objects cannot annihilate themselves in this way. Rocks and oceans do and can do nothing that will suffice to bring themselves to nothing. If a rock is pulverized as a result of rolling down a mountainside in an avalanche, or an ocean is evaporated by exposure to unusual heat, this is best accounted for by saying that they were acted upon by something other than themselves, not that they acted. Animate beings, however, may be able to so act. A bird might kill itself by flying at speed into a window's clear glass, and if you think that birds are just bodies, it will thereby have annihilated itself. Birds, however, are unlikely to intend to do what I've just described (if indeed it's proper to say that they intend to do anything); they annihilate themselves, if they do, as a side effect or by-product of intending something else. We human beings can certainly do likewise: we can kill ourselves without intending to do so, though whether this amounts to self-annihilation depends upon whether human beings are just bodies. But we are unlike birds (and perhaps also unlike all other embodied animate beings) in that we can also kill ourselves by intending to do so, just as we can inflict many other kinds of damage upon ourselves by intending to do so. But self-annihilation does not require that it be intended in order that it occur; all that's required is that an agent act in such a way as to bring it about.

So we now have our question before us, clear and vivid: Can you, human being that you are, so damage yourself that you bring yourself to nothing? Is there anything you can do to rid the cosmos of yourself definitively and finally, leaving only your traces to ornament it? Can you annihilate yourself? There are elements in Augustine's thought that strongly suggest this possibility.

An Augustinian Vision

The standard Augustinian picture of what happens to us when we die goes like this: earthly life ends with physiological death, the death of the body. This is the first death,[3] and it is defined as the separation of the soul from the body and the body's consequent loss of life. Immediately following this is an interim period that will last for each separated soul from the moment of the first death to the moment of the general resurrection and the Last Judgment, which will be inaugurated by Jesus Christ's second coming. This means that for some the interim will be very long and for others very short. This interim will be disembodied: souls exist in it without bodies of any sort. Augustine finds this puzzling because it is axiomatic for him that a human being is by definition an embodied soul, which is to say neither just a soul nor just a body.[4] Any existence that a disembodied soul has, therefore, must be shadowy, a half-life. He calls the place of this interim existence an *abditum receptaculum*,[5] "a secret refuge," and does not speculate much about its nature. In this secret refuge separated souls await the resurrection of their bodies, and they do so with either pleasure and tranquility or restless suffering, according to the nature of their lives prior to the first death. The good will find the interim pleasurable, an anticipation of heaven; the bad will find it distressing, an anticipation of hell; and there may be some who, although they suffer in the interim, will nonetheless finally enter heaven. Their interim suffering, unlike that of those destined for hell, is purificatory,[6] and what Augustine says about this contributed to the much later development of a doctrine of purgatory. Separated souls in the interim, therefore, are not properly speaking in either heaven or hell. Interim existence, because it is bodiless, can be no more than a shadowy anticipation of heavenly or hellish existence. The imprecise, tentative, and speculative nature of Augustine's discussions of this part of postmortem existence reflects what he thinks about the nature and feel of disembodied existence for human beings. It is questionable for him that your separated soul in the interim is really you; it is certainly not fully you.

The interim state comes to an end with the general resurrection and the Last Judgment, at which every separated soul is reunited with its body, judged by God to be worthy of heaven or hell, and sent immediately thereto. At that moment begins a changeless and endless mode of embodied existence—an eternal mode of existence in the full and proper sense of that term. And Augustine thinks that every separated soul, without exception, enters upon one or another of these destinies. The *anima*, the soul, was created immortal,[7] and these two embodied destinies are, he thinks, the only final possibilities for each individual soul. He places enormous emphasis, therefore, upon the resurrection of the body. The body with which your separated soul will be reunited at the general resurrection will be *your* body, in some sense identical with the body that died in the first death; but it will also be significantly unlike that body, and the exact nature of the likenesses and unlikenesses proved matter for endless speculation. Will the resurrected body necessarily be of human shape? Will it be gendered? Will it be like the earthly body at twenty, or forty, or sixty? What will happen to the hair and nail clippings of which the earthly body was divested so often? What about human beings who died as small children or in the womb—what will their resurrected bodies be like?[8]

Augustine likes to say of those resurrected for hell that they have undergone the second death, a death in which the soul is definitively separated from God. This is the last moment in the life of the damned, for thereafter, strictly speaking, there are no more moments: there is only a changeless, eternal expanse of embodied suffering. Two polemical concerns arise for Augustine out of this picture of hellish existence. The first concerns the idea of bodies that can endure eternal suffering: Does this idea make sense? Is it not the case that bodies are by definition temporal, transient, and therefore incapable of enduring eternal suffering? Augustine has answers to this difficulty that need not detain us.[9] The other polemical question is pressed by those Christians who are uneasy about the idea of eternal suffering without chance of change. Why does this come about? How can it be avoided? Does it make sense? Augustine has answers for these problems, too, even if not entirely satisfying ones.[10] I shall not pursue those discussions here.

This sketch of Augustine's views (and they are not only his: they are largely agreed on by all late-antique Christians) about what happens to us when we die yields the following picture for the hell bound: they sin here below; their first death separates them from this body into a shadowy interim period of anticipatory suffering; at the general resurrection they are reunited with their bodies and consigned to hell, which is their second death. There they suffer for eternity. The same picture, mutatis mutandis, applies to the heaven bound. And there is no one else: all human beings are either hell or heaven bound. None will be annihilated, from which it follows that none can annihilate themselves.

But Augustine undercuts this view in much of what he writes about the soul and its capacity for self-diminution by means of sin. He thinks that each human being is in part constituted by a soul, which is to say a noncorporeal, rational, free, and internally complex entity, self-related on the model of God's triune self-relation. The rational soul, because it is God's image, participates more fully in God than does any creature, and to say that each human being is an embodied rational soul is therefore to attribute to each of us a high dignity. To say that the soul is free is at least to say that it is the bearer of certain powers or capacities, the particular exercise of which is not fully determined by agents or circumstances other than itself. Among these powers are, most notably, the capacity to know, which carries with it the capacity to argue, to judge, and to evaluate; the capacity to identify, to desire, and actively to seek particular goods, and to understand itself as doing so; and the capacity to form habits or dispositions.

Augustine also thinks that the soul's capacities can be exercised well or badly. We can identify as a good what is not a good; we can desire what we should not; what seems to us knowledge can be error; and so on. The freedom of the rational soul is, therefore, in part a freedom to diminish and damage the human being of which it is a proper part, and it is essential to Christian orthodoxy to claim that every human being is, since the Fall, damaged, in part by its inheritance and in part by its own free actions.[11] Damage is diminishment, the partial obscuring of the divine image in which the human being essentially consists. On this understanding, self-annihilation would occur when the divine image was erased. Anything that then remained would be a trace, not the human being itself. If the soul's defining properties listed so briefly in the preceding paragraph are severally necessary and jointly sufficient for its existence, then the irretrievable loss of any one of them will mean its annihilation. Were a particular soul to become so damaged that it lost, irretrievably, freedom, the capacity to know, and the capacity to form dispositions and act upon them, it would, simply, cease, and with it would cease the human being of which it was a part. No one of these capacities could be damaged to the point of irretrievable loss without similar damage to the others, in much the same way that no one of the body's vital systems (respiratory, sanguinary, neuronal) can be damaged to the point of irretrievable loss without concomitant damage to the others.

It is essential to Christian orthodoxy to claim that we can damage ourselves. This is what the doctrine of sin is about. When we sin, we avert our gaze from God and from the radiant weight of God's glory that is evident in creation. We turn ourselves away, that is, from what is toward what is not, from the good that is God to the *privatio boni* that is God's absence, also known as evil. In doing so we become less than we were, which is to say that we participate less fully in God than we otherwise would have. We are diminished by our sin. This way of describing sin's nature and effects is both scriptural and philosophical. It assumes and hinges upon a particular, broadly Platonist, understanding of what it is for particulars (me, you, tables, trees) to exist, an understanding that construes the existence of each particular in terms of the participation in God—the *plenum*, the *ipsum esse subsistens* (to use Thomist language)—appropriate to its nature. A rational soul's sin, on this view, damages it by removing it from such participation and taking it toward the *nihil*, that absence from which it came and which is the only possible direction in which such removal can tend. The assertion of a self-willed autonomy, for instance, paradigmatic as it is of all sin, decreases the soul that asserts it exactly because it is successful in its goal, namely to avert the soul from God and to make it self-dependent, which is to say dependent upon something less than God, its creator and sustainer.[12]

The depiction of sin's damage by way of images of ontological loss, of decrease in being, is everywhere in the fathers of the church. Augustine depicts it often, and lyrically:

> [The rational soul] does many things because of perverse desire, as though it had forgotten itself. It sees in an interior way certain beautiful things which are in that more eminent nature which is God. And although it should keep still so that it might enjoy them, it wants instead to make them subject to itself, and not to be like him [God] because of him, but to be what he [God] is all by itself.

And so it turns away from him [God] and slips and slides into what is less and less, which it imagines to be more and more. Neither itself nor anything else suffices for it as it moves away from that one [God] who alone suffices. In its destitution and difficulty, it becomes excessively intent upon its own actions, and upon the disquieting delights it gets from them.[13]

This is diminution toward nonexistence, the dying fall of a diminuendo that will (or may) end in silence. It involves error—the sinner takes to be more what is in fact less—but it also and more importantly involves will or intention: the sinner wants to move away from God and toward himself, and he does what is necessary to bring this about.

The language of destitution (*egere, egestas*) is scriptural.[14] Augustine is echoing the story of the Prodigal Son from Luke's gospel, and that story, uniquely in the New Testament, uses the language of substance (*substantia*, Greek *ousia*) to depict the process of loss involved in sin. What the prodigal demands from his father (from God) is the portion of *substantia* due him. This is (Augustine thinks) to demand ownership or control over what he is: your *substantia* is what you essentially are, what makes you you. It is a gift freely given by God, and to demand it for yourself is to make it less than it is by turning it into an object wholly owned instead of a gift freely received. The result is loss, and not just the simple loss of an object but rather a cumulative process of loss, loss piled upon loss ("[the soul] slips and slides into what is less and less"), loss tending exactly toward nothing. The prodigal becomes destitute: he has consumed his substance (*dissipavit substantiam suum . . . omnia consummasset*, Luke 15:13–14) until there is almost nothing left. And this, surely, is just what it would mean to go out of existence altogether: to be devoid of *substantia* is to be annihilated. The prodigal turns back from the brink: he repents and has his substance returned to him as a result. His destitution leaves him still the capacity for repentance, a sole remaining human capacity as he lives with the pigs and eats what they eat. And when he exercises that capacity, everything else—all the rest of his substance—is returned to him by the merciful father.[15]

This language of loss and diminution clearly suggests the possibility of coming to nothing, of annihilation *stricto sensu*. That is what gives it the undeniable power it has. For Augustine, as for most of the fathers of the church, the possibility of self-annihilation is suggested by an ontology of participation and gift. On this view, the fact *that* you are is sheer unmerited gift, and *what* you are is a participant in God. Sin is the rejection of the gift, and thereby the rejection of participatory being. The result is loss of a properly ontological sort, and it is a loss that proliferates and multiplies as the sinner, the loser, attempts to grasp ever more firmly what is not there at all: the illusion of a mode of being independent of God. This proliferative loss eats away at the soul, causing the progressive loss of its distinctive properties (freedom, choice, judgment, understanding, virtuous habit, and so on) to the point where the soul returns to that from which it came: *nihil,* nothing, the void, simple absence. The prodigal approaches this condition. All that's left to him is the capacity to repent and ask the father to be given once again the substance he has consumed. Were he to have lost that capacity too, he would have ceased to be, for that was the last remaining capacity that distinguished him from the pigs, the last remaining property that distinguished him from nonhuman existence. When the body is sufficiently corrupted, it dies; when the soul is sufficiently corrupted, it ceases to be. In both cases, what's left is the trace, or what Augustine calls the *vestigium.* For the body that means decaying material components; for the soul it means psychic detritus of various sorts. But in either case, it means annihilation on the definition in play here.[16]

Augustine, along with most other Christian thinkers, does not accept this conclusion, even though his language and his ontological assumptions suggest that he might—suggest, that is, not only that the soul's definition permits the possibility that it could come to nothing but also that much about the soul and its powers makes it inevitably tend toward the nothing from which it came. He is representative of most Christian thinkers in this refusal, but unlike many he often uses language that undercuts this refusal even when it is being explicitly offered. Consider the following passage:

> The human soul is truly said to be immortal, but it nevertheless has its own kind of death. To call the soul immortal is to say that it does not cease to live and to experience, no matter how little. But the body is mortal because it can be abandoned by all life since it does not at all live from itself. The death of the soul happens, therefore, when God abandons it, just as that of the body happens when the soul abandons it. And so the death of both together, which is to say of the whole human being, occurs when a soul deserted by

God deserts the body. For then the soul does not live from God, and the body does not live from the soul. In this way there occurs the death of the whole human being, which the authority of divine speech calls the second death.[17]

The central analogy that Augustine uses to link the first death with the second in this passage is that of desertion or abandonment. When the body is abandoned by the soul, it is left behind completely and irreversibly. That is what abandonment means. When the body is left in this way, death is the result, as Augustine explicitly says. This death is the death of the body; it is also, in the terms of this essay, the annihilation or bringing to nothing of the body. The body's lifelessness just is its annihilation. All that's left of a soulless body (as anyone who has seen dead bodies knows very well) is the physical trace. The dead human body is no longer a *corpus humanum*, a human body, at all; neither is it a corporeal substance. It is detritus, to be scattered, pulverized, buried, or burned. By analogy, one might expect Augustine to say, when God has completely or irreversibly abandoned the *anima humana*, the human soul, it too is brought to nothing, annihilated. Augustine does say that the soul dies, and he gives no reason in the quoted passage not to read God's desertion of the human soul in the same way as the soul's abandonment of the human body. If it were to be read in the same way, the conclusion would be that the soul bereft of God is no longer a human soul, because among the things that defined it as such was exactly God's presence to it as sustainer of it in being. Without that, whatever remains is a trace—not a corporeal trace, as with what's left when the soul abandons the body, but rather a noncorporeal trace, psychic detritus without any principle of identity that could permit it to continue in being.

On this interpretation, the second death would be the bringing of the soul to nothing, its annihilation. And the plausibility of this reading is deepened by recalling the pervasiveness in Augustine of emphasis upon the idea that the *anima humana* is brought into being out of nothing and has a constant tendency to damage itself by losing being, by tending toward the nothing from which it came. A soul bereft of God would necessarily be nothing, for only God's graceful act brought it into being, and only God's graceful act sustains it in being. Without these, it comes to nothing. The second death does to the soul what the first death does to the body: brings it to nothing.

But Augustine resists this conclusion, in the passage quoted and consistently elsewhere. And he does so even though the grammar of his thought strongly supports it. "The human soul is truly said to be immortal," he says, which is to say that it never ceases to live (*vivere*) and to experience (*sentire*). But why is this so? Why is it necessary to say that an *anima humana* related to God as a dead body is to a soul separated from it continues to be a subject of experience, and does so without end? What sustains, in Augustine and in the later tradition, the view that the human soul is necessarily immortal, no matter what damage it does to itself?

The Impossibility of Self-Annihilation

Augustine and Aquinas

Augustine, in his early work *De immortalitate animae*, notes that it is hard to say why the *animus*,[18] the human soul, should not come to nothing (*ad nihilum cadere*), since it is clear that it is subject to defects (*defectus*), and this suggests at least that it can be reduced in being, for defect is loss, and loss repeated and magnified might eventually bring the loser to nothing.[19] But then he goes on to give reasons why this cannot be so: why, that is to say, the soul cannot annihilate itself.

First, he says that the soul must be immortal because it is the locus for reason and order (*ratio, disciplina*), and since these never perish, it must also be the case that the *anima* does not perish.[20] This argument appears to assume that if x is the locus for y, y cannot exist without x—on that reading, the relation "is the locus of" would be one of necessary conditionality: without x, no y. Allowing that understanding, all that follows from this first argument is that at any time some soul must exist, not that each and every soul must always exist.[21]

The second argument is that even bodies extended in space cannot come to nothing, and how much more is this the case for souls, which are *melior et vivacior* (better and more lively, more alive) than bodies.[22] Augustine thinks that bodies cannot come to nothing because however small the parts into which they are divided, there is always something left—a version of Zeno's paradox of motion. But this is an understanding of what it is to come to nothing at odds with that in play in this essay. Augustine means only that once a body has existed there will always be traces of it, and that if this is true of bodies it must also be true of souls. This is right, but it is quite compatible with the view that particular bodies (and, by extension, particular souls) can come to nothing. A human body does so when it ceases to live, no matter what traces are left behind. This second argument, too, does not achieve what Augustine would like it to.

Augustine also several times makes use of an argument for the soul's immortality from our natural and universal desire for immortality. To be happy (*beatus*, blessed) is what everyone wants, he says—a claim that goes back at least to Aristotle and that Augustine asserts from the beginning to the end of his career. But the desire for happiness entails desire for immortality: "For a person to live happily, he must live."[23] And since it is the case, Augustine thinks, that we are *beatitudinis capax*, we must also be *immortalitatis capax*.[24] This argument, however, does not show that each human being is inevitably or necessarily incapable of annihilation; it shows only that each human being possibly has an existence that does not come to an end. This claim is certainly essential to the grammar of fully Christian thought: without it there is no orthodoxy. But it is far from requiring the stronger claim that each human being is inevitably or necessarily beyond annihilation, and it is quite compatible with conditional immortality.[25]

Augustine does not sufficiently distinguish between the thesis that every soul is possibly immortal and the thesis that every soul is necessarily so. He wants to claim the second, but the reasons he gives for doing so are not probative. The tension I've indicated remains unresolved in Augustine. He certainly wants to say that annihilation does not and cannot occur for any human being, but he also wants to say that we can always move ourselves toward nothingness by self-diminution. And there the matter remains for him. Both threads are prominent in the fabric of his eschatological thought, but it is far from clear that a garment woven from both can hold together.

Aquinas, on this matter as on so many an inheritor and elaborator of Augustine's thought, takes the same substantive position as Augustine on the essentials—that every human being is an embodied rational soul; that the rational soul survives the death of the body and can temporarily exist (though not as a human being) in a disembodied state;[26] and that each rational soul is reunited with its body at the general resurrection and thereby becomes a human being for eternity in either heaven or hell—but uses a more precise (and in some respects more problematic) technical terminology to explain and defend the position, and more specifically the part of it that asserts the impossibility of annihilation for any human being.

In discussing whether the soul, the *anima* (also called *anima rational*, *anima humana*, or *anima intellectiva*, terms effectively synonymous for the purposes of this discussion), can come to nothing, Aquinas usually asks whether it can be corrupted, which is to say whether *corruptio* is possible for it, whether it can become *corrupta*. Corruption, in turn, is defined as something's transformation or alteration (*transmutatio*, *mutatio*) away from being and toward nonbeing.[27] Corruption may be complete, in which case the thing corrupted ceases to be, as when formed matter loses its form in the death of an animate creature or the pulverization of an inanimate object;[28] or it may be partial, as when the corrupted thing loses some of its being, as in the amputation of a limb from an animate body or the removal of some part of an inanimate one. And he understands the *anima humana* as an intellectual substance (*substantia intellectualis*), sometimes referred to simply as *intellectus*.[29] Our question as it presented itself to Aquinas, therefore, was: Is it possible for intellectual substances in general and the human soul in particular to undergo corruption, whether partial or complete? He answers both no and yes, and the two answers can be reconciled only with some difficulty.

The dominant answer is the negative one. Corruption is contrary to the definition of an intellectual substance, Aquinas thinks, which means that intellectual substances are not and cannot be subject to it. If every intellectual substance subsists in its own essence,[30] which is a standard definition offered by Aquinas, this is just to say that existing is proper to it and that it is not dependent upon anything external to or other than itself. It follows from this definition that substances of this kind cannot lose being,[31] which, put differently, is also to say that they have no potential whatever for nonbeing.[32] Once such things are, they necessarily continue to be. They cannot be reduced or brought to nothing by anything other than themselves, and there is nothing intrinsic to themselves that permits or forces them to tend toward nonbeing. Were there anything of this sort, the incoherent result would be *separetur a seipsa*,[33] that it would become separated from itself.

This is a piece of broadly Aristotelian metaphysics. If a particular substance (a particular existent that bears properties) is noncorporeal, this means that it has no necessary dependence upon anything corporeal.[34] For a particular substance to be intellectual, capable of having knowledge, is for it to be noncorporeal. And the human soul is, by definition, an intellectual and therefore noncorporeal substance, from which it follows that it has no necessary dependence upon anything corporeal. The final move is then to say that corruption belongs only to bodies, to the corporeal. This series of definitions yields the following summary position, of which Aquinas says that it is the one *quam fides nostra tenet*, the one held by our faith: "That the intellective soul [the soul capable of understanding] is a substance not dependent on a body; that there are as many intellective substances as there are bodies; that they continue as separated [substances] when [their] bodies are destroyed without passing into other bodies; and that in the resurrection each [separated soul] assumes again a body numerically identical with the one it had laid down [at death]."[35]

Aquinas here (and in many other places) affirms inevitable immortality of a particular sort. What provides the possibility of such immortality for each human being is that one part of that human being, the soul, does not die when another part of it, the body, dies. But it is not the kind of immortality that permits passage of that soul into new and different bodies. No, a particular soul exists in only one of two ways: either as embodied in one and the same body ("numerically identical," *idem corpus numero*),[36] or as "separated," not embodied at all. But each and every intellective soul must necessarily, once it comes into existence, continue to exist in one of these two ways because of the impossibility, given the kind of thing it is, that it can be corrupted.

That is Aquinas's negative answer to the question of whether an intellectual substance—a soul—can undergo corruption. It is the dominant answer. But there is also a positive answer.

Consider the following claim, made by an objector: "Furthermore, everything that comes from nothing is capable of returning to nothing. But the human soul is created out of nothing, and is therefore capable of returning to nothing. And so it follows that the soul is corruptible."[37] Aquinas answers that, yes, of course it's true that whatever came from nothing can return to nothing "unless it might be kept in being by the hand of the one who rules it. But it is not said to be a corruptible thing because of this; [it would be so described] if there were some principle of corruption intrinsic to it. It's in this sense that 'corruptible' and 'incorruptible' are essential predicates."[38]

Aquinas acknowledges here that the human soul is *vertibile in nihil*, capable of returning toward nothing, which is to say capable of approaching annihilation. He squares this with his earlier insistence that the human soul is by definition incapable of being corrupted by claiming that calling something "corruptible" is claiming that it is essentially so, while to say the human soul can be brought to nothing if God does not continue to preserve it in being is to attribute the soul's loss of being not to itself but to something extrinsic to it. And since this is not to predicate essentially, it follows that even if we allow that the soul can be brought to nothing by God's action (or inaction), this does not amount to saying that the soul is corruptible. Fair enough. The upshot, though, is that even though on Aquinas's usage it remains proper to say that the human soul is not corruptible, this remains quite consistent with the claim that the human soul can be brought to nothing.[39]

The most direct and clear treatment by Aquinas of these difficult questions is in q. 104 of the first part of the *Summa theologiae*. This question discusses God's *conservatio* of the cosmos, and the first point made there is that yes, of course, every creature must be "conserved," maintained or kept in being, by God. If it were not, it would cease to be: *sine eo* [sc. Deo] *esse non possit*.[40] All creatures (and this includes us) receive *esse* from God as the air receives light from the sun: so long as the sun shines (God conserves), the air is full of light (beings continue to be); when the sun doesn't shine (God ceases to conserve), darkness falls (beings cease to be).[41] But human beings, since we are (on Aquinas's view) embodied rational souls (which, for the reasons already canvassed, have no natural capacity for nonbeing), can come to nothing only if God ceases to conserve us. God's so ceasing would be both necessary and sufficient for our ceasing to be.

Next, Aquinas asks whether God is able to return any creature to nothing (*aliquid in nihilum redigere*), and he answers that God's freedom means that he could at any time take any creature out of existence.[42] Just as he is not constrained by the necessity of his nature to create anything in the first place but does so freely, so he is not constrained to conserve any particular creature. Any one of us (or all of us) could, therefore, come to nothing. It's worth noting that this position contradicts Augustine's. For him, the *anima Deo deserta* does not cease to be; for Aquinas, anything *Deo deserta* would have to come to nothing.

But q.104 doesn't end at that point. Having established that God's ceasing to conserve would be both necessary and sufficient for any human being's coming to nothing, he goes on to ask whether as a matter of fact anything is brought to nothing. And the answer to this is no. In rational creatures *non est potentia ad non esse*,[43] as already noted, and God will not cease to conserve any of us because to do so would not make his free and graceful gift evident (*non pertinet ad gratiae manifestationem*).[44] The conclusion is that no rational creature comes to nothing because the only condition that could bring this about lacks *convenientia*: it is, that's to say, something God wouldn't do, something inappropriate to his nature.

Aquinas is forced in this question to approach a self-contradiction. In the response to one objection he says that creatures possess intrinsically (*ex seipsa*) a tendency toward nonexistence;[45] in another place he says that creatures have no potential for nonexistence.[46] It is possible with some work to resolve this apparent contradiction, but the presence of the two claims in the same question does dramatize the tension in Aquinas's position. On the one hand we have no tendency toward (no possibility of) coming to nothing because we are immaterial substances, and such, by definition, lack such tendencies. But on the other hand, being created out of nothing as we are, we must have such a tendency, and this is again because of the kind of being we are.[47] So we are beings who in one respect find nonbeing impossible and in another tend toward it.

Aquinas's position is of course not compatible with the claim that we can bring ourselves to nothing. For him, were any one of us to be brought to nothing, this would have to be because of something God did or did not do. This yields an important difference between Thomistic and Augustinian thought. For Aquinas (and so also for Thomists), our nature as (in part) intellectual substances makes it impossible for us to damage ourselves so that we tend toward nonexistence. And for Augustine and Augustinians, such talk is unavoidable: it is the only proper construal of sin. This difference will dispose Augustinians toward taking the possibility of self-annihilation more seriously than Thomists are likely to do.

Augustine denies that our propensity toward and capacity for self-annihilation is ever brought to term, but he leaves it unclear why. Aquinas denies that we have any such capacity, while affirming that we would indeed be brought to nothing if God were to desert us.

Augustine, as I've shown, defines damnation, the second death, in exactly these terms with the formula *totius hominis mors est cum anima Deo deserta deserit corpus*. The verb here, *deserere*, is worth comment. *Serere* means to link, connect, couple, or join; *de-serere* therefore means most fundamentally to unlink, decouple, separate, disconnect, and then, by extension and intensification, to abandon, desert, depart from. Augustine, ever sensitive to verbal connotation and echo, means all this. When God deserts us—and God does desert the damned—we are truly bereft, left deserted and destitute, left with nothing but ourselves. And if you came into being out of nothing and are kept in being only by God's continued presence and caress, then to be left with nothing but yourself is in fact to be left with nothing. Aquinas agrees that if we were deserted by God we would come to nothing, but he denies that God ever in fact deserts us: all of us, even the damned, are conserved, kept in being, exactly because God always and inevitably remains present to us.

Neither Augustine's position nor Aquinas's is satisfactory. Augustine's unsatisfactoriness lies in his unwillingness to have the courage of his convictions and draw the conclusion not only that we have the capacity to take ourselves out of existence but that God permits some of us to do so. Aquinas's unsatisfactoriness lies in his unwillingness to permit us even the capacity to act in such a way as to corrupt—move from being toward nonbeing—ourselves. There is, I think, a better way, a position that permits affirmation of the possibility of self-annihilation, and, following Augustine's definition of the second death, of self-annihilation as identical with damnation. To that I'll turn in the final section of this essay, but first—at least for Catholics—some comment on magisterial teaching on this question is necessary.

The Magisterium

The magisterium has consistently claimed that the soul, and with it the human being, is immortal, and has sometimes clearly defined as doctrinal error the view that it is or may be mortal. Such magisterial teaching, however, has not usually made a clear distinction between the thesis that every soul—and with it every human being—is necessarily incapable of coming to nothing and the thesis that every soul—and with it every human being—is possibly incapable of coming to nothing. There are also magisterial texts that appear, by their tendency toward the view that there are two, and only two, final ends (eternal bliss and eternal suffering), to rule out the possibility of annihilation.

Prominent among magisterial texts of this latter kind is *Benedictus Deus*, a Constitution promulgated by Benedict XII in 1336.[48] Benedict's central purpose in this text was to exclude the possibility that the saved are elsewhere than heaven and the damned elsewhere than hell during the period between their deaths and the day of the final and general judgment. Instead, those who die *in actuali peccato mortale* descend at once (*mox*) to hell, where they suffer the pains of hell until, at the day of judgment, they appear embodied before Christ to get what's finally coming to them, which is eternal embodied life in either heaven or hell (with numerous qualifications in the former case about purgatorial suffering). Benedict's interest here is not in the possibility (or impossibility) of annihilation; it is only in emphasizing the importance of thinking, first, that everyone's final end is set (though not necessarily that it is known to them) at their death; that there is no lag between death and the experiential beginning of that end; and that among the possible ends is endless embodied suffering. This last point does not contradict my suggestion that annihilation is possible; it would do so only if the categories into which Benedict divides human beings were exhaustive, which the Constitution does not say. It does contradict the view that the only two eternal ends possible for us are the beatific vision and annihilation, but since the Constitution does not say that as a matter of fact anyone meets the conditions for eternal embodied suffering, it remains compatible with the view that, first, annihilation is possible, and, second, that no one in fact suffers eternally. In this it is typical of magisterial texts on hell and damnation; and many scriptural and magisterial texts affirm the possibility that no one is damned much more forcefully than the bare possibility of this provided by a strong reading of *Benedictus Deus*.[49]

But the question of magisterial teaching on the possibility of hell's emptiness is not the central issue here, for every position on that question is neutral to the question of whether annihilation for some is possible. Of more interest is what the magisterium has to say about immortality, whether of soul or person; for if all persons are necessarily immortal, then annihilation is not possible.

And on that question there are some interesting materials, among which is the discussion at the eighth session of the Fifth Lateran Council, held on 19 December 1513, of the mortality of the soul.[50] The council fathers identified as among the *perniciosissimi errores* introduced by the ancient enemy the view that the *anima rational* (also called the *anima intellectiva*) is mortal (*quod videlicet mortalis sit*). In opposition to this view, the council fathers claimed that the soul is *immortalis*, quoting Matthew 10:28 ("They cannot kill the soul") and John 12:25 ("Whoever hates his soul in this world will keep it in eternal life"), and saying that if the soul were not immortal Christ's promises of eternal reward and punishment would be empty and the saints would be *miserabiliores cunctis hominibus*.

What's rejected here, it seems, is the view that the soul is necessarily mortal, that it belongs to its definition to cease to be. This is principally because, were this true, the eternal rewards and punishments spoken of by Christ would not be possible. The scriptural verses quoted say that no one other than you can kill your soul[51] and that there is an eternal reward for those who merit it. These claims certainly entail the falsity of the claim that the soul is necessarily mortal, necessarily capable of being annihilated. But they are neutral with respect to the claim that the soul is possibly capable of annihilation, which is to say that there are circumstances under which it may come to nothing. The Fifth Lateran's claims are, then, at least prima facie compatible with the position that self-annihilation is possible, as they are also compatible with the position that it is not actual.

The *Catechism*, too, is explicit in its support of the claim that the soul is immortal, which it glosses to mean that " [the soul] does not perish when it separates from the body at death, and it will be reunited with the body at the final Resurrection."[52] Authorities quoted in support of this claim are the Fifth Lateran, already discussed; Paul VI's *Sollemnis professio fidei* (1968), which merely says that human beings (*homines*) are created by God with spiritual and immortal souls;[53] and *Gaudium et spes*, a document from the Second Vatican Council that uses the same phrase.[54] These texts, while explicit and clear and most naturally read to rule out the possibility that any human soul can come to nothing, are *obiter dicta*. Their claims about the soul's immortality (and again, the distinction between the soul's necessary mortality and its possible or conditional mortality is not made) occur almost by the way, in contexts in which the argumentative focus is elsewhere. But the texts do show at least that it is almost a routine rule of composition that whenever the *anima humana* is mentioned it must be characterized as *spiritalis* and *immortalis*.

In 1979, the Congregation for the Doctrine of the Faith issued a brief "Letter on Certain Questions Concerning Eschatology."[55] It was prompted, it claims, by a concern that the church's teachings about eternal life have been to some extent undermined in the minds of the faithful—that even where they are still believed, they are not paid much attention. It reiterates the church's central claims on these matters, among which is the following: "The Church affirms that a spiritual element survives and subsists after death, an element endowed with consciousness and will, so that the 'human self' subsists, lacking, however, for a while, the complement of its body. To designate this element, the Church uses the word 'soul,' the accepted term in the usage of Scripture and Tradition."[56]

This is a clear affirmation that the soul continues after death. The Congregation's main interest in affirming this, however, is to combat, not the view that the soul (and therefore the human being) is conditionally immortal, but rather the view that it is not possibly immortal, that no interim disembodied state is possible. The document goes on to emphasize the importance of keeping the word *soul* as a lively item of churchly vocabulary; of avoiding doctrinal positions that "would render meaningless or unintelligible" prayers offered for the dead together with other modes of relating the living to the dead; and of avoiding claims about what happens to people when they die that would render incoherent the doctrine of the Assumption. None of these matters has any direct bearing on the question of conditional immortality.

The letter continues: "In fidelity to the New Testament and Tradition, the Church believes in the happiness of the just who will one day be with Christ. She believes that there will be eternal punishment for the sinner, who will be deprived of the sight of God, and that this punishment will have a repercussion on the whole being of the sinner. She believes in the possibility of a purification for the elect before they see God, a purification altogether different from the punishment of the damned. This is what the Church means when speaking of Hell and Purgatory."[57] The phrases of relevance here are those that treat hell. These phrases, especially "eternal punishment for the sinner," can be read in such a way as not to contradict the view that the ordinary meaning of damnation is annihilation. What, after all, could be more punishing for a being made for the eternal happiness of the *visio Dei* than to eternally lack that delight? Such lack would certainly be entailed by annihilation. And this interpretation is certainly compatible with the phrase "this punishment will have a repercussion on the whole being of the sinner." However, it must be admitted that the reading just suggested is unlikely to be the one the Congregation had in mind. It is much more likely that the term *punishment,* thrice repeated in the paragraph quoted, was intended to imply that the damned continue to exist and to suffer, not that they go out of existence. However, the surface of the text does not immediately rule out the view that some human beings may go out of existence. The letter certainly does not make the distinctions between conditional and necessary immortality necessary for full discussion of this topic.

There is, then, little conciliar teaching of direct relevance to conditional immortality, and what little there is has other interests. Other magisterial teaching is somewhat more expansive, but even here, although there is considerable interest in rejecting the view that immortality is impossible for human beings and in affirming the view that damnation is possible, there is not much that speaks directly to annihilation as a form of (or as coextensive with) damnation. It remains possible for a Catholic thinker to speculate along these lines, as I shall now do.

Self-Annihilation Redivivus: A Speculative Position

So, what have we?

First, there is a consistent, persuasive, and elegant Augustinian (and in my view properly Christian) position according to which we can annihilate ourselves. This position begins from three axioms. The first is that we have been brought into being by God from nothing, which means that we exist only as participants in God. This is the doctrine of creation as it should be rendered. The second is that we actively and inevitably seek to return to the nothing from which we came by attempting to extricate ourselves from participation in God. This is the doctrine of sin as it should be rendered. And the third is that there is nothing about us or about God that requires our inevitable failure at the annihilation we constantly attempt. From these axioms it follows that we may succeed, and that some of us may already have succeeded, which is to say that some human beings who once existed no longer do.

This Augustinian view may be extended easily in the following direction. Suppose damnation is defined as the definitive and irreversible success of the sinner at prosecuting the project of sin. That project, recall, is extrication from participation in God. Complete success at this would simply mean nonexistence, for participation in God is the only kind of existence there is; and if the success were not only complete but irreversible, the upshot would be a final nonexistence, annihilation without the possibility of reversal by new creation. Such a definition of damnation yields annihilation as a synonym. To be damned, definitively and irreversibly extricated from participation in God, would be to be brought to nothing. And so it would follow that if hell is populated by the damned, hell would have to be empty because those who have been brought to nothing populate nowhere.

Notice that this position is not the same as most varieties of universalism. Those doctrines typically (perhaps always) assume that there are two and only two final destinies, heaven and hell, and that each human being will occupy one or another of them for eternity. To say that hell is empty on ordinary universalist assumptions, then, means that everyone is or will be in heaven. But to say that hell is empty on annihilationist assumptions means that those not in hell aren't necessarily in heaven either. They may instead have come to nothing.

There is another important difference between hell's emptiness on universalist assumptions and the same on annihilationist assumptions—at least according to the speculative version of annihilationism on offer here. On this version of annihilationism, it belongs to the very definition of hell that it be empty. If hell is the place of the damned, and the damned are those who have taken themselves out of existence, then hell must be the place of no one.[58] It would be incoherent to suppose otherwise. For universalists, however, hell's emptiness does not belong to the definition of hell. It is, for them, not incoherent to suppose hell inhabited. And even for those (few, perhaps none) who think universalism not just true but necessarily so, the necessity of hell's emptiness is not derived from the definition of hell together with a particular understanding of damnation's nature; rather, it is typically derived from a complex set of connections among particular understandings of God's nature and human nature.[59]

Annihilationism of the stripe under consideration here is also quite compatible with intense and long-lived postmortem sufferings for those whose habits and character make this appropriate. It is also, interestingly, compatible with the view that not all of those undergoing such postmortem sufferings are assured that they will end—though they are assured that while they continue they could end, whether in heaven or annihilation.[60] This is just to say that the sufferings after physiological death of those who do not at once begin to know as they are known are always open to either of the two ends mentioned. Experienceable suffering must always be open to ending by repentance or annihilation; it cannot by definition be irreversible, as are the sufferings of those in Augustine's or Dante's hell. A human being *Deo deserta* would, just because of that, be nonexistent. Those who suffer after death would be sure neither of their final salvation, as are those in purgatory, nor of their final extinction. They would be, instead, like the prodigal among the swine, vastly reduced, in agony, but capable always of penitence that would issue in penance and forgiveness. To lose the capacity for such penitence would exactly be to be brought to nothing, to be *Deo deserta*.[61]

This speculative annihilationism envisages only two final destinies: annihilation and full participation in God; or, to describe the same two differently, self-caused final and irreversible separation from God, and final acquiescence to God's offer of that blissful participation in himself that is beatitude. If, as the tradition almost universally asserts, the second coming of the Lord Jesus Christ, the resurrection of the body, and the Last Judgment together mark the final separation of sheep from goats, then there will be no resurrection for damnation, and Augustine's speculations about the nature of physical bodies fitted for eternal suffering will be relegated to their proper place, which is as theologoumena derived from a flawed eschatology. What there will be is resurrection for eternal life.

Before the final separation of sheep from goats (which will mean the goats' annihilation), there is as much scope as you like for suffering and torment, whether in this life (where it cannot be denied) or after physiological death. But this suffering will be of two kinds only: first, purificatory (purgatorial) suffering, belonging to those whose final beatitude is certain (though not necessarily to them) and who need to suffer only as do those seeking the healing of a diseased body by surgery; and second, open-ended suffering, belonging to those who have not yet either irrevocably damned themselves or irrevocably consented to God's offer of salvation. They suffer as did the prodigal among the swine.

I present this view not as the correct one, the one Christians ought to hold, but rather as a view that Christians would do well to entertain. I entertain it myself, taking it to have many advantages and on the whole to be preferable to its major competitors. I do no more than entertain it, however, because I take it that no fully detailed eschatology can have the kind of credibility that demands assent from Christians.[62] Some eschatological claims do demand such assent, being sufficiently deeply rooted in scripture and tradition that they form part of the grammar of orthodoxy. Among these I would include the doctrine of the resurrection of the body, with its concomitant anthropological claim that no human being can exist as such absent a body; the doctrine that eternal beatitude is possible for each human being; and the doctrine that productive and loving relations are possible between the dead and the living. But beyond that, all is speculation, and even the claims just mentioned are capable of many different construals. The history of Christian thought about the postmortem destinies of human beings is a series of attempts, often beautiful and inspiring, sometimes grimly terrifying, to put these non-negotiable elements together into pictures and systems. These pictures ought, without exception, to be entertained rather than taught as dogma, and for the most part the Catholic Church both represents and advocates this modesty with respect to eschatological speculation. It may be that Protestants are, in general, somewhat less modest about these matters.

What are the main objections to the speculative annihilationism I've presented here?

The first, and for most Christians I expect the most pressing, is that one thing or another in the tradition's authoritative sources—scripture, and (for Catholics) magisterial tradition—contradicts and thus rules out one or more of the central claims of this variety of annihilationism. I shall not say more about objections of this sort here. My brief comments above on (Catholic) magisterial teaching show that I take the annihilationism entertained here to be at least possibly compatible with that teaching. And since I take that teaching to be a proper (though partial) development of what's said and implied by scripture on these matters, the same applies to that. Scripture presents, on my view, no clear, unambiguously detailed picture of what happens at death, and those who think it does typically labor under a set of dubious hermeneutical assumptions. Objections of this sort are important, therefore, but I do not think it likely that they will lead to the conclusion that the speculative annihilationism I'm entertaining should as a matter of principle not be entertained.

A second set of objections might center upon the idea that annihilationism does not treat free human action with sufficient moral seriousness. If, it might be said, I can annihilate myself by sinning, then I do not have to live with the consequences of my sin, and this makes my sin less morally serious than would be the case had I to suffer its consequences eternally.[63] This objection will be powerful for some. They will think that coming to nothing doesn't count as an eternal consequence of moral seriousness, or that at least it counts as less of one than would eternal torment of body and soul. Who, such objectors might say, wouldn't choose annihilation over torment? The answer, of course, is that many would not. Many find the idea of coming to nothing vastly more frightening—and, hence, more serious—than the idea of eternal torment. Consider Philip Larkin's lines:

The mind blanks at the glare . . .
. . . .
. . . at the total emptiness for ever,
The sure extinction that we travel to
And shall be lost in always. Not to be here,
Not to be anywhere,
And soon; nothing more terrible, nothing more true.[64]

Nothing more terrible . . . Larkin's understanding of the void of annihilation is, I expect, quite widely shared. For those who do share it, the objection under discussion here will not carry much weight. If, then, as I think, one of the criteria that ought to be used to discriminate eschatologies that ought to be entertained from those that ought not is the seriousness they give to human action here below, application of this criterion will not suffice to show that speculative annihilationism ought to be rejected.

A third objection might say that it is always better for persons to continue in being, even without possibility of salvation, than for them to go out of being by means of self-annihilation. Perhaps—though my confidence in my own or anyone else's capacity to judge which of two dreadful alternatives like these is better in God's eyes is sufficiently small that the "perhaps" needs emphasis. But even if, *per impossibile*, it were to be established that it is better for someone to be damned than to cease to be, it still does not follow that God would not permit self-annihilation. There are many cases in which God does not prevent (and thus permits) the occurrence of a state of affairs worse than other possible states of affairs—for example, Eve's sin, and all subsequent sins. If, then, God would not and does not permit self-annihilation, it must be for reasons other than that damnation is in his eyes better. And it remains obscure, to put it mildly, what such reasons might be. Aquinas thinks, as already noted, that God's permission of self-annihilation would lack *convenientia* because it would not make God's grace manifest. But judgments about what does and what does not lack *convenientia* are notoriously difficult to assess.

A fourth set of objections might appeal to ideas about justice and punishment. We saw above that magisterial teaching often uses this language, and scripture certainly does. An objector might say that divine justice requires that God punish sinners for their sin and that such punishment requires at least that the one receiving it continue in being so that its flavor can be agonizingly tasted. There are large and difficult questions here, not least about God's nature and the nature of punishment. These questions are certainly worth pursuing, but it is clear enough at first blush that if punishment is defined as the loss of some good that would otherwise have been possessed, a loss produced as direct result of the actions of the one punished, then annihilation fills the bill just as well as eternal suffering. The good lost—beatitude—is the same in both cases, and the losing of it is a loss greater than which none can be conceived. To claim that pain experienced is, for the sufferer, worse than annihilation returns us to the previous objection, which I've already suggested is not remotely decisive. The only other difference in play might be one of agency. Perhaps, the objector might say, God must be involved as direct agent of punishment, one who requires and brings about pain rather than annihilation; and since speculative annihilationism makes the principal agent of annihilation the sinner rather than God, and annihilation does not involve pain, this is a disadvantage for speculative annihilationism.

This is a deep and important objection, but it cannot finally be sustained, I think—though all I can do in a single paragraph is indicate the most pressing reasons why this is so. Sin, the averting of sinners by their own actions from God's loving face, has nothing whatever to do with God. It is an absence, a horror, a grasp after nothing that succeeds in moving the graspers toward what they seek. God has nothing to do with the privation, the absence, that sinners seek. He cannot. He is the God who spoke the beautiful cosmos into being out of nothing, and his causal involvement in attempts to return it to nothing is and must be exactly zero. For God to inflict pain, eternally or temporarily, upon nothing-seekers would be for him to recognize an absence as a presence and to respond to it as though it were something.[65] What he does instead is to enter into and pass through that absence by incarnation, crucifixion, and resurrection, thus remaking the cosmos away from the absence introduced into it by sin and toward the harmony of ordered beauty. The doctrine of the harrowing of hell, implicit already in the Apostles' Creed, can stand as a symbolic representation of this view: God makes and remakes; he does not unmake, and to inflict pain as punishment would be to contribute to unmaking. An objector who wishes to defend the necessity of God's agency in pain-producing punishment for those who attempt to unmake themselves is insufficiently serious about what it means to say that God is creator and redeemer, and therefore all too likely to make of God a local idol engaged in a cosmic battle with dark forces. Better, altogether more Christian, to say that the only thing God does for sinners is to remake them (by baptism, by killing the fatted calf to return their substance to them) when and whenever they ask, and that the only thing sinners can do for themselves is unmaking. *Necesse est quod anima Deo deserta in nihilum cadat*; and since God does not change, remove himself, punish, or condemn to hell, this must occur by the sinner damaging himself sufficiently that God no longer sustains him—and perhaps can no longer sustain him.

Notes

I'm very grateful to the following people for making useful comments on this paper at various stages of its composition: C. Brown, J. T. Burtchaell, R. Hütter, D. Jeffreys, J. D. Kiernan-Lewis, N. Marinatos, A. Plantinga, P. Reasoner, R. Reno, C. Taliaferro, K. Yandell. None of them should be held responsible in any way for its many shortcomings. I'm honored and pleased, too, that the essay should appear in a volume commemorating the life and work of Phil Quinn. He was a first-rate philosopher with an abiding interest in the philosophy of religion in general and in the meaning and defensibility of Christian doctrine in particular: *requiescat in pace*.

1. The earliest Christian thinker to have defended a version of conditional immortality was probably Arnobius of Sicca at the end of the third century.

Self-Annihilation or Damnation? 111

2. The topics broached in this paragraph circle around the difficulties of individuation and composition: Where does one thing end and another begin? How (if at all) can we tell the difference between one thing and another? Are all such tellings tellings only? What is the proper account to give of the relation "being a proper part"? These are among the most difficult conceptual questions, and while they can be resolved (I think) for animate beings, I do not see that they can be resolved for inanimate creatures. On this see, inter alia, Peter van Inwagen, *Material Beings* (Ithaca: Cornell University Press, 1990).

3. There were debates about whether everyone has suffered or will suffer this death. Most, Augustine included, excepted Enoch and Elijah from the first death upon the basis of scriptural evidence (Gen. 5:21–24; 2 Kings 2:9–12): they, it was thought, were taken directly into heaven without dying. Some also excepted Mary. And some also thought that those who had not undergone the first death at the time of Jesus's second coming and the almost-simultaneous general resurrection would not need to die. On this latter point, see *De civitate dei* 20.20.

4. "Homo non est corpus solum vel anima sola sed qui et anima constat et corpore [referring to Gen. 2:6]. Hoc quidem verum est [Augustine is discussing the view of an opponent with whom he agrees on this point about what a *homo* is] quod non totus homo sed pars melior hominis anima est, nec totus homo corpus sed inferior hominis pars est. Sed cum est utrumque coniunctum simul, habet hominis nomen." *De civitate dei* 13.24. Augustine goes on to explain that we can refer to either the body or the soul as (a) man, but that when we do so it is good to recall that we are speaking synecdochically.

5. *Enchiridion* 29.109.

6. *De civitate dei* 21.26; *Enchiridion* 18.69.

7. "Tamen non sic mori potuerunt [Augustine is writing of the rebel angels, but he goes on to apply the same point to *homines*] ut omni modo desisterent vivere atque sentire quoniam immortales creati sunt, atque ita in secundam mortem post ultimum praecipitabuntur iudicium ut nec illic vita careant, quando quidem etiam sensu, cum in doloribus futuri sunt, non carebunt." *De civitate dei* 13.24.

8. Augustine catalogs and discusses these disagreements in *De civitate dei* 22.12–21.

9. This problem is analyzed at length in the first half of book 21 of *De civitate dei*.

10. They are discussed in the second half of book 21 of *De civitate dei*.

11. All Christians would except Jesus's human soul from this claim about damage, and some would also except Mary's. But for the rest, damage is unavoidable.

12. The doctrine of participation is a difficult one and a matter of controversy among Christians both as to whether it belongs to Christian thinking at

all and, among those who think it does, as to which of its several versions is to be preferred. In my view, some version of it is unavoidable if a fully Christian distinction between creator and creature is to be maintained, but this essay is no place to argue that point. Essential reading on the idea of participation includes Craig A. Boyd, "Participation Metaphysics in Aquinas's Theory of Natural Law," *American Catholic Philosophical Quarterly* 79 (2005): 431–45; W. Norris Clarke, S.J., "The Meaning of Participation in St. Thomas," in *Explorations in Metaphysics: Being-God-Person* (Notre Dame: University of Notre Dame Press, 1994), 89–101; Oliver Davies, *The Creativity of God: World, Eucharist, Reason* (Cambridge: Cambridge University Press, 2004), chs. 1–2 (for a critique); Cornelio Fabro, *La nozione metafisica di partecipazione secondo San Tommaso*, 2nd ed. (Turin: Società editrice internazionale, 1950); Louis Geiger, *La participation dans le philosophie de S. Thomas Aquin*, Bibliothèque Thomiste, no. 23 (Paris, 1942); Fran O'Rourke, "Aquinas and Platonism," in *Contemplating Aquinas: On the Varieties of Interpretation*, ed. Fergus Kerr, O.P. (London: SCM Press, 2003), 247–79; Kenneth L. Schmitz, *The Gift: Creation* (Milwaukee: Marquette University Press, 1982); Ferdinand Ulrich, *Homo Abyssus: Das Wagnis der Seinsfrage* (Einseideln: Johannes Verlag, 1961); John F. Wippel, "Thomas Aquinas and Participation," in *Studies in Medieval Philosophy*, ed. John F. Wippel (Washington, DC: Catholic University of America Press, 1987), 117–58.

13. "Multa enim per cupiditatem pravam, tanquam sui sit oblita, sic agit. Videt enim quaedam intrinsecus pulchra, in praestantiore natura quae Deus est: et cum stare debeat ut eis fruatur, volens ea sibi tribuere, et non ex illo similis illius, sed ex se ipsa esse quod ille est, avertitur ab eo moveturque et labitur in minus et minus quod putat amplius at amplius; quia nec ipsa sibi, nec ei quidquam sufficit recedenti ab illo qui solus sufficit: ideoque per egestatem ac difficultatem fit nimis intenta in actiones suas et inquietas delectationes quas per eas colligit." From *De trinitate* 10.5.7. Compare *De trinitate* 12.9.14. See also *De immortalitate animae* 7.12, in which Augustine explicitly says that the soul can tend toward nonexistence *(id ipsum esse minus habet, quod est deficere)* and that the extent to which it does so is the extent to which it approaches the *nihil*. For an equally lyrical display of evil as nothing, see Jean-Luc Marion's discussion of the devil as "l'idiot absolu," the one who has become "l'absolu négatif de la personne," in *Prolégomènes à la charité*, 2nd ed. (Paris: Éditions de la Différence, 1991), 36, 38. The essay from which these quotations were taken was written in 1979.

14. In saying this I mean that it echoes the Latin versions of scripture that were familiar to Augustine. For him, the authoritative scriptural texts were Greek (the Septuagint for the Old Testament and the original Greek for the New), but he read and knew these mostly in Latin versions, of which there was more than one current in his time. He had an interesting exchange of letters with Jerome on the propriety of making new translations of the Old Testament

from Hebrew rather than Greek, a procedure to which he objected on the principal ground that the Greek text of the Old Testament had been treated as authoritative by the authors of the New.

15. Augustine often uses the language of Luke 15 to describe the nature and results of sin. See, e.g., *Confessiones* 2.3.5–2.10.18. In my interpretation I draw upon Jean-Luc Marion, *God without Being: Hors-Texte* (Chicago: University of Chicago Press, 1991), 95–102; Danuta Shanzer, "Pearls before Swine: Augustine *Confessions* 2.4.9," *Revue des Études Augustiniennes* 42 (1996): 45–51; H. Derycke, "Le vol des poires, parabole du péché originel," *Bulletin de Littérature Ecclésiastique* 88 (1987): 337–48.

16. Augustine gives a very clear exposition of the logic of loss, damage, and annihilation in *Confessiones* 7.12.18.

17. "Anima humana veraciter immortalis perhibeatur, habet tamen quandam etiam ipsa mortem suam. Nam ideo dicitur immortalis, quia modo quodam quantulocumque non desinit vivere atque sentire; corpus autem ideo mortale, quoniam deseri omni vita potest nec per se ipsum aliquatenus vivit. Mors igitur animae fit cum eam deserit Deus, sicut corporis cum id deserit anima. Ergo utriusque rei, id est totius hominis, mors est cum anima Deo deserta deserit corpus. Ita enim nec ex Deo vivit ipsa nec corpus ex ipsa. Huius modi autem totius hominis mortem illa sequitur quam secundam mortem divinorum eloquiorum appellat auctoritas." *De civitate dei* 13.2. In referring to the *divinum eloquium* Augustine has in mind the use of the phrase *mors secunda* in Rev. 20:6.

18. Augustine sometimes uses *animus* and *anima* interchangeably. When he does make a distinction between them, it is to restrict *animus* to the human soul while using *anima* for any kind of soul (angelic, animal, vegetable).

19. Augustine, *De immortalitate animae* 7.12.

20. Ibid., passim.

21. Augustine here assumes, probably, the existence of a single world-soul, on something like Plotinus's model. This was an assumption he came later to reject. Without some such assumption, the argument makes little sense.

22. *De immortalitate animae* 8.15.

23. "Ut enim homo beate vivat, oportet ut vivat." *De trinitate* 13.8.11.

24. I summarize here the version of the argument given in *De trinitate* 13.8.11, but essentially the same argument is found in many other places.

25. Aquinas also makes use of this argument, but he typically does so in a more modest fashion by saying that our natural desire for immortality (endless existence) is a *signum*, a sign, of the truth that our souls are intellectual substances and therefore necessarily incapable of coming to nothing. See, inter alia, *Summa contra gentiles* 2.55.13; *Quaestiones de anima* 14, corpus; *Summa theologiae* 1.75.6, corpus.

26. On this Thomas strikingly writes, in commenting on 1 Cor. 15:17–19, "Anima autem cum sit pars corporis hominis, non est totus homo, et anima mea non est ego." Quoted in Jean-Pierre Torrell, O.P., *Saint Thomas Aquinas*, vol. 2, *Spiritual Master* (Washington, DC: Catholic University of America Press, 2003), 257 n. 12. See also Brian Davies, O.P., *Aquinas* (New York: Continuum, 2003), 110.

27. For this definition, see *Scriptum super libros Sententiarum* 2.19.1, ad 1; *Summa contra gentiles* 2.55 throughout but esp. 2.55.3, 2.55.7.

28. *Summa contra gentiles* 2.55.1–3. Thomas does say (in *Summa contra gentiles* 2.55.4) that corruption never produces absolute nonbeing, but by this he means that a trace always remains, not that the thing itself does.

29. For this usage, see *Compendium theologiae* 84.

30. "Intellectus . . . substantia subsistens in suo esse." From *Compendium theologiae* 84.

31. "Impossibile est igitur quod ipsae [formae] esse desinant." *Summa contra gentiles* 2.55.3.

32. See *Summa contra gentiles* 2.55.5, 2.55.14 ("Proprium naturis intellectualibus est quod sint perpetuae"). Compare *Quaestiones de anima* 14, corpus: "Si ergo sit aliqua forma quae sit habens esse, necesse est illam formam incorruptibilem esse."

33. This phrase is from *Summa theologiae* 1.75.6, corpus, where Aquinas is discussing *utrum anima humana sit corruptibilis*. Étienne Gilson glosses this with his customary lucidity in *The Christian Philosophy of St. Thomas Aquinas*, trans. L. K. Shook (1956; repr., Notre Dame: University of Notre Dame Press, 2002), 188.

34. "Anima intellectiva habet esse absolutum, non dependens ad corpus." *Scriptum super libros Sententiarum* 2.19.1, corpus.

35. "[Q]uod anima intellectiva sit substantia non dependens ex corpore, et quod sint plures intellectivae substantiae secundum corporum multitudinem, et quod destructis corporibus remanent separatae, non in alia corpora transeuntes sed in resurrectione idem corpus numero quod deposuerat unaquaeque assumat." *Scriptum super libros Sententiarum* 2.19.1, corpus.

36. A great deal could be said about what, for Aquinas, makes a body at a particular time numerically identical with a body at another time. But those are debates beyond the scope of this essay.

37. "Praeterea omne quod est ex nihilo est vertibile in nihil. Sed anima humana ex nihilo creata est. Ergo vertibilis est in nihil. Et sic sequitur quod anima sit corruptibilis." *Quaestiones de anima* 14, obj.19.

38. "Nisi manu gubernantis conservetur. Sed ex hoc non dicitur aliquid corruptibile, sed ex eo quod habet in se aliquod principium corruptionis. Et sic corruptibile et incorruptibile sunt praedicata essentialia." *Quaestiones de anima* 14, ad 19. Fundamentally the same point is made at *Scriptum super libros Sententiarum* 2.19.1, ad 7; *Summa theologiae* 1.50.5, ad 3; 1.75.6, ad 2.

39. It's interesting to note, too, that Aquinas's way of responding to this objection commits him to the claim that being created out of nothing is not essential or proper to the *anima humana*. This is what makes it possible for him to speak of the human soul as an intellectual substance without also speaking of it as brought into being *ex nihilo* by God. This is to give altogether too much independence to *natura*—Augustine's epigram about the Pelagians, that the enemies of grace hide themselves in the praise of nature (*Contra duas epistolas Pelagianorum* 2.1.1), begs for application.

40. *Summa theologiae* 1.104.1, corpus.

41. Aquinas takes the point and some of the arguments from Augustine, *De Genesi ad litteram* 4.12.22–23.

42. I omit comment on Aquinas's discussion of whether God conserves mediately or immediately in *Summa theologiae* 1.104.2: interesting but irrelevant to my purposes here.

43. *Summa theologiae* 1.104.4, corpus.

44. Ibid., 1.104.4, corpus.

45. "Sic igitur Deus non potest esse causa tendendi in non esse; sed hoc habet creatura ex seipsa inquantum est de nihilo." Ibid., 1.104.3, ad 1.

46. "In eis [sc. in creaturis] non est potentia ad non esse." Ibid., 1.104.4, corpus.

47. It's interesting to note that most scholarly treatments of Aquinas on the soul's immortality pass over almost in silence the claim that we have a capacity for extinction because we are created *ex nihilo*. Herbert McCabe's "The Immortality of the Soul: The Traditional Argument," in *Aquinas: A Collection of Critical Essays*, ed. Anthony Kenny (Notre Dame: University of Notre Dame Press, 1976), 297–306, is entirely representative in this respect.

48. I've consulted the Latin text in H. Denzinger and A. Schönmetzer, eds., *Enchiridion Symbolorum*, 36th ed. (Rome: Herder, 1976), §§ 530–31.

49. A representative scriptural text is 1 Tim. 2:4, which says that God wants everyone to be saved—implying, with only a little conceptual work, the possibility of that result. A representative recent magisterial text on the subject is John Paul II's *Redemptoris missio*, §§ 9–10 (text available in seven languages at www.vatican.va), where "the real possibility of salvation in Christ for all mankind" is affirmed. The best argument for universal salvation's possibility can be found in Hans Urs Von Balthasar's *Dare We Hope "That All Men Be Saved"? With a Short Discourse on Hell* (1987; repr., San Francisco: Ignatius Press, 1988). This work spawned a vast and polemical response in all the major European languages, which still continues.

50. I've consulted the Latin text in Norman P. Tanner, ed., *Decrees of the Ecumenical Councils* (London: Sheed and Ward, 1990), 605–8.

51. This is the surface meaning of the clause from Matt. 10:28 quoted above. The whole verse ("And do not be afraid of those who kill the body but cannot kill the soul; rather, be afraid of the one who can destroy both soul and

body in Gehenna," NAB) does appear to say that the soul can be killed. Augustine would interpret this to refer to the soul's second death, which on his view is not identical with its annihilation.

52. *Catechism of the Catholic Church*, 2nd ed. (Washington, DC: U.S. Catholic Conference, 1997), § 366.

53. Paul VI, *Sollemnis professio fidei*, § 8, www.vatican.va.

54. *Gaudium et spes* § 14, in Tanner, *Decrees*, 1077.

55. I quote from the English version given at www.catholicculture.org/docs. I have not seen the Latin text.

56. Congregation for the Doctrine of the Faith, "Letter on Certain Questions Concerning Eschatology," § 3. J. Neuner and J. Dupuis Neuner, in *The Christian Faith in the Doctrinal Documents of the Catholic Church*, 7th ed. (New York: Alba House, 2001), 1026–27 (where a partial English version of the letter can be found), note that the Latin version of this letter published in *Acta Apostolicae Sedis* contains a clause—"interim tamen complemento sui corporis carens"—absent from that published in *L'Osservatore Romano*. I include this clause in the version quoted above (it is not in the version given at www.catholicculture.org) because the *AAS* version bears official doctrinal weight. The difference between the two versions is interesting, however. It indicates that giving a precise account of what happens in the interim state was a difficulty for the Congregation in 1979 in much the same way and for much the same reasons as it had been for Augustine 1,600 years earlier.

57. "Letter," § 7.

58. It's worth noting that on the position I'm elaborating and entertaining here, the fairly settled view of the church that we know the devil to be damned and yet still to exist requires modification. The direction of the modification, however, should be toward considering what is meant by speaking of the devil's existence, and on this I would incline toward the picture sketched by Marion in *Prolégomènes à la charité*, ch. 1.

59. If there is a version of universalism with which annihilationism of the kind considered here is compatible, it is a possibilist (preferably middle-knowledge) variant, according to which damnation is not possible, and annihilation is possible, though as a matter of fact no one is annihilated.

60. This was C. S. Lewis's view. He thought that the postmortem sufferings of hell may come to be seen, retrospectively, as those of purgatory if you leave hell. If you don't, they will always have been hellish. See Lewis, *The Great Divorce* (New York: Macmillan, 1946), 39, 67.

61. Again, Lewis approaches this view in *The Great Divorce*. During a discussion about whether a grumbling woman will cease grumbling long enough to take the chance of repentance being offered her, the angelic interlocutor says that this is possible "if there is a real woman—even the least trace of one—still there inside the grumbling" (74). But if not, if she's become nothing but

a grumble and no longer a grumbler, there's nothing there to be saved. The same point is made in the depiction of the damned Bonaparte as nothing but a rant (20–21).

62. For useful commendations of deep epistemic modesty in this sphere, see the Congregation's 1979 "Letter" and the preface to Lewis's *Great Divorce*.

63. See Jerry L. Walls, *Hell: The Logic of Damnation* (Notre Dame: University of Notre Dame Press, 1992), 136–38, for a discussion of this point.

64. Lines from Philip Larkin's "Aubade" (1977), in Larkin, *Collected Poems*, ed. Anthony Thwaite (London: Faber and Faber, 2003), 190.

65. The pain that we suffer is always the result either of the damage to which the Fall subjected the cosmos or of the particular sins that we commit in that damaged cosmos. God does not punish us, if that means inflicting pain upon us in retribution for wrongs we have done. The only sense in which he can be said to punish us is that we, because we are damaged and sinful, may find God's caress painful. But such pain is epiphenomenal to love and has the presence of damage—which is the presence of an absence—as its necessary condition. God, therefore, does not and cannot intend the infliction of pain and has no causal implication with its occurrence. Pain is, without remainder, the felt component of absence being reduced by presence.

Part Three
Political Philosophy

Five

Moral Foundations of Liberal Democracy, Secular Reasons, and Liberal Neutrality toward the Good

Robert Audi

A comprehensive political philosophy should provide an account of the normative basis of the form of government it favors. It should also show how the normative basis it articulates can justify a constitutional structure. In that light, it will support a range of standards not only for evaluating laws and public policies but also for the ethics of citizenship on the part of individuals. The form of government in question here is liberal democracy, and my central questions are how it may best be seen to be morally grounded and how, given a plausible moral grounding, it may conceive the good of citizens. Must a liberal democracy be, for instance, neutral with respect to all goods other than those that must be maintained in order for citizens to be genuinely free and to have basic political equality? Or may it seek to promote human flourishing of various specific kinds?

These questions are not only of great theoretical interest. They also bear on many problems important in the current climate of nation building, in which constitutions must be constructed, new laws framed, and sound standards of political conduct articulated and internalized. There is a particular urgency about achieving a sound conception of liberal democracy today. The rise of terrorism is forcing the democracies of the Western world—those commonly considered liberal by any plausible definition—to weigh civil liberties against considerations of safety and to try to balance the costs of military and police power against those of social welfare.

A single paper cannot fully answer any of these questions. What it can do is present one plausible way in which liberal democracy may be morally grounded and defend, on that basis, some major elements in a position on how such a form of government may grant a special place to a certain broad conception of human flourishing. I will begin with a sketch of a theory of normative foundations of liberal democracy and, building on that, present a conception of the limits of liberal neutrality and a related view of political obligation.

An Approach to the Moral Grounding of Liberal Democracy

There are many ways to provide a normative grounding for liberal democracy, and in earlier work I have detailed a number of them.[1] They have much in common, in part because of their common object: to justify democracy's two fundamental commitments. One commitment is to the freedom of citizens; the other is to their basic political equality, symbolized above all in the practice of according one person one vote. Kant put this dual commitment of liberal democracy even more strongly. He suggested that standards of freedom and equality are the only moral ones deserving a place in the constitutional structure of a morally sound political system: "It is a fundamental principle of moral politics that in uniting itself into a nation a people ought to subscribe to freedom and equality as the sole constituents of its concept of right, and this is not a principle of prudence, but is founded on duty."[2]

Given the two fundamental commitments—which we might call the libertarian and egalitarian commitments—it is plain that a liberal democracy must respect the autonomy and political rights of persons. A vote can represent a citizen's political will only if it is autonomous. This entails that it is not only uncoerced but also free of the kinds of manipulation and rights violations that would prevent its appropriately representing the values of the voter.

If democracy may be conceived as a government *of*, *by*, and *for* the people, none of this should be controversial. The *for* here carries great weight. Conceiving a democracy as *for* the people suggests that, in a certain way, a democracy—and this certainly applies to a liberal democracy—is *individualist*. It does not view the political structure of society as subordinated to the good of a sovereign, to a class of society, or even to the glory of God, if that is conceived as incompatible with the earthly flourishing of people in society. Religious ideals and other normative standards may inspire a liberal democracy, but it must not subordinate the welfare of individuals to that of any privileged person(s), any deity, or, especially, any abstraction.

A liberal democracy may be called simply a free democracy, but *liberal* adds something important. It is not here a political term that contrasts with *conservative*. Rather, a liberal democracy is one that promotes liberty, as opposed to maintaining the minimum level of freedom required for autonomous voting by the populace. Beyond this, it characteristically encourages political participation and supports institutions, political and cultural, that foster both political participation and diffusion of power. These include a free press, a legal system that protects individuals and enforces contracts, and a system of public education. The term *liberal democracy* is too contested and varied in usage to permit precise definition, but nearly any prominent conception will provide for the elements just noted.[3]

Kant's conception of a morally sound political system, as expressed in the quoted passage, is not only normative but also moral. One might think that a plausible normative grounding of liberal democracy would have to be moral. But, given the presupposition of certain shared ends among citizens, a rationale can be provided from an instrumentalist point of view.[4] I believe that instrumentalist theories of reasons for action are seriously deficient.[5] But even apart from that, my interest here is in a moral grounding. I have already cited Kant as a source of one such grounding, and there is no question that Kantian ethics has the resources to provide the basis of a moral argument for liberal democracy as the best form of government. The same holds for utilitarianism as developed by Mill and later utilitarians. Virtue ethicists can also frame an argument for this. So can proponents of a natural-law perspective, and any of these approaches can be combined with a theology.

All of these approaches are theoretical in a sense in which not every moral approach need be. If we can identify a moral position that appeals wholly or mainly to less controversial basic standards, this will be an advantage in providing a moral foundation for liberal democracy. If, in addition, its basic standards are largely common to the other plausible moral approaches, that will be an additional advantage. My own recent work in ethics has convinced me that such a *convergence strategy* is viable and that a version of intuitionism meets the criteria just stated. Even in the form in which W. D. Ross cast intuitionism in 1930,[6] it provides a set of basic everyday moral principles that can be—and commonly are—used as guides to moral conduct.

Ross proposed, as morally fundamental, a list of prima facie duties: duties of fidelity (promise keeping, including honesty conceived as fidelity to one's word); reparation for one's wrongdoing, as where one repairs damage one did to someone's property; justice (particularly rectification of injustice, but also what we might call equitable distribution of benefits and burdens); gratitude; beneficence; self-improvement; and noninjury.[7] Let us first consider just the position consisting of the principles calling for fulfillment of these duties. I propose to leave aside the often associated controversial claim that the principles are self-evident. We then have something one might view less as a theory than as a kind of ethical common-sensism.

A great deal must be said to clarify and defend intuitionist ethics, and I have undertaken that task elsewhere.[8] Here I presuppose the revised and expanded intuitionist position defended there. It centers *both* on the Rossian principles just listed and on two others that go well with the ideals of liberal democracy. One states a prima facie obligation to enhance and preserve freedom; the other states a prima facie obligation to treat people respectfully in the manner of our actions, where this is roughly a matter of how we do what we do rather than of what actions we perform. The contrast may also be described as holding between *duties of matter*, which range over types of acts, and *duties of manner*, which call for morally appropriate ways of fulfilling the former duties. If, for instance, I must direct a student's research project, there are moral constraints on how I may do this: in communicating evaluations, in intoning my advice, even in controlling facial expressions. There are myriad ways to err here; there is also the possibility of an admirable style of interaction.

The use to be made of these ten principles will depend chiefly on a broad interpretation of them in which they are widely accepted even by people who might justify them in ways quite different from those I myself employ. Given their broad scope and wide sociopolitical applicability, we may certainly hold that they are a good basis for framing two closely related kinds of evaluative criteria important in political philosophy. First, we need *establishment criteria:* standards that enable us to judge whether a form of government, such as democracy as opposed to benevolent monarchy, is desirable. Second, we need *performance criteria:* given an actual government, we need a way to evaluate its performance. If, for instance, an envisaged form of government permits officials to be unjust (e.g., dictatorial) to citizens or to injure them, it is to that extent bad; if it encourages beneficence and self-improvement among them, it is to that extent good. The same kinds of criteria apply to actual governments.

Since intuitionists stress benevolence, they can use some of the same arguments to support the desirability of liberal democracy that a utilitarian would take to favor liberal democracy as a form of government. Given the intuitionist stress on justice and on preservation and enhancement of liberty, they can use some arguments that Kantians (including contractarians) would offer in support of liberal democracy. Given the large role intuitionism accords to virtue, both in helping others and as a target of self-improvement, it can use some arguments that virtue ethics might offer.[9] In practice, even a good government is mixed, having some bad points as well as good ones. In appraising a government, intuitionists will consider its overall merits in the light of all the relevant facts available. There is no formula for a correct decision.[10]

My main concern here is not with framing a detailed case to show that, on moral grounds, liberal democracy meets sound establishment criteria; it is to sketch a plausible way in which this might be done from an intuitionist standpoint and then to explore the extent to which a democracy viewed as morally well grounded in that way must be neutral with respect to the good. Performance criteria, then, are of more direct concern here than establishment criteria. I will assume that liberal democracy can be morally well grounded on the basis of being most likely to enable individuals to fulfill the requirements of the intuitionist principles in question (at least given an adequately educated citizenry). The plausibility of this assumption should be supported by much of what is said in the remainder of this paper. In assessing the neutrality question, however, we need not assume an ideal case. I will offer a more detailed argument for my position.

One might object that if the proposed intuitive principles are common to all the plausible ethical theories, and particularly if they are in any sense self-evident, there should not be so much moral disagreement, including even disagreement on whether the principles themselves are true. Let me suggest a line of reply to this objection. Even if there should be persisting disagreement on the truth or status of the Rossian principles as general standards of conduct, there need not be disagreement, in particular cases of decision, about the basic moral force of the considerations cited in those principles. For instance, whether or not we accept the principles expressing a prima facie obligation to keep promises and to avoid injuring others, we might, both in deciding what to do ourselves and in criticizing others, take a person's promising to do something as constituting a moral reason to do it, or the fact that running through a crowd to catch a train would knock others down as a reason not to do that. I call such agreement *in* reasons for action *operative agreement*. This is a practical kind of agreement that does not presuppose any discussion of reasons or even reflection on them. It does not require agreement *on* reasons, for instance on some principle to the effect that there are moral reasons to keep promises.

Agreement in reasons also does not require agreement on the magnitude of the force of the elements that constitute the reasons relative to that of the force of other considerations. Consider the view that killing people by poisoning their water supply with pesticides is worse than—hence prohibited by a stronger moral reason than—not treating them for the typhoid that some of them have acquired from polluted water they have already drunk. We can agree that both acts are wrong even if we differ about which is worse.

Agreement *on* reasons is a higher-order, theoretical kind of agreement. This kind of agreement also admits of degrees and comes in various kinds. We can agree that a factor, such as avoidance of lying to a friend who asks a slightly impertinent question, justifies this action, or even that it is a good reason for the action, even if neither of us can formulate, or we cannot both accept, a principle that subsumes the case. In this way, a moral principle can be like a rule of linguistic usage: we can be guided by it without being able to formulate it, and we may, at least initially, reject a formulation that describes our own practice.

It is true that, as in linguistic matters, once we begin to discuss a case in detail, particularly if we disagree and reflect on the issue, we may ascend from citing reasons for our position to formulating principles that we think support us, or undermine those who disagree with us, or both. But the fact that those who agree *in* reasons can move quickly to disagreement on them—sometimes without noticing the different level of discourse—does not undermine the distinction I am making.

If we look at moral practice rather than moral theory, we can find the most important kind of consensus needed to support the intuitionism I propose in the role I give it here. It may at least be argued that the truth and noninferential justifiability of the relevant principles best explains the high degree of consensus among people of very different backgrounds in wide segments of their everyday moral practice, and particularly in their spontaneous, intuitive moral judgments and morally relevant inferences, say from the judgment that the act of running over of a child is negligent to the conclusion that it is being wrong. Police brutality is universally abhorred, normal persons everywhere want freedom of movement and of speech, and a right to vote seems to be wanted even by those who do not take the trouble to exercise it.

To be sure, even if the suggested intuitive principles are virtually universally accepted or at least universally acceptable, the obligations they express can conflict. You may be obligated to help one person just as you find that you must keep a promise to another. Such conflicts of duties—in this instance, between beneficence and fidelity—have led to the question whether there is any general theory available to help us in cases of conflicting intuitions. Here I suggest the possibility of deriving those moral principles from, or integrating them in terms of, something more general or both. Even if they are self-evident and hence are not in *need* of justification, they may admit of it.[11] We can both treat the intuitive principles (or similar ones) as a morally autonomous framework for judging a form of government and embed them in some way in a wider theory, such as a Kantian one. This is a strategy I have developed elsewhere;[12] here I simply point out its availability. A moral grounding of liberal democracy does not depend on it.

If we do not pursue such a unifying strategy, is the intuitionist approach reduced to an eclectic position that has no distinctive character?

I think not: the idea that the wide-ranging moral principles in question are intuitively knowable (or at least justifiedly believable on the basis of reflection on their content) is defensible quite apart from any theory that unifies them. Indeed, unless there were some such principles, we would have too little basis for accepting a more general theory in the first place. If we did not find some kinds of behavior prima facie obligatory or impermissible, we would have too few definite intuitions to warrant accepting a general moral theory. Would we even be inclined to construct, say, a utilitarian or Kantian theory if we did not have intuitive paradigms of good and evil, right and wrong? I believe, then, that a carefully constructed intuitionist approach to political justification, with or without the help of a more general theory, is among the procedures we may reasonably use in attempting to ground liberal democracy. Any plausible intuitionist position will embody principles that tend to support according individuals the kind of extensive liberty and the basic political equality central to liberal democracy.

The Religious Neutrality of Liberal Democracy

Like any of the normative positions—at least any of the nontheological ones—that provide for a plausible grounding of liberal democracy, intuitionism is (except in limited ways) religiously neutral. Negatively, it does not favor any particular theology or religious position. Positively, however, it would imply the moral wrongness of certain extreme forms of religious conduct: any kind that, like ritual human sacrifice and ceremonial mutilation of children, violates intuitive standards for the protection of persons. This is the kind of limited neutrality that defenders of liberal democracy have generally considered appropriate. It provides for great diversity in styles of life, but prohibits (non-self-defensive) harms to other persons.

Even religious freedom, then, *may* be limited in some ways by a morally well-grounded and liberal democracy that is appropriately neutral in matters of religion. This point is probably not controversial, but there is disagreement concerning the degree to which a liberal democracy may *promote* the practice of religion as such, provided it does not prefer one religion over another.[13] Suppose that a majority of the people want national observance of religious holidays or, say, compulsory religious education in the schools. Must this be objectionable? The observance might be as minor as closure of government offices.

Moreover, one might provide for religious children to be instructed only in their own denominations and by people approved by authorities in those denominations, and, for the nonreligious, one might provide religious education that, being simply *about* religion, is essentially secular.

Such educational programs have existed in democratic countries. They are not directly in conflict with a plausible requirement of separation of church and state, and in any case it is arguable that no such requirement is needed for a sound liberal democracy.[14] (In some forms, as in England, its rejection may have at most a slight effect on the realization of democratic ideals.) As to compulsory religious education in the schools, although it may be conducted in a way that expresses a state preference for the interests of religious citizens over those of nonreligious citizens, it need not be. Religion is historically of immense importance; and it can be so important, not only in international relations, but also in the lives of many citizens, that requiring certain kinds of nonconfessional religious education can be defended as necessary for informed citizenship. The greater the interaction within a state between different religious groups, and the greater its involvement with countries that differ significantly in religion, the better the case for required religious education in the schools.

In religious education, however, and—even more important for this paper—in moral education, there can be at most a limited neutrality toward conceptions of the good: roughly, of human flourishing. Under the heading "conceptions of the good," I have in mind especially the standards for what elements make life worth living and should underlie people's basic choices. Should a liberal democracy promote, for instance, such favorite candidates for major roles in the good life as friendship, knowledge, artistic expression, athletic skills, the beauty of the environment, physical and psychological health, and spirituality in general, even if not religion? John Rawls, among others, has argued that the liberal state should be neutral with respect to what he called "comprehensive" views of the good.[15] Although I do not believe he made at all precise what sort of conception this is, I will assume that a view of the good encompassing even the items just cited would count as comprehensive. I want now to explore this position in the light of the broad moral standards central for intuitionist ethics and commonly affirmed by many who hold other ethical theories or none at all.

Liberal Neutrality toward the Good

There is a wide range of views regarding the extent to which a liberal democracy may be committed to a large-scale conception of the good for human beings. One view is that no such conception is appropriate and that a religiously based conception of the good is simply a special case of one. A less restrictive view is that some presuppositions about the good may be commitments of a liberal democracy but that religious conceptions are not among them. It is true that there are theories, and general conceptions, of the good for human beings that are not an appropriate basis for the underlying structure of law in a liberal democracy, but the almost unrestricted exclusion of conceptions of the good favored by some neutralists is excessive.

To be sure, if one thinks of morality as an institution directed essentially toward preventing or reducing evils,[16] it is natural to suppose that the framing of laws, especially those defining the liberties and political powers of citizens, should share this goal. Such a view of morality may be one (or even the main) route to the libertarian version of liberalism. For libertarianism (as I interpret it), the overriding concern of government should be to protect people from harm. Liberty is limited, then, only by this aim, not by, for instance, the needs of the sick or unemployed, which are widely seen to necessitate substantial taxation of those who are financially well off.

Suppose for the sake of argument that this negative conception of morality is correct at least as regards constitutional matters. We would still need an account of harms or of some even wider range of evils that can justify limitations on the freedom of citizens, for liberal democracy is clearly committed to supporting the maximal liberty citizens can exercise without certain harms (or a substantial likelihood of them).[17] Thus, even if a liberal state could be neutral toward the good, it could not be neutral toward the bad. It could not, then, be *value-neutral*.

There is, however, no sharp distinction, and perhaps no distinction in practice as opposed to principle, between a government's restricting liberty as a way to preventing harm and its doing so as a way of promoting some good. Consider education. Compulsory education is essential to prevent the harms attendant upon ignorance. But education is surely one kind of good, and it is in practice impossible to provide in a way that makes it effective in preventing harm yet is not inherently good. Even apart from that, can we reasonably design a required curriculum appropriate to a liberal democracy without making quite comprehensive presuppositions as to what counts as good human functioning, what skills are needed for good citizenship, and what is worth knowing for its own sake? Surely not. Indeed, early education is typically so deeply influential in the remainder of a person's life that we should consider very carefully what goes into the elementary school curriculum and, equally important, what values and attitudes it is likely to engender in students. In determining the content and manner of compulsory education, there may be a huge range of values, including positive ones, toward which it is virtually impossible (and not unnecessary) for the state to be neutral.

A strong neutralist might reply that government should promote human well-being but might characterize it in terms that are, as regards intrinsic goodness, value-neutral. This approach is represented by John Rawls's appeal to "primary goods," such as respect and economic security, which he takes every rational person to want but—given his commitment to a decision-theoretic concept of rationality—does not view as intrinsically good.[18] They are presumptively universal instrumental goods, being on everyone's route to desire satisfaction. However, Rawls posits nothing as worth desiring for its own sake, hence as an initial, basic constraint on rational decision.

Using this kind of decision-theoretic strategy, welfare liberalism can claim to be as neutralist toward intrinsic goodness as libertarianism. In my view, that claim is at best a surface truth. Primary goods are functional equivalents of intrinsic goods, at least on the assumption that there is no need to argue about them as providing noninstrumental reasons for action. Moreover, in their name the state can do much the same things it can do in the name of intrinsic goods.[19]

Suppose, then, that we do not assume that there are some kinds of things that are intrinsically good. Suppose further that we tie the goods suitable as a basis for structuring a liberal democracy to human nature—at least in the sense that we assume there are some things every rational person wants (where rationality is understood in the content-neutral, instrumentalist sense). Given how much our desires can be influenced by fashion, circumstance, and demagoguery, and given the growing specter of a technology that can alter our very genes, one wants moral and political theories that, in an overall way, at least, can provide standards for judging human desires independently of what they happen to be in a particular cultural and sociopolitical setting.[20] We must not allow social justice to be at the mercy of the contingencies of desire. Even if we can trust nature, we cannot in general trust its manipulators.

On the intuitionist view I defend, freedom, justice, noninjury, and beneficence are taken to be basic sources of reasons for action and, indeed, for its restriction when it would conflict with them. Let me clarify one of these elements that is particularly pertinent to the question of the limits of liberal promotion of the good. In characterizing beneficence, Ross listed improvements in knowledge, pleasure, and virtue as its main aims. Any of these three and any of the other constitutive aims of the standards that intuitionists affirm could be explicated at length, but for our purposes it suffices to say that there is a core of elements in each that are widely agreed to provide reasons for action and, in that sense, to have normative authority. Scarcely anyone would deny that, for instance, the fact that an action that would enhance the enjoyment or, especially, reduce the suffering of others is a reason (though of course not necessarily an overriding reason) to do it. This applies to governmental action as well as to individual action.

If, as I think plausible, this point about the normative authority of considerations of beneficence is not only correct but a priori, its footing is very solid indeed. Our justification for accepting the kind of beneficence principle in question need not depend on prior premises, even though such principles may be supported by them.[21] But here my concern is only to bring out that in governmental as well as individual actions there is little disagreement on the point that reducing human suffering is a reason for action, in the normative sense entailing that such a reason can justify an action and *will* if there are no counter-reasons.

In resisting this line of thought, one might reply that, although any plausible theory of the basis of liberal democracy affirms at least two values as essential constituents in such a society, namely, liberty and basic political equality, the state should be neutral on every other value and particularly toward overall conceptions of the good. This reply is at best of limited force. For just as we need some account of the good to decide what burdens to impose on the freedom of students, we will need some account of the bad to determine limitations on the freedom of citizens in general. We need some kind of account or theory of the bad, especially of the kinds of harms or evils that warrant certain *restric-*

tions of liberty, as well as a theory of competence to vote in order to determine eligibility.

Particularly in relation to determining justified restrictions of liberty, it is plain that some things will be functionally intrinsic evils, but I suspect that some will also be functionally intrinsic goods. Recall compulsory education, which surely is a requirement for ensuring competence to vote, especially at the legislative level. The educational requirements for competent judges are higher still. One may certainly seek to design a political structure in which the state is as nearly neutral as possible about the good, but even if (as Kant seemed to do in the passage quoted above) one affirms only the values of liberty and basic political equality as governing standards, there are drastic limits to how far this can go.

If there are limits, should we not stop with the most restricted conception of governmental commitment to the good that accords with these two constitutive values of liberal democracy? To answer this, we need at least two distinctions, which I will take in turn.

One distinction is between neutrality in matters of taste and plan of life and neutrality in matters of basic value and basic moral standards. The kinds of basic moral standards and fundamental values expressed by the intuitive moral principles I have introduced accommodate a wide range of tastes and plans of life. Indeed, governmental support for the kinds of values and moral principles in question enhances the potential for pluralism; it does not impose conformity.

The second distinction we need here is between structural neutrality—roughly, neutrality at the constitutional level—and policy neutrality. A liberal *state* need not, and I think should not, be neutral about such values as freedom, justice—distributive as well as retributive—education, and the provision of health care at some appropriate level, but it should be neutral (within the limits of protection of the population) about the aesthetic preferences of citizens in their own dwellings, their choice of friends, and their vacation preferences. This is a structural point, concerning the state and not a particular government within a state at a given time.

A liberal-democratic *government*, by contrast with a state and taken at a particular time and place, need not be neutral in matters on which the state should be: matters left open by a sound structure, such as the architectural style of government buildings or even the proportion of funds directed toward education as opposed to upkeep of national parks. Note, too, that governmental neutrality about something, such as who one's friends should be, does not imply neutrality about promoting the *conditions for enjoying* that kind of thing, in this case friendship, as a human good. Neutrality about what conduct constitutes the exercise of a freedom does not imply neutrality about the conditions for its preservation.

Overall, then, I do not see that the strong neutrality thesis—the view that a liberal democracy cannot presuppose any large-scale view of the good—is sustainable. Even the value commitments needed for determining the *scope* of liberty and the proper means of maintaining basic political equality seem to require recognition of some definite human goods as well as the evils that a good government seeks to prevent. There are many ways in which a liberal-democratic government should be neutral, but the strong neutrality thesis goes beyond them. A well-founded liberal society requires a commitment to at least this: ideals of free democracy, in a sense implying one person, one vote; autonomy, in the sense of self-determination in a context of extensive liberty; respect for persons, implying at least equal treatment before the law and a legal system nurturing self-respect; and material (including psychological) well-being.

Am I, then, proposing a version of what is often called *perfectionism*, a theory that takes the democratic state to be properly structured so as to realize certain ideals of the good? The term *perfectionism* is misleading in suggesting a maximizing standard. I am not proposing any such standard, and intuitionists have characteristically rejected maximization views in favor of the position that overall moral judgment (and, by implication, overall normative judgment in general) is a holistic matter and not fully appraisable in any quantitative fashion. There are elements in my view that could be claimed to imply that it is a "moderate perfectionism,"[22] but even this term is misleading. My emphasis has been on *certain* kinds of goods and evils that, within the moral limits set by the constitutive ideals of liberal democracy and the ten principles of obligation I have sketched, should guide a liberal democracy. The overall position is a version of liberalism and, perhaps in part for that reason, is at best misleadingly called a kind of perfectionism.

Granted, it is easy for any morally grounded liberalism to go too far, especially in interpreting psychological well-being. Someone might, for instance, argue for a requirement of religious observances by all citizens as part of a realization of our psychological and social good. This pattern is not entailed by any notion of psychological well-being compatible with the moral standards I have sketched as plausibly grounding liberal democracy; any notion that entailed it would be at odds at least with the religious neutrality standard governing the liberal state. Still, one can go beyond the minimal premises needed for guiding the achievement of justice alone without becoming committed to a theory of the good that is unduly restrictive. Compulsory education illustrates this point. One could take it to be a good, and certainly to be crucial for avoiding myriad evils, quite apart from a theory, as opposed to an intuitively plausible standard, of the good.

Political Obligations in Liberal Democracies

So far, I have been arguing that a wide range of substantive value commitments is compatible with the kind of neutrality appropriate to a liberal-democratic state. I have indicated, for some of those values, how they are implicit in the two constitutive ideals of liberal democracy. Other values I have taken to be supported by intuitively compelling moral principles. My focus has been, not on citizens as such, but on the state. A full-scale theory of liberal democracy, however, should provide a basis for an account of political obligation. I take this to be not the obligation (if there is one) to establish government in the first place but rather the prima facie obligation to obey the law once there is a government to enact laws, and, more generally, to cooperate in policies framed by government agencies. I cannot offer such an account here, but I can sketch the bearing on political obligation of the moral principles I have proposed as good grounds for liberal democracy.

One might think that if, as I have suggested, there are moral reasons to favor liberal democracy as a form of government, then there is no political obligation outside such a society. This would not follow. A benevolent monarchy could have and perhaps deserves greater loyalty among subjects than exists in most democracies. It could see to their welfare, respond to their complaints, and respect their freedom in selected political matters; this could be sufficient for at least some political obligation. I will, however, make two presuppositions: first, that given the moral reasons favoring liberal democracy, together with Hobbesian considerations about the nastiness of life outside a well-ordered human society, governments will inevitably arise among peoples; second, that, especially in liberal democracies, political obligation will have a basis not just in what the state does for citizens but also in how citizens are related to one another. How, in this light, should we account for obligation to a liberal-democratic government, and in particular to its laws?

One way to understand my inquiry is to ask whether the same kinds of grounds that legitimate governmental reasons for political action—above all for establishing laws and public policies—can legitimate reasons for action on the part of individuals, especially political actions such as voting for candidates for public office. There may be no one principle among the intuitive ones I have suggested that provides for an answer here, but taken together they seem to provide as good an answer as we are likely to find.

Consider first the duties of veracity and fidelity to promises, and, for clarity, make two assumptions. First, we are talking about a "just state," in the sense of one that at least approximates fulfillment of the values appropriate to liberal democracy so far defended; and second, the obligations we must account for are prima facie rather than absolute. In establishing a liberal democratic form of government, founders will make mutual promises to abide by its constitution or laws. Once such a government is in place—the case of most interest here—some citizens will make similar promises.

We might also countenance implicit promises and, with perhaps equal intuitive plausibility, we might say that in our conduct in obeying the law, and in criticizing those who do not, we give rise to a legitimate expectation of obedience, one that carries a prima facie obligation to act accordingly. It is true that we can criticize conduct without promising to observe a standard prohibiting it; but to criticize it and not ourselves observe such a standard at least tends to bespeak *hypocrisy*. We are in the neighborhood of breaking a promise, even if not clearly doing it. The intuitive ideal of fidelity to one's word goes beyond keeping promises and avoiding lies.

Beyond this, there is also the duty of justice: it is a clear injustice to benefit knowingly from the obedience of others while allowing them to be deceived in expecting a similar obedience on one's own part. Disregard for the law also tends to harm others: it goes against the duty of beneficence even if it does not harm, but only potentially burdens, others, and it tends to limit, certainly not to preserve, the liberty of others.[23]

All this could be illustrated in many ways, and there are other ways in which the intuitive principles may imply political obligations. Rather than elaborate on this dimension of the problem, I want to recall a general point that supports the overall direction of the argument. Although I am prepared to defend the epistemic autonomy of the intuitive principles—to argue that they commend themselves to reflection in a way that makes them acceptable without supporting premises—I also maintain that they can be defended by appeal to premises. These may be drawn from a variety of points of view: Kantian, utilitarian, virtue-ethical, and theological.

What so highly commends the principles for understanding liberal democracy is that the grounds of action they identify are, for virtually everyone who has no skeptical or other theoretical reason to disagree, plausible or indeed compelling. Even if they are not, as Ross held, self-evident (which is not to say obvious), they are eminently *reasonable*.[24] They articulate a basis for identifying reasons for action that have independent normative force; and the reasons have that force even when they are political, whether institutional, as in the case of reasons for governmental action, or individual, as in the case of citizens' reasons for acting in their political capacities.

Political obligations differ from obligations to individuals as such in that they may be owed to others as public officials or to others as citizens who have justified claims to one's fulfilling those obligations. This is not to say that political obligations are always wholly *impersonal*. They do go with politically definable roles, but we may know our governors personally. Political obligations may also overlap general moral ones: we may have special obligations of noninjury to fellow citizens, but we also have obligations not to harm people in general. The point is that the basis of political obligations essentially depends not just on moral considerations but also on political relationships.

Political obligations are, however, like other obligations in admitting of conflict. A prima facie obligation to obey a law may conflict with an obligation to others as citizens. Perhaps we can see that obedience would harm them, as with serving in a brutal police force. Perhaps our obligation to preserve liberty for all citizens requires opposing a government and thus conflicts with our political obligation. This conflict is especially likely to come to the fore when, as in the present climate in much of the world, the threat of terrorism may lead to widening police powers and restricting the free movements of citizens. Can anything usefully general be said here about resolution of such problems?[25]

A presupposition of my case for a moral foundation for liberal democracy is that the moral obligations are not only *inalienable* but also ineliminable given the presence of their grounds. We therefore have them (even if they are overridden) under any conditions. We have them independently of the political system we are in, and we cannot renounce them. If the promissory grounds of my obligation to serve in the military are intact (e.g., I have been given no waiver), I have the obligation; and even if the obligation can be overridden (say, by gross injustice in the conduct of a war I am to fight in), I cannot simply renounce it, as someone to whom I have made a promise *can* free me from the obligation by indicating that the action is no longer needed (thereby eliminating the ground of the promise).

Moreover, at least insofar as political obligations can be morally grounded, we cannot take them to be always secondary to moral obligations. For instance, the obligation to serve in the military in a just war might override the obligation to keep a promise to join someone in a project. Political obligations may also conflict: a legislature may face a conflict between its obligation to uphold liberty and its need to do thorough and sometimes intrusive screening of applicants for pilots' licenses and passports.

Where there is a conflict between political obligations, the constitutive ideals of liberal democracy have a special place: considerations of liberty and basic political equality will be the strongest source of a case for nonfulfillment of a political obligation. A regime that represses its people's liberty does not merit one's loyalty. One that disproportionately gives power to a minority should be opposed and merits at most limited loyalty. One that restricts liberty for heightened security against threats from terrorists or criminals or even hostile foreign governments must be scrutinized and, in some cases, resisted.

It cannot be denied that the promotion of one democratic ideal, such as liberty or basic political equality, can conflict with the preservation or extent of another, such as security or economic freedom to spend money in support of political candidates. Here, as with nonpolitical obligation, we may not say that one of the conflicting obligations or values automatically takes priority over the other. In political as in ethical matters generally, practical wisdom is essential for resolution of such conflicts. The same holds where a religious obligation conflicts with a political one, say where one's religious opposition to assisted suicide conflicts with a legal duty to tolerate it. In a free society, however, one may oppose the law that generates the obligation. Here we encounter a question, not of the state's obligation of neutrality, but of the individual citizen's.

In this domain, I propose a principle that reflects an appropriate religious neutrality while at the same time accommodating religious convictions. It is the *principle of secular rationale*: "In liberal democracies, citizens have a prima facie obligation not to advocate or support any law or public policy that restricts human conduct, unless they have, and are willing to offer, adequate secular reason for this advocacy or support."[26] This is supportable by the kinds of general moral considerations I have pointed to in grounding liberal democracy. These are secular in the sense that their justificatory authority does not depend on the existence of God—or on denying it—or on religious scriptures or the views of religious authorities as such. The principle requires neutrality in the limited sense that it calls for a religiously neutral reason for conduct that restricts the freedom of citizens, but it also respects religious liberty in, first, making the obligation that it articulates only prima facie and, second, allowing religious considerations to play a significant role.

The notion of a prima facie obligation needs elaboration here. For one thing, prima facie obligation is by its very nature defeasible. But in this case we can say more: there is a moral right, and in liberal democracies there should be a legal right, not to adhere to this principle. Because I think it clearly possible to do something morally criticizable even when one has a right to do it, I have no hesitation in affirming this. I take rights to protect one from a certain kind of coercion, but not from moral criticism.[27] Morality asks far more of us than simply acting within our rights.

I have argued in great detail elsewhere for the appropriateness of this and related principles of political obligation in relation to religion and politics.[28] My present concern is mainly to point out that even this fairly strong neutrality principle is consistent with a quite rich view of the good. Religious well-being can even be taken to be an important element in human flourishing. It may be central in the flourishing of many even if, for some, human flourishing of a different kind is possible on the basis of other elements.

Indeed, the principle of secular rationale is quite consistent with a plausible counterpart that is addressed not to citizens in general but to citizens whose religions have (as do, for instance, Christianity,

Judaism, and Islam) ethical standards that apply to large segments of sociopolitical conduct. This *principle of religious rationale* says: "In liberal democracies, such religious citizens have a prima facie obligation not to advocate or support any law or public policy that restricts human conduct, unless they have, and are willing to offer, adequate religiously acceptable reason for this advocacy or support,"[29] where the criteria of adequacy are objective in the same way as in the case of the principle of secular rationale, but the criteria of religious acceptability are internal to the religion in question and may or may not be objectively adequate, depending on the character of that religion.

What is ruled out by the principle of secular rationale is not this and similar principles but only taking religiously grounded reasons as a basis of coercion or other limitations of liberty *without* adequate independent support from adequate reasons grounded, as are those essential to the intuitionist framework I have sketched, in secular considerations. We can support laws and policies that facilitate religious freedom and religious association, for instance, without doing so for religious reasons. Just as, without a taste for painting, one can regard the enjoyment of paintings as a good for those who value them, one can, without being religious, regard people's religious activities as an element of human good for them. The application of the principle of secular rationale, then, can be guided by universally applicable moral principles that articulate a framework of values and obligations ascertainable by the use of reason.[30]

Conclusion

To draw together the main strands of this paper, I have argued that liberal democracy can be justified from the moral point of view and that this can be best seen by setting aside ambitious theories of the good or the right and pursuing what I have called a convergence strategy: going to the core intuitive principles apparently common to all our best ethical theories. These principles do require religious neutrality on the part of a liberal democracy—though not indifference to religion—but do not require neutrality toward the good. Indeed, they require a rich enough notion of the good to provide a rationale for reasonable compulsory education, for a humane (beneficent) health care system, and for promotion of liberty and of rational political participation.

To be sure, both liberal neutrality and views of the good permissibly taken by a liberal state may differ at constitutional, judiciary, and legislative levels (the judiciary operates, of course, on many levels). The lower the level, the less the obligation of neutrality, other things being equal. There is also a limited obligation of neutrality on the part of individual citizens in a liberal democracy: they may properly promote religious flourishing, but they should not, without adequate secular reason, such as may be implicit in the intuitive principles that can ground liberal democracy in the first place, restrict the liberty of fellow citizens. This moderate limitation does nothing to undermine the point that liberal democracy can not only can countenance, but depends on recognition of, a plurality of considerations as constituting reasons for action, and that it can be a realization of a rich and tolerant conception of the good.

Notes

Earlier versions of this paper were given at the Becket Institute conference "The Publicity of Reasons, Normative Authority, and Religious Liberty," at St. Hugh's College, Oxford, at the University of Helsinki, and at the University of Northern Colorado. For helpful comments on earlier versions, I thank Joan Donovan, Robert Frazier, Simo Knuuttila, Daniel Robinson, Jack Lee Sammons, and Raimo Tuomela.

1. See, e.g., Robert Audi, *Religious Commitment and Secular Reason* (New York: Oxford University Press, 2000). This book is a basis for several points made in this paper.

2. Immanuel Kant, "To Perpetual Peace: A Philosophical Sketch," in *Perpetual Peace and Other Essays*, trans. Ted Humphrey (Indianapolis: Hackett, 1983), p. 133.

3. The most influential conception of liberal democracy to emerge in the second half of the twentieth century is that of John Rawls. See, e.g., John Rawls, *Political Liberalism* (New York: Columbia University Press, 1993) and *The Law of Peoples* (Cambridge, MA: Harvard University Press, 1999).

4. Audi, *Religious Commitment*, pp. 3–30, indicates an instrumentalist rationale for liberal democracy.

5. See Robert Audi, "Prospects for a Naturalization of Practical Reason: Humean Instrumentalism and the Normative Authority of Desire," *International Journal of Philosophical Studies* 10 (2002): 235–63, for a detailed critical assessment of instrumentalism.

6. See W. D. Ross, *The Right and the Good*, ed. Philip Stratton-Lake (New York: Oxford University Press, 2003).

7. Ibid., p. 21.

8. See Robert Audi, *The Good in the Right: A Theory of Intuition and Intrinsic Value* (Princeton: Princeton University Press, 2004), which offers a full-scale intuitionist ethical theory.

9. In speaking of the desirability of a liberal democracy as a form of government, I am presupposing a populace sufficiently educated to be capable of informed self-government. It is difficult to specify the level of freedom and education required, and perhaps there can be conditions under which, if a certain kind of liberal democracy is instituted for a population falling short of this standard, progress leading to its satisfaction is a reasonable expectation. These matters must be left aside in this paper.

10. Ross, *Right and the Good*, pp. 6–47, appeals to practical wisdom to argue that no alternative theory, such as utilitarianism or Kantianism, is in a position to do better.

11. See, e.g., Audi, *Good in the Right*, pp. 40–79.

12. See ibid., pp. 80–120.

13. See Robert Audi and Nicholas Wolterstorff, *Religion in the Public Square: The Place of Religious Convictions in Political Debate* (Lanham, MD: Rowman and Littlefield, 1997), in which the authors debate the kind of religious neutrality appropriate to liberal democracy.

14. The case of English monarchy is a good example of a candidate for a prima facie sound liberal democracy with only a limited separation of church and state. See also Audi, *Religious Commitment*, pp. 98–99, for reasons to think that a voucher system is compatible with a liberal democracy; see also Wolterstorff's contributions to Audi and Wolterstorff's *Religion in the Public Square* for a different range of reasons for permitting state support of private religious education.

15. Rawls, *Political Liberalism*.

16. See, e.g., Bernard Gert, *Morality: Its Nature and Justification* (New York: Oxford University Press, 1998), for a plausible defense of this negative conception of morality. But see Robert Audi, "Rationality and Reasons in the Moral Philosophy of Bernard Gert," in *Rationality, Rules, and Ideals: Critical Essays on Bernard Gert's Moral Theory*, ed. Walter Sinnott-Armstrong and Robert Audi (Lanham, MD: Rowman and Littlefield, 2002), p. 73, which critically discusses Gert's view and argues that his theory is not as negative as he makes it sound.

17. John Stuart Mill's famous harm principle is a prominent example of the kind of view in question. See John Stuart Mill, *On Liberty* (New York: Penguin Books, 1982).

18. John Rawls, *A Theory of Justice*, rev. ed. (Cambridge, MA: Harvard University Press, 1999), p. 79. See also Robert Audi, *Moral Knowledge and Ethical*

Character (New York: Oxford University Press, 1997), pp. 195-216, for an examination of the neutrality of the conception of rationality Rawls describes.

19. It should not be thought, however, that even an intuitionism committed to a priori principles determining reasons for action must posit intrinsic goods in the (G. E.) Moorean, apparently Platonic realist sense objectionable to certain moral theorists. An objectivist, rationalist moral epistemology can be minimal in its ontological commitments. See Audi, *Good in the Right*, pp. 40-79, for a defense of the view that intuitionism can be quite minimal in its ontological claims.

20. I am of course implicitly rejecting an instrumentalist conception of rational action and of practical reason in general. See Audi, "Prospects for a Naturalization," for support of this position.

21. See Audi, *Good in the Right*, pp. 80-120, for a case to establish that the possibility that the moral principles in question are both self-evident (hence a priori) and capable of being evidenced and unified by something more general.

22. For a plausible version of a moderate perfectionism, see Joseph Chan, "Legitimacy, Unanimity and Perfection," *Philosophy and Public Affairs* 29 (2000): 5-42; for a detailed critique of this essay, see Thaddeus Metz, "Respect for Persons and Perfectionist Politics," *Philosophy and Public Affairs* 30 (2001): 417-42. Although he supports some elements in a moderate perfectionism, Metz proposes an "open perfectionism" in which citizens are free to emigrate. This is an important freedom, but the right to it is not absolute, and a significant problem for any liberal democracy—and one that I cannot discuss here—is how to accord it. People with certain obligations within a state (as well as those guilty of certain crimes) should not be allowed unrestricted exercise of the right. The question is fruitfully compared with that of conditions for conscientious exemption from military service.

23. Civil disobedience is not ruled out as morally impermissible by anything said here, in part because the obligation to obey the law is prima facie. There are also special categories of persons whose obligations toward the law are different from those of citizens in general. Lawyers are included. For an indication of the complexity of their political obligations, see W. Bradley Wendel, "Civil Obedience," *Columbia Law Review* 104 (2004): 363.

24. Reasonableness is a stronger normative category than rationality. See Robert Audi, *The Architecture of Reason* (New York: Oxford University Press, 2001), pp. 135-70, for a brief account of what constitutes reasonableness.

25. There is one area of tension in liberal democracy that I can only mention in passing. It concerns science policy, especially in government and major institutions. Terrorist threats—as well as the profit motive—may lead to insufficient restrictions, for instance in weapons development or genetic engineering; on the other hand, insufficient governmental neutrality can lead to

unwarranted restrictions on medical research. For extensive discussion of the role of science and science policy in democratic societies, see Philip Kitcher, *Science, Truth and Democracy* (New York: Oxford University Press, 2001).

26. See Audi, *Religious Commitment*, p. 86. Votes are included, of course, and the principle applies differently to people depending on their roles (e.g., as governmental officials or ordinary citizens) and on the degree of coercion involved. A prima facie obligation is of course defeasible.

27. See Audi, *Religious Commitment*, pp. 59–78, which argues this point, and indeed the stronger point that even certain duties (such as beneficence) can be violated within one's rights; Robert Audi, "Wrongs within Rights," *Philosophical Issues* 15 (2005): 121–39.

28. See Audi, *Religious Commitment*. But see Wolterstorff's contribution to Audi and Wolterstorff's *Religion in the Public Square* for a contrasting view.

29. See Robert Audi, "Religiously Grounded Morality and the Integration of Religious and Political Conduct," *Wake Forest Law Review* 36 (2001): 251–78, which states this principle and provides a preliminary defense of it.

30. It might seem that (perhaps on grounds of equal treatment) fairness toward religious citizens would require that nonreligious citizens have and be willing to offer adequate religious reasons for the same range of conduct as is covered by the principle of secular rationale. Philip L. Quinn suggests this objection, though he does not think either the latter principle or the proposed one acceptable. Philip L. Quinn, "Religion and Politics, Fear and Duty," in *Philosophy of Religion for a New Century*, ed. Jeremiah Hackett and Jerald Wallulis (New York: Springer, 2004), pp. 307–28. But it is a mistake to assume epistemic parity here. The kinds of secular reasons in question—above all, moral, evidential, logical, and instrumental ones—are such that it is appropriate to expect all rational persons to recognize them, at least at the level of agreement in reasons and in responding to them in guiding their everyday thought and action. Indeed, these reasons are such that, apart from a normal responsiveness to them—the possession of natural reason, in one terminology—people need medical or remedial assistance. I might add that secular reasons of the kinds in question seem common to all the major religions, which is one reason why, for religious people, the secular rationale principle is not unduly burdensome.

Six

Egalitarianism without Equality?

Paul J. Weithman

Like, I expect, many other people, I am drawn to democratic egalitarianism in large part because it seems to me to fit so well with my religious convictions. Democracy's ethos of equal respect for all seems to me to be among the proper political and cultural expressions of the universal love my religion enjoins. Egalitarian principles of distributive justice seem to me to be among the proper ways of expressing the demands for justice found throughout the Hebrew and Christian scriptures.

If I try to be more specific about just what I mean by talking of a good fit between my religious and my political convictions, I am led to the following. Both a democratic ethos and egalitarian principles seem to me somehow to be underpinned by two claims: the claim that human beings are by nature equal and the claim that our natural equality must be expressed in our social and political relations. The first of these claims seems to me to be one of which my religion contains at least the elements of an account, in the form of claims about our common paternity and destiny.

But on examination, the connections that seem to me to be in place among democratic egalitarianism, the two claims I have said underpin it, and religious accounts of human equality all appear rather loose. Even if we suppose, as I will, that my version of Christianity is committed to the equality of all people, it is far from clear exactly how that commitment supports the ethical and distributive commitments of democratic egalitarianism. *Pace* some recent work by Jeremy Waldron, it is also far from clear that any such underpinning is needed.[1] For there are reasons to think that egalitarian principles of distributive justice can be sustained, or at least publicly sustained, without the support of the sort of robust account of natural equality that I have suggested religion can provide.

Some of those reasons depend upon Rawlsian arguments about the political character of political philosophy. According to those arguments, egalitarian principles can derive all the public justification they need from ideas to be found in political culture. Deeper religious justifications are not necessary. Other reasons depend upon the very challenging claim that our egalitarian convictions about distributive justice do not depend upon the value of equality at all. Here I shall ignore the first set of reasons for thinking that egalitarianism can get by without robust ideas of human equality and shall concentrate on the second. Let me begin by trying to state my concerns more precisely.

The Fairness Conditional

I am concerned with the distribution of an important class of socially created goods that I shall refer to as "basic social benefits." Basic social benefits are those goods that together constitute the so-called currency of egalitarian justice. They are the goods with the distribution of which distributive justice is most fundamentally concerned. For now I shall remain noncommittal about what the currency of egalitarian justice is, though later I shall say something about what I believe to be one of the currency's more important denominations. I shall also suggest the need to distribute some basic social benefits differently than others— to use the currency of egalitarian justice to, as it were, make change. But for the moment we can take the currency to be Rawlsian primary goods, preference satisfaction, opportunities for welfare, access to advantage, or Sen and Nussbaum's capabilities.

The questions that concern me are how these basic social benefits should be distributed and why.[2] By saying that I am attracted to egalitarian principles, I do not mean that I am attracted to the equal distribution of these benefits. I am, however, attracted to the claim that departures from equal distribution must be justified, so that there is a presumption in favor of equal distribution. I want to ask how that presumption can be defended and among what class of beneficiaries it holds.

It is natural to think that the presumption in favor of equal distribution is justified by the moral importance of some form of equality. And it is natural to think that the appeal to equality will not drop out when the most basic premises of the argument for egalitarianism are brought forward. Much political philosophizing in the democratic tradition—as well as much street-level political discourse—encourages the thought that equality is not just of moral importance but of *fundamental* moral importance. While arguments and pleas for greater equality may often rely on premises about other values as well, such as liberty and fraternity, the moral importance of equality is not generally explained by reference to these other values. Rather, the value of equality seems to be sui generis. And so if we think that the presumption of equal distribution is justified in part by the moral importance of equality, it will also be natural to think that some appeal to equality will be part of the deepest justification available.

Some philosophers, however, have asked whether the value of equality really is fundamental in egalitarian thinking about distributive justice. They have argued instead that an egalitarian distribution is justified because it serves other moral and political values. Some of these philosophers have maintained that the presumption in favor of an equal distribution of basic social benefits is supported by a requirement that procedures for distributing those benefits be fair, together with premises about the requirements of fairness and about who is owed fair treatment. I shall call the argument these philosophers offer for the presumption of equal distribution "the argument from procedural fairness." The philosophers who offer this argument deny that equality is fundamental in egalitarian thinking about distributive justice because, they claim, the value of equality does not figure in the argument from procedural fairness in any fundamental way.

T. M. Scanlon has thought about the argument from procedural fairness especially deeply. In an important essay he provides the "schematic form" of that argument.[3] According to Scanlon, the argument relies upon a premise to the effect that beneficiaries of a distributive scheme have claims to enjoy the benefits the scheme distributes. What makes the argument an argument *from procedural fairness* is its reliance on a conditional claim about what follows if the beneficiaries' claims to benefit are prima facie equal and if the distributive scheme is to be fair. I will call that conditional "the fairness conditional." The fairness conditional, as Scanlon states it, says:

> If all the members of a certain group have a prima facie equal claim to benefit in a certain way, then a fair procedure for distributing such benefits must (in the absence of special justification) result in equal benefits.[4]

Let me recast the fairness conditional a bit more formally. More formally stated, the conditional says:

> If all members of group G have a prima facie equal claim to benefits B, then if there is no special justification for departing from equal distribution, a fair procedure for distributing such benefits must result in equal benefits for members of G.

Thus the form of the argument from procedural fairness for equal distribution is:

(1) [The formalized version of the fairness conditional.]
(2) All members of group G have a prima facie equal claim to enjoy benefits B.
(3) There is no special justification for departing from equal distribution.

Therefore

(4) A fair procedure for distributing benefits B must result in equal benefits for members of G.

And if we assume that the benefits must be fairly distributed, we arrive at the conclusion that benefits must be distributed equally among members of G.

Egalitarianism without Equality? 149

With this schematic form in hand, we can see the form of the argument from procedural fairness for a presumption of equal distribution. That argument form is:

(1) [The formalized version of the fairness conditional.]
(2) All members of group G have a prima facie equal claim to enjoy benefits B.

Therefore

(3) If there is no special justification for departing from equal distribution, a fair procedure for distributing benefits B must result in equal benefits for members of G.

And if we assume, again, that benefits must be fairly distributed, we arrive at the conclusion that they must be distributed equally unless there is some special justification for doing otherwise. I take this conclusion to express a presumption in favor of equal distribution.

Scanlon's reliance on arguments from procedural fairness places him firmly in the line of egalitarian thought that Derek Parfit dubs "deontic egalitarianism."[5] Scanlon is certainly not alone among deontic egalitarians in thinking that egalitarianism (either actual or presumptive) is somehow required by people's equality of claims and the demands of fair treatment.[6] In fact, he thinks that arguments from procedural fairness are frequently if implicitly invoked to support egalitarian conclusions in a great deal of political philosophy and workaday political thinking.[7] I shall take him at his word and suppose that these arguments are of sufficiently general use and interest that they merit close attention.

Scanlon's treatment of these arguments is noteworthy because he has laid out the connections between procedural fairness, equality of claims, and egalitarian conclusions especially clearly and economically and because he has most explicitly drawn the provocative conclusion that equality itself plays a minimal role in egalitarian thinking. But I am less concerned with the details of Scanlon's own discussion than I am with the soundness of arguments from procedural fairness and with their implications, if any, for the role equality plays in justifying the presumption of equal distribution.[8]

Once we see the form of arguments from procedural fairness, however, we might wonder why their proponents think that such arguments do not appeal, or do not fundamentally appeal, to the moral value of equality. It is not immediately clear what might count as a fundamental appeal to the value of equality. Scanlon sometimes implies that, when he says he is not appealing to equality in a fundamental way, what he means is that his arguments for egalitarian outcomes do not depend upon the premise that an equal outcome is for that reason a better outcome.[9] Sometimes, however, Scanlon seems to be saying something more. When he lays out the schematic form of arguments from procedural fairness, he stresses that "what [such arguments] have in common is not that all men and women are created equal" but that they all rely on what I have called "the fairness conditional." This remark suggests that, when he denies he is appealing to equality in a fundamental way, Scanlon is not merely denying that he relies on the claim that an equal distribution is a better distribution simply because it is equal. He is also denying that he relies upon claims about human equality to provide or to support premises in his arguments for egalitarian outcomes. What interests me is the question of whether arguments from procedural fairness show that egalitarian conclusions can indeed by adequately supported without appealing to such claims.

It might seem that arguments from procedural fairness do depend upon the premise that those who are to benefit from the distributive scheme in question are equal in an important respect—namely, they have prima facie equal claims to benefit. If the fairness conditional is true, then this form of equality has important consequences. So the argument's reliance on the assertion that beneficiaries are equal in this respect seems to imply that it *does* rely on the importance of preserving or respecting that form of equality—hence that it does appeal to the value of equality in a fundamental way.

Proponents of arguments from procedural fairness like Scanlon deny this conclusion. They do so because of what they think makes the antecedent of the fairness conditional true. They think that even when the antecedent of that conditional is true—even when members of some group do have prima facie equal claims to benefit—the prima facie equality of their claims does not itself depend upon further claims about human equality. I shall ask what does ground the prima facie equality of claims below in the section "Participation and Equal Claims." But I want to begin asking about arguments from procedural fairness by asking about the truth of (1), the fairness conditional.

Consequent Blockers

At first glance, the fairness conditional might seem implausible because it might seem to prove too much. The antecedent of the conditional refers to parties with prima facie equal claims to benefits. But now consider members of some group G whose prima facie claims are undefeated. It might be thought that when their claims are undefeated, (3) is true and there is no justification for departing from equality. Conjoined with an appropriate instance of (2), which asserts the antecedent of the fairness conditional, the conditional might then be thought to support, not just the *presumption* of equal distribution of benefits among members of G, but the equal distribution of benefits among them *tout court*. This conclusion may seem worrisomely strong, for it is far from obvious that those who have ultima facie equal claims to benefit should get equal benefits. Since I am supposing for the sake of argument that the relevant instance of (2) is true, the problem seems to be due to the strength of the fairness conditional.

The support that the fairness conditional seems to provide for the stronger conclusion is illusory. The illusion arises from misconstruing the phrase "in the absence of special justification." More specifically, it arises from the mistaken thought that such justifications can provide only reasons for denying that parties who have prima facie equal claims have ultima facie equal claims. For if that is the only sort of reason such justification can provide, then (2) plus the conditional will indeed imply that there cannot be any compelling reason for departing from an equal distribution among those with ultima facie equal claims.

In fact, the phrase *special justification* must refer to considerations of two very different sorts. It must refer to what we might call *antecedent defeaters*, which defeat prima facie equal claims to a benefit. It must also refer to *consequent blockers*.

Consequent blockers in this case are justifications for deviating from an equal distribution of benefits even when the antecedent of the fairness conditional is satisfied (and the parties really do have prima facie equal claims to benefit), when there are no considerations that defeat those prima facie claims, and when the distributive scheme is supposed to be fair. Of course, the availability of consequent blockers does not show that the fairness conditional is false, since—I am maintaining— the conditional allows for the possibility of consequent blockers by including the clause about special justification. The point of construing *special justification* as referring to consequent blockers is to make provision for cases in which we want to deny claims to equal benefits without denying that the fairness conditional is true, that the scheme for distributing benefits must be fair, or that the parties in question have ultima facie equal claims to benefit.

Consider an example. Rawls thinks citizens of a well-ordered society have prima facie equal claims to primary goods, and he thinks there is a presumption in favor of equal distribution. Yet he famously thinks that fair distributive schemes may yield unequal distributions of income and wealth. He thinks an unequal distribution is justified by the fact that when inequalities function as incentives, all parties are better off under an unequal distribution than they are under an equal one. Just how this justification functions depends upon just what is meant by *prima facie equal claims;* I shall say more about that in the next section. For now, let me say simply that I think the incentives justification does not function to defeat citizens' prima facie equal claims to primary goods. Indeed, I believe Rawls thinks these prima facie claims are undefeated in the well-ordered society, so that citizens of well-ordered societies have not just prima facie but ultima facie equal claims to the benefits of social cooperation.[10] And so I think the function of the justification must be to block the inference *from* citizens' ultima facie equal claims *to* the conclusion that income and wealth should be equally divided.

What does this conclusion show about arguments from procedural fairness?

If the conclusion is correct, then an argument from procedural fairness could be used to vindicate Rawls's presumption that all primary goods should be distributed equally among those with prima facie equal claims. Someone using that argument could then maintain that the presumption is rebutted in the case of income and wealth because, while the only special justification for departing from equality (namely, Rawls's incentives argument) leaves those claims intact, it blocks the inference to the consequent of the relevant fairness conditional (which would require equal distribution).

Another example of a consequent blocker is the special justification for departing from equal distribution that can be based upon special features of some of those among whom benefits are to be distributed, such as physical handicaps. Though I am primarily interested in the distribution of what I called "basic social benefits," the fairness conditional is not restricted to such benefits. It applies to any benefits whatever. To see how a special justification based on physical handicaps can function as a consequent blocker, consider the claims that citizens have to the benefits of a national park such as Yosemite. I assume that all citizens have prima facie equal claims to those benefits. I also assume that physical handicaps do not defeat those prima facie claims. For reasons that I hope will become clearer when I ask just what it is to have equal claims, I think that we treat differently abled citizens as equals only if we deny that disabilities defeat prima facie equal claims to benefits. And so I shall assume that differently abled citizens, as such, have ultima facie equal claims to the benefits of Yosemite.

What follows from this depends in part upon just what citizens have equal claims *to*. I would argue that the most appealing answer—more appealing than *enjoyment* of Yosemite or the *opportunity to enjoy* Yosemite—is that the benefit to which citizens have equal claim is *access* to Yosemite. If this is so, as I shall assume it is, then unless we allow for a consequent blocker, the fairness conditional implies that a fair procedure for distributing that benefit would give citizens equal access to Yosemite.

The problem with this implication is that differently abled citizens cannot be granted equal access to all of Yosemite. There are some ways of accessing parts of the park, such as climbing the face of El Capitan, that are not open to those with certain physical disabilities. And so granting equal access to Yosemite is simply not possible. Unequal access is reasonable in this case. In the absence of a consequent blocker, an argument from procedural fairness could be used to establish rights of equal access. But the impossibility of granting equal access to differently abled citizens justifies the unequal distribution of access and blocks the implication that equal access must be granted.

When I introduced the idea of consequent blockers, I said they allow us to provide for cases in which we want to justify the unequal distribution of benefits while asserting the truth of the fairness conditional and maintaining both that the distributive scheme must be fair and that citizens have ultima facie equal claims. The examples I have discussed do just that. Rawls's incentives argument justifies the unequal distribution of income and wealth by a distributive scheme that fairly takes account of citizens' ultima facie equal claims to primary goods. The impossibility of granting equal access to Yosemite justifies unequal access while allowing us to maintain that access must be distributed fairly and that differently abled citizens have ultima facie equal claims to access.

The distinction between consequent blockers and antecedent defeaters therefore makes it possible to defend fairness conditionals against the charge with which I opened this section, the charge that they prove too much in cases in which we do not wish to deny ultima facie equality of claims to benefit. By doing so, the distinction enables us to blunt what looked like a powerful objection to arguments from procedural fairness. But what of the claim that considerations of fairness, rather than some fundamental claim about equality, account for the presumption in favor of equal distribution?

At this point it may be said that by construing the presumption of equality as requiring only that departures from equality be justified, I have construed the presumption too weakly. It might be thought that even in cases in which there is a justification for departing from equality, we intuitively think that the ideal of equality has a special place. For example, in cases in which citizens have ultima facie equal claims to benefit and in which distributive procedures must be fair, we may still suppose that the presumption of equal distribution requires more than that there be no departure from equal distribution without some special justification. The presumption might also be thought to require that, even in the presence of such a justification, the ideal of equal distribution should play a privileged role in determining what the right distribution is. Perhaps it will be thought to require that, in the presence of a consequent blocker, we should try for the most reasonable approximation of equal distribution.

Whether this thought is plausible depends upon what makes an approximation reasonable. What makes an approximation reasonable in the example of the differently abled, it might be said, is that the degree of access provided to all citizens reasonably balances the interests of the disabled in accessing the park against the interests of those whose access and enjoyment would be impeded by the presence of ramps and the exclusive dedication of parking space. And what makes the distribution of income and wealth in Rawls's well-ordered society a reasonable approximation of equal distribution, it might also be said, is that it reasonably privileges the interests of the least advantaged.

One difficulty with this line of thought is that, by referring to the reasonable approximation of equal distribution, it seems to contain an unnecessary shuffle. Instead of saying that we should reasonably approximate equal access and that such an approximation is reached by reasonably balancing the interests of differently abled citizens, why not simply dispense with the idea of an equal distribution of access altogether in this case? Why not say simply that striking such a balance just is the right thing to do when citizens who have ultima facie equal claims to a socially generated benefit differ in their capacity to enjoy or access it? And why not say that reasonably balancing the interests of citizens in a well-ordered society just is the right thing to do when there is a justification for departing from the equal distribution of income and wealth?

My suggestion, then, is that we eliminate the shuffle by rejecting the thought that equal distribution has a privileged role in determining what the right distribution is in the presence of consequent blockers. The presence of consequent blockers does not imply that there is not a presumption of equal distribution; it implies that that presumption is overridden. My suggestion is therefore compatible with retaining the presumption of equal distribution among parties who have prima facie equal claims. It is also compatible with using the fairness conditional to argue for that presumption. And so it is compatible with the truth of the fairness conditional.

But by allowing so much work to be done by the notion of a reasonable balance of interests, my suggestion about how to eliminate the shuffle raises questions about just what work the idea of procedural fairness does. Perhaps the fundamental principle at work when distributive questions must be settled is a principle requiring that fair distributive procedures strike a balance of the interests of those with prima facie equal claims that none of the claimants could reasonably reject.[11] And perhaps what the fairness conditional does is express a requirement of reasonability in cases in which those prima facie equal claims are undefeated and in which there are no consequent blockers.

When the idea of procedural fairness was introduced to help justify egalitarian outcomes, it may have seemed that that idea was being taken as primitive. If my speculations in the previous paragraph are correct, however, then this is a misunderstanding. If those speculations are right, then procedural fairness is not primitive; instead it is a species of reasonability. The distinction between antecedent defeaters and consequent blockers showed how to maintain the truth of the fairness conditional because the distinction can be deployed to show that the conditional does not prove too much. But while the fairness conditional may be true, its truth may depend upon other, more fundamental considerations.

This line of thought does not try to turn the tables on proponents of arguments from procedural fairness, for it does not conclude that equality is more fundamental than fairness. But it is an attempt to beat these philosophers at their own game by showing that if procedural fairness is more fundamental to our thinking about distributive justice than equality is, then reasonability is more fundamental still. Even so, these philosophers might think that understanding procedural fairness in the way I have suggested is in the spirit of their view, for understanding the idea that way still makes it possible to account for the presumption of equal distribution without fundamental appeal to the value of equality. I now want to argue that we may need to make such an appeal to justify some egalitarian outcomes that are intuitively appealing. I will do so by shifting my attention from the plausibility of the fairness conditional to the meaning of the conditional's antecedent, which I will take up in the next section, and to the conditions under which the antecedent is true, which I will take up below in the section "Participation and Equal Claims."

Equal Claims to Benefit

The antecedent of the fairness conditional is satisfied when members of a given group have prima facie equal claims to benefit. What is it to have prima facie equal claims to a benefit?

I shall assume for the sake of argument that we understand what it is for two or more people to have *claims* on some benefit. But while we may also think that we understand the idea that they have claims that are prima facie *equal*, the idea of claims that are prima facie equal is very puzzling on closer examination. I will not puzzle over the idea long, nor will I answer the question of what it is to have prima facie equal claims. I will, however, puzzle over this question long enough to suggest some possible answers and to raise further questions about arguments from procedural fairness.

One way in which A and B can have prima facie *equal* claims is for them to have *identical* claims, where by *identical claims* I mean that they have claims with identical grounds. For example, two people who have identical lottery tickets bearing winning numbers have prima facie equal claims to the payoff. Two people who have performed identical work have prima facie equal claims to wages.[12] When people have prima facie equal claims of this sort, it does seem plausible that, in the absence of further considerations, fair distributions of the payoff or the wage pool will result in their receiving equal benefits.

So if we take it that A and B have prima facie equal claims just in case they have identically grounded claims, it would be easy to establish a presumption of equal distribution using an argument from procedural fairness. This will seem like a strong point in favor of this analysis to those who find arguments from procedural fairness intuitively compelling. The problem with our understanding prima facie equality of claims in this way is that, while identity of grounds may be sufficient for having prima facie equal claims, it can hardly be necessary. It is too easy to come up with cases of people who seem, intuitively, to have prima facie equal claims to benefit but whose claims are differently grounded.

A different analysis of *prima facie equal claims* may seem more promising: perhaps A and B have prima facie equal claims to benefit just in case a fair distributor of the benefit does not have reason to benefit one of them more than the other in the absence of special considerations. This may seem promising because if we adopt it, then—as with the suggestion about identically grounded claims—arguments from procedural fairness are easily used to establish a presumption of equality. For if it is established that A and B have equal claims in this sense and that the distributive scheme should be fair, then it would indeed follow, in the absence of special considerations, that the two should receive equal benefits.

One problem with this suggestion may seem to be that it simply helps itself to a distinction that is very difficult to make out. To see the problem, note first that tenability of the suggestion depends upon our being able to draw the distinction between (i) reasons for denying that A and B had prima facie equal claims in the first place and (ii) those "special considerations" that would justify an unequal distribution between A and B in spite of their having prima facie equal claims. Among the "special considerations" in set (ii) are presumably considerations that override the prima facie equal claims of A and B. So the tenability of the suggestion depends upon our ability to distinguish reasons of kind (i) from kind (ii), those reasons for differentially benefiting A and

B that presuppose but override their prima facie equal claims. It is by no means clear how this distinction is to be drawn. So the intuitive plausibility the suggestion seemed to enjoy is in fact purchased with a promissory note that may be very difficult to redeem.

I do not think that this objection is as telling as it may seem to be. For I do not think we should expect intuitions and intuitively obvious distinctions alone to take us far in understanding what it is for people to have prima facie equal claims. Instead, I suggest that the idea of prima facie equal claims, the conditions under which people have such claims, and the considerations that defeat or override those claims are all most likely to be understood only in the context of a philosophical theory in which these various notions play a role. If it is not immediately clear how to draw the distinction between the sets of reasons that I discussed in the previous paragraph, we should remain open to the possibility that the distinction can be made clear by a theory of justice or of equality the whole of which strikes us as plausible.

The suggestion now under consideration is that A and B have prima facie equal claims to benefit just in case a fair distributor of the benefit does not have reason to benefit one of them more than the other in the absence of special considerations. I have said that we should not expect our intuitions alone to take us far in understanding what it is for people to have prima facie equal claims. Insofar as I have intuitions that bear on this suggestion, they incline me to think that the suggestion is not the right way to understand what it is for A and B to have *prima facie equal claims to benefit*. Rather, they incline me to think that this is a way to understand what it is for A and B to have *prima facie claims to equal benefit*. For it strikes me that, if prima facie there is no reason for a fair distributor to give A more than B, then this fact bears not on the equality or inequality of their claims but on how much A and B have claims to. If that is so, then it is no wonder that mistaking it for the way to understand *prima facie equal claims to benefit* makes it so easy to demonstrate a presumption of equal distribution.[13]

What is it, then, for parties to have prima facie equal claims to some benefit? Let me just mention a number of possibilities. Perhaps A and B have prima facie equal claims to benefit just in case, prima facie:

- Their claims to benefit must be equally taken into account.
- Their interests in the benefit must be equally taken into account.

- There is no reason to satisfy one's claim at the expense of the other's.
- It would be wrong to satisfy one's claim at the expense of the other's.
- The distribution of the benefit must be justifiable to them as free and equal.
- The distribution of the benefit must be such that they could not reasonably reject it.

These various attempts to understand the prima facie equality of claims to benefit are obviously not equivalent. My aim here is not to decide which one, if any, is correct. In the remainder of this section, I want to show how these understandings of the prima facie equality of claims confirm the need for consequent blockers. In the next, I want to raise questions about the conditions under which people might have prima facie equal claims, however the nature of such claims is to be understood.

First, there may be considerations that override prima facie equal claims to benefit, understood in one of these ways, and that may thereby justify an unequal distribution among people with prima facie equal claims. These are considerations I referred to earlier as antecedent defeaters. If the benefits in question are shares of what I called basic social benefits, then it is the job of a theory of justice to identify the considerations that can serve as antecedent defeaters. Perhaps, according to the right theory of justice, prima facie equal claims to basic social benefits are defeated if able-bodied persons who have those claims refuse to contribute to the social product because they prefer to spend their days surfing. In that case, though prima facie the surfers' and the nonsurfers' interests in the social product should (for example) have equally been taken into account, the fact that the surfers have refused to work overrides the need to take equal account of their interests. Ultima facie, the nonsurfers' interests in the basic social product may be given priority.

But once we survey the possible ways of understanding what it is to have prima facie equal claims, we can see why antecedent defeaters cannot be the only considerations that justify departures from an equal distribution of benefits. For there may be cases in which we think an unequal distribution is justified but in which we do not want to say that there are considerations that defeat prima facie equal claims to

160 Paul J. Weithman

benefit—now understood in one of the foregoing ways. Thus there may be cases in which we think an unequal distribution of benefits is justified but in which we do not want to say that the need to take equal account of the beneficiaries' interests has been overridden or that the considerations that justify unequal distribution also make it the case that the distribution need not be justifiable to the beneficiaries as free and equal. Instead we want to maintain that though an unequal distribution is justified, parties have ultima facie—as well as prima facie—equal claims to benefit.

Rawls's incentives argument, for example, provides reason for departing from the equal distribution of income and wealth. But it does not provide a reason to deny that citizens' interests in the primary goods need to be taken equally into account or that the distribution must be justifiable to them. The impossibility of providing differently abled citizens equal access to Yosemite furnishes a reason for providing unequal access. But, I would maintain, it does not provide a reason for denying that the interests of the differently abled must equally be taken into account when benefits are distributed.

It is important to maintain that the prima facie equality of claims is undefeated in these cases—it is important to maintain that claims in these cases are ultimate facie equal—because to have a claim on socially created benefits is to have a status in the scheme that creates and distributes those benefits. In the case of some distributive schemes, equality of status is something about which beneficiaries may care deeply. To deny that some people have that status and to assert that they are only prima facie equal claimants may be deeply hurtful or insulting, especially if the features of their persons or behavior that are said to override the prima facie equality of claims are features that they value highly or over which they have no control.

Thus I believe Rawls thinks it would unjustifiably denigrate the least well off in the well-ordered society if they were said to have claims that were not ultima facie equal to those of the better off—if, say, their interests would not need to be given the same weight as those of the better off—simply because they did not have the ability to occupy positions that people normally need incentives to fill.[14] I believe it would unjustifiably denigrate disabled citizens to say that their disabilities defeat the prima facie equality of their claims to access public parks. Allowing physical disabilities and the considerations appealed to in the incentives argument to function as consequent blockers makes it possible to justify unequal distributions while avoiding such unjustifiable denigrations of claimants' status.

Participation and Equal Claims

What establishes that people have prima facie equal claims, understood in one of the ways I have canvassed? What, that is, establishes that (2) is true and that the antecedent of the fairness conditional is satisfied?

For possible answers, I return to Scanlon. Scanlon writes that the "antecedent [of the fairness conditional] is true in an important range of cases—e.g. that participants in many cooperative ventures do have prima facie equal claims to the benefits produced."[15] An especially important example of a cooperative venture in which participants have prima facie equal claims, Scanlon continues, is "the case of the basic institutions of society." Moreover, Scanlon clearly implies, it is participation in the basic institutions of society that *confers* prima facie equality on claims to benefit.

In this section I want to focus on the example of society's basic institutions. I shall assume that the phrase *basic institutions of society* denotes what Rawls's phrase *the basic structure of society* denotes. I shall also assume that we know what institutions the phrase denotes. Finally, I shall assume that the basic institutions of society, taken together, are a cooperative venture that produces and distributes basic social benefits. What I want to query is the assertion that participants in society's basic institutions have prima facie equal claims to basic social benefits in virtue of their participation.

That assertion is difficult to assess without knowing (i) just what the conditions of participation are and (ii) who satisfies those conditions. Perhaps we can make some headway in answering (i) and (ii) by seeing how the truth of the assertion would advance the case that proponents of arguments from procedural fairness wish to make. I said early on that some philosophers think considerations of procedural fairness—rather than the moral value of equality—justify the presumption in favor of equal distribution of basic social benefits and sometimes justify equal distribution itself. They deny that the value of equality plays a fundamental role in justifying the presumption or in justifying an equal distribution because they think that arguments from procedural fairness do not appeal to the moral value of equality in any fundamental way. I take it that what proponents of arguments from procedural fairness have in mind is the following.

A presumption in favor of equal distribution does not depend, or does not depend exclusively, upon the brute goodness of equality as a property of distributions. Rather, it depends, or depends as well, upon considerations of procedural fairness together with the fact that beneficiaries have prima facie equal claims. Beneficiaries' prima facie equality of claims does not depend upon their natural equality as persons. Rather, their having those claims depends upon something they have done—namely, take part in the venture that produces the benefits to be distributed. The question is what they would have to have done—what participation would have to be—to ground such claims. If the answer is that persons with the claims must have played some productive part in the cooperative scheme that produces the benefits, then arguments from procedural fairness need not appeal to the value of equality. For while showing that participants have prima facie equal claims on the basis of what they have done may require us to appeal to moral values about earnings, desert, or the legitimacy of expectations, these values do not seem to be rooted in the value of equality.[16]

Suppose for the moment that the answer to (i) is: a participant in a cooperative venture is someone who takes part in the production of the benefits to be distributed. Let us turn to (ii). Who participates?

For purposes of ideal theorizing about basic institutions, we might simply assume that every citizen in a society participates in those institutions. We might then assert that everyone's participation entitles her to partake of the benefits produced, maintaining—as Scanlon says—that participation gives one a prima facie equal claim to partake of those benefits. We can then ask what principles of justice must be satisfied by the distribution of those benefits among participants with prima facie equal claims.

I do not want to engage in ideal theory here. Instead I want to ask whether arguments from procedural fairness can support what egalitarian intuitions we may have about *actual* societies such as the contemporary United States. Actual societies are especially difficult for those who think arguments from procedural fairness can support the egalitarian outcomes we favor because, when we reason about actual societies, we are forced to question idealizing assumptions and stipulations that we might make for purposes of ideal theorizing. One assumption we are forced to question is the assumption that every citizen of an actual society is a participant in its basic social institutions. Once we question it, we are forced to revisit (i), the question of just what participation is.

I will not try to formulate a set of necessary and sufficient conditions for participation here.[17] Instead, I shall just suppose—as seems to me very plausible—that participation is a demanding notion. In particular, I shall suppose that being a productive member of one's society requires opportunity, ability, and motivation to take part in basic social institutions. And so I shall suppose that someone does not participate in the basic institutions of his society if he is involuntarily without meaningful work for long periods of time or if having been raised in social conditions of violence and deprivation has left him permanently alienated from the society in which he lives. These suppositions open the possibility that there are some citizens of actual societies, such as the contemporary United States, who do *not* participate in their societies' basic social institutions.

Let us call the opportunity, ability, and willingness to participate in one's society "the social conditions of participation." These conditions are themselves socially created goods. To say that the willingness or the ability to participate is produced and distributed by society's basic social institutions may seem to stretch the notions of production and distribution. But conditions of poverty, violence, and social disintegration can produce profound and permanent alienation from one's society, an alienation in virtue of which one believes that putting forth effort to participate in one's society is hopeless or is otherwise not worthwhile. The conditions that produce such alienation are themselves the result of how society's basic social institutions are configured. So while saying that the willingness to participate is itself socially produced may be elliptical, it is not inaccurate. That opportunity and ability also depend upon the configuration of basic institutions seems even clearer.

Being a productive member of one's society is a very great good. This is true in part because being productive is inherently satisfying.[18] It is also true because, in societies such as the contemporary United States, being rightly regarded as a productive member of one's society is a precondition for the respect of one's fellow citizens. The social conditions of participation are therefore very important goods. (And the philosopher who says participation entitles one to a prima facie equal claim is thereby committed to regarding them that way.) Indeed, I shall assume they are so important that they count among basic social benefits if anything does. My intuition is that there is at least a presumption that these goods—the social conditions of participation in one's society—should be equally distributed. I also have the intuition that that presumption can be overridden by only a very limited class of considerations. The questions I now want to pose are how those conclusions can be supported and, in particular, whether they can be supported without fundamental appeal to equality.

It is tempting to support the conclusion with an argument from procedural fairness. Such an argument would begin with the relevant instance of the fairness conditional. It would include the premises that everyone in society has prima facie equal claims to the social conditions of participation and that the procedure for producing and distributing these conditions must be fair. The challenge facing someone who wants to pursue this line of thought lies in the difficulty of establishing the second premise, which says that everyone in society has a prima facie equal claim to the conditions of participation. Why should we think that that premise is true?

Not everyone can have such claims in virtue of their being participants in a cooperative venture that produces and distributes those conditions, for I have supposed that in actual societies not everyone participates. There are some who do not. Among these are some who do not do so because they have been denied the social conditions of participation. The fact that they have been denied these conditions is one of the injustices of actual societies that needs remedying. An argument for remedying it cannot, however, depend upon the grounds that those who have been denied the social conditions of participation are participants.

Perhaps it will be said that having prima facie equal claims to the social conditions of participation in a society simply follows from, or is part and parcel of, equal citizenship in that society. The basic idea behind this reply is that citizenship is not simply a legal status. It is a moral status in this sense: to have the status of a citizen in a society just is or includes the entitlement to make claims on that society, including claims to basic social benefits. When a society commits itself to the equality of citizens, part of what it commits itself to is the prima facie equality of those claims. Thus the step in the argument from procedural fairness with which I am now concerned—the step according to which citizens have prima facie equal claims to the conditions of participation—is true simply because of what it is to be a citizen.

I am supposing that the presumption in favor of an equal distribution of the social conditions of participation is a presumption that is very difficult to override. If citizenship itself confers prima facie equality of claims to those conditions, then we can see why the relevant argument from procedural fairness establishes a presumption that is so strong. For arguments from procedural fairness establish equality of claims in the absence of special considerations. I have argued that those special considerations should be divided into antecedent defeaters and consequent blockers. It seems plausible that only a small number of very powerful considerations could serve as antecedent defeaters—as considerations that defeat the antecedent of the relevant fairness conditional by defeating the prima facie equality of claims.

This seems plausible, in turn, because it seems plausible that only a small number of very powerful considerations can defeat the prima facie equality of citizenship to which contemporary liberal democracies like the United States are theoretically committed. It also seems plausible that only a relatively small number of powerful considerations could serve as consequent blockers, though I admit that this would be more difficult to show. The assertion that prima facie equality of citizenship confers prima facie equality of claims to the social conditions of participation thus helps to show, not only why there is a presumption in favor of equal distribution of those conditions, but also why the presumption is so strong. That it does so may seem to tell in favor of the assertion.[19]

But proponents of arguments from procedural fairness face a serious difficulty if they assert both that citizens have prima facie equal claim to basic social benefits simply in virtue of their citizenship and that arguments from procedural fairness do not appeal to the value of equality in any fundamental way. To see that difficulty, let's recall why arguments from procedural fairness seem so plausibly to account for the presumption that socially created goods, such as basic social benefits, should be equally distributed and to do so without appeal to the value of equality.

Those arguments include the relevant versions of the fairness conditional as premises. The apparent soundness of the arguments from procedural fairness depends upon the fact that the second premises of those arguments—the premises that assert the antecedents of the fairness conditionals—seem to be true in the case of cooperative ventures, such as the cooperative ventures that produce basic social benefits. Those premises seem to be true in such cases because it seems plausible that someone gets a prima facie equal claim to the benefits of a cooperative scheme when she is one of the people who cooperate to produce those benefits.[20] Arguments from procedural fairness thus seem to justify presumptions of equal distribution because it seems so plausible that those who take part in cooperative schemes thereby earn prima facie equal claims to the benefits produced. These arguments seem to support presumptions of equality without appeal to the value of equality because, as I suggested earlier in this section, appeals to earnings do not seem to be appeals to equality.

By suggesting that participation in society has somewhat demanding requirements, I raised the possibility that some citizens in actual societies such as the United States do not participate in the cooperative scheme that produces basic social benefits. I thereby raised the possibility that some citizens in those societies do not earn prima facie equal claims. A philosopher who wants to maintain (as I do) that there is still a presumption in favor of distributing some of basic social benefits equally, and who also wants to maintain (as I do not) that arguments from procedural fairness explain that presumption without fundamental appeal to equality, can still insist that people *have* such claims. I have suggested the grounds he might bring forward for his insistence. But if I am right about the requirements of participation, then this philosopher cannot maintain that all the citizens who *have* those claims have *earned* them.

The shift from *earning* to *having* is significant, for it seems that proponents of arguments from procedural fairness are able to maintain that they do not appeal to the value of equality because they maintain that participants in cooperative ventures earn their prima facie equal claims. Once they fall back on the claim that citizens simply have prima facie equal claims in virtue of their citizenship, these philosophers may seem to be making a fundamental appeal to the moral value of equality after all. In particular, they seem to be making a fundamental appeal to the moral significance of equal citizenship.

Equal Claims without Equality

An adequate reply to this objection would have to show why citizens have prima facie equal claims and to do so without fundamental appeal to equality. Is such a reply available?

We can imagine a number of arguments for the assertions that equal citizenship confers prima facie equal claims and that among the benefits citizens have prima facie equal claim to are the social conditions of participation. One such argument might begin from the claim that political power is properly thought of as the power of citizens who are free and equal. When society exercises that power to regulate the production and distribution of basic social benefits, the exercise of that power must be justified to those whose power it is. So the production and distribution of those benefits must be justifiable to citizens as free and equal. To say this is just to say that citizens have prima facie equal claims, on one of the understandings of *prima facie equal claims* that I listed in the section "Equal Claims to Benefit." A different argument might begin from my earlier claim that being an equal claimant is a valued status. To deny that citizens are prima facie equal claimants, it might be argued, is unjustifiably to denigrate their status as citizens.

Neither of these arguments as it stands is sufficient to answer the objection, for both seem to make fundamental appeal to some value of equality. The latter derives citizens' prima facie equality of claims from the imperative to respect their status as equal citizens. The former derives it from the claim that citizens are free and equal coholders of society's political power. Furthermore, it is not obvious that the former argument is valid, for it is not obvious—without either additional premises about the relationship between citizens and the government that exercises their power or additional premises about what that power is exercised to do—that the exercise of citizens' power must be justifiable to them.

A different reply to the objection begins from the proposition that society's basic institutions have a profound impact on citizens by the ways they provide or fail to provide citizens with the incentives, opportunities, and abilities to participate in their society. Because the productive and distributive effects of a society's basic institutions have so profound an impact on its citizens, there is a prima facie case for taking citizens' interests in those effects equally into account in assessing how the social conditions of participation are produced and distributed.[21] To say that there is a prima facie case for taking these interests equally into account is just to say that citizens have prima facie equal claims to the conditions of participation, on one understanding of what it is for people to have prima facie equal claims. So the second premise of the relevant argument from procedural fairness—the premise according to which citizens have prima facie equal claims to the social conditions of participation—might be thought to follow from plausible claims about how profoundly citizens are affected by their society's basic institutions.

The profundity-of-effect reply seems also to imply that even nonparticipant citizens have prima facie equal claims to basic social benefits, since their life prospects are as profoundly affected as those of participant citizens. The reply therefore furnishes the missing premise in a procedural fairness argument for the presumption of equal distribution among participant and nonparticipant citizens. The fact that it does so might be thought to tell in favor of the reply, since this is a presumption that needs to be justified once we drop the idealizing that all citizens are participants.

My own view is that some version of the profundity-of-effect reply is correct: it is the profundity of the impact of social institutions on people's fundamental interests that creates prima facie entitlements to the benefits those institutions create and distribute. But there are difficulties with the reply, at least from the point of view of those who deny that fundamental appeals to equality are needed to justify the presumption of equal distribution.

One problem with the version of the reply that I offered a couple of paragraphs ago is that it is difficult to tell whether that version appeals to the value of equality or not. This is because that version of the reply masks the need to explain what it is about citizenship that confers a prima facie equal claim by some of the language the reply employs. That reply refers to the opportunities citizens have to participate in *their* society and to how societies are affected by *their* society's basic institutions. The use of the possessive suggests that being a citizen makes one a joint possessor or perhaps a joint owner of the basic institutions of the society of which one is a citizen. This relation of shared possession or ownership might, in turn, be thought to ground citizens' prima facie equality of claims to basic social benefits, including claims to the conditions of participation. If this is so, then what does the work in what I have called the "profundity-of-effect reply" is not the profundity of effect at all but a set of claims about citizenship and possession or ownership. The nature of possession or ownership, why possession or ownership follows from citizenship, and why possession or ownership confers prima facie equality of claims are not spelled out. When they are, there may well be an appeal to equality after all.

Another problem with the reply arises from the fact that those who want to deny the importance of fundamental appeals to equality must restrict the class of those with prima facie equal claims—the membership of what I referred to as "group G" when I laid out the schematic form of arguments from procedural fairness. The restrictions they need may be hard to sustain without making some very unrealistic assumptions.

If we assume that we are theorizing about a nation-state that is isolated from all others and that is composed only of citizens, the effects of a society's basic institutions on resident noncitizens and on those who live in other societies can be left out of account. Once we drop the assumptions, however, these effects cannot be ignored. That the effects of a society's basic institutions on its resident noncitizens are profound is obvious. Those institutions determine the opportunities and benefits available to resident noncitizens, the burdens that can be imposed upon them, the liberties they enjoy, and the conditions under which they can gain citizenship.

The effects of a society's basic institutions on residents of other societies can be, and often are, profound as well. The policies a society makes about the extraction and depletion of natural resources, its distribution of externalities such as pollution across national borders, the patterns of consumption that its economy allows and encourages, and the ways in which its economic demands influence what other economies have incentives to produce all have profound effects on the lives of those in other societies. The profundity-of-effect reply therefore opens the possibility that nonresident citizens and residents of other societies have claims on basic social benefits that are prima facie equal to those of citizens. It thus opens the possibility that arguments from procedural fairness could be used to support the presumption of distributing those benefits—or some of those benefits—across borders.

I believe that there is a presumption in favor of distributing some basic social benefits equally even across borders. Among the plausible candidates for this presumption, I would argue, are political influence over the extraction and consumption of valuable resources that are scarce and nonrenewable and influence over the creation and imposition of externalities such as pollution and greenhouse gases. Perhaps other people will think that other basic social benefits enjoy this presumption in addition or instead. I am prepared to grant that the presumption in favor of equal distribution depends upon the prima facie equality of claims to benefit that are had by those among whom the benefit should be distributed. I am also prepared to grant that this prima facie equality of claims depends upon some form of the profundity-of-effect argument. The interests of those among whom benefits are to be distributed have prima facie equal claims to benefit because they are profoundly affected by schemes that distribute those benefits.

It may still be that special considerations—in the form of antecedent defeaters, consequent blockers, or both—defeat the presumption in favor of equal distribution.[22] I do not want to ask what those special considerations might be. Instead, I want to ask whether the prima facie equality of claims can be established without appealing to equality in some fundamental way. The answer, I believe, is that it cannot. Anyone who maintains that persons who are profoundly affected by a society's basic institutions have prima facie equal claims to some of the social benefits it generates must explain why effects on those persons matter and why they matter enough to generate prima facie equality of claims among all those affected. The explanation can only be that effects generate prima facie equal claims among those affected because all those affected are equal, so that effects on some count every bit as much as effects on others.

So long as our attention is restricted to citizens of a single society or to those who live in a single society, it may be possible to support the equality of those affected by appealing to their equal citizenship or to their shared membership in a single society. The commitments to the equality of citizens—or, more broadly, to the equality of members—may be thought to be among the fundamental commitments of liberal democracy and so not to be in need of any further justification. Once we ask about why those across borders are equal, however, appeals to equal citizenship and equal membership no longer suffice. In this case, what is needed is an appeal to human equality. It is because human beings are of equal worth and matter equally that a society's profound effects on their life prospects can ground prima facie equal claims. The question is how these claims about equal human worth can be defended. It is the need to answer this question that opens the space for appeal to religious accounts of human equality.

Dropping the Idealizing Assumptions

Let me conclude by taking stock. First, arguments from procedural fairness most strongly support a presumption of equal distribution among all and only citizens when the crucial premises of those arguments are based on three assumptions, namely that societies are composed exclusively of participants, that those participants are all citizens, and that societies exist in isolation. Second, as those assumptions are progressively dropped, proponents of procedural fairness arguments are driven from the claim that citizen-participants in a cooperative scheme *earn* their prima facie equal claims to the benefits they produce by participating in that scheme to the premise that persons *have* prima facie equal claims to the benefits produced by a cooperative scheme in virtue of the scheme's effects on their life prospects. Third, the move from the former claim to the latter widens the class of claimants from participant-citizens to all citizens of a given society, then to all the residents of that society, and finally to many of those affected, whether resident or not. Successively dropping the idealizing assumptions thus opens the possibility that at least some of the benefits created by a society's basic institutions—its economic benefits and opportunities, for example, or political influence over its extraction of nonrenewable resources and its distribution of externalities—may have to be distributed equally across borders in the absence of special considerations because those across borders may have prima facie equal claims.

The three assumptions are idealizing assumptions. They are assumptions that it would be natural for a philosopher to make if he were building an ideal theory of justice or domestic justice. Indeed, I believe they are assumptions Rawls makes to facilitate just such a project. Given these assumptions, it may be possible to articulate and defend egalitarian principles of domestic justice without appealing to metaphysically robust claims about human equality. But it does not follow from this that such claims about human equality—and religious accounts of those claims—have no place in other defenses of egalitarianism.[23]

Notes

This paper was drafted for the conference "Religion and Equality" held at the Einstein Forum, Potsdam, Germany, on June 10–12, 2004. I am grateful to Phil Quinn for helpful comments on an earlier draft.

    1. Jeremy Waldron, *God, Locke and Equality* (Cambridge: Cambridge University Press, 2002).

    2. Quine once waggishly remarked that the two questions with which political philosophy concerns itself are "Who gets what?" and "Says who?"

3. T. M. Scanlon, "The Diversity of Objections to Inequality," in *The Difficulty of Toleration: Essays in Political Philosophy* (Cambridge: Cambridge University Press, 2003), p. 206.

4. Ibid., p. 208 (emphasis in original).

5. Derek Parfit, "Equality or Priority," in *The Ideal of Equality*, ed. Matthew Clayton and Andrew Williams (New York: Palgrave Macmillan, 2002), pp. 81–125, esp. p. 84.

6. See Ronald Dworkin, *Sovereign Virtue: The Theory and Practice of Equality* (Cambridge, MA: Harvard University Press, 2000); also Stanley Benn, "Egalitarianism and the Equal Consideration of Interests," in *Equality*, ed. J. Roland Pennock and John W. Chapman, Nomos 9 (New York: Atherton Press, 1967), pp. 61–78, esp. pp. 67ff.

7. For an example of a reliance on what I have called "the fairness conditional," see Stuart White, *The Civic Minimum* (Oxford: Oxford University Press, 2003), p. 38.

8. Thus Scanlon tries to catalog the diversity of reasons for objecting to inequality, only one of which is that it sometimes violates the demands of procedural fairness. I will not attend to his other reasons here.

9. Scanlon, "Diversity of Objections," p. 208.

10. I assume Rawls thinks that citizens of a well-ordered society have prima facie equal claims to a stock of primary goods sufficient to develop and exercise their moral powers. If Rawls also accepts the fairness conditional, he is committed to the conclusion that primary goods should be distributed equally in the absence of special considerations. He is in fact committed to that conclusion; see the statement of the "general conception of justice" in *A Theory of Justice* (Cambridge, MA: Harvard University Press, 1999), p. 54. The question is whether the special considerations to which Rawls appeals to justify the unequal distribution of income and wealth are considerations that he thinks defeat citizens' prima facie equality of claims. I have asserted that they are not. Substantiating this assertion would require more exegetical work than I can undertake here. For a passage that could, I believe, be exegeted to substantiate it, see the important paragraph on equality and the difference principle in John Rawls, *Collected Papers*, ed. Samuel Freeman (Cambridge, MA: Harvard University Press, 1999), pp. 230–31. The paragraph is found in Rawls's essay "Some Reasons for the Maximin Criterion."

11. For the idea of reasonable rejectability, see T. M. Scanlon, "Contractualism and Utilitarianism," in *Utilitarianism and Beyond*, ed. Amartya Sen and Bernard Williams (Cambridge: Cambridge University Press, 1982), pp. 103–28.

12. Of course two people cannot have *numerically* identical tickets, nor can each of two people do *numerically* identical jobs. The use of the word *identical* in talk of identical grounds is like the use of that word in talk of identical

twins. In such cases, we predicate identity of two subjects in virtue of their being identical in a respect to which identity unproblematically applies.

13. Phil Quinn has noted another difficulty with the suggestion under consideration. If that suggestion were followed and the analysans were substituted for the antecedent of the fairness conditional, then the notion of fairness would do crucial work in both the antecedent and the consequent of the (newly parsed) conditional. Quinn raises the possibility that that substitution, if warranted, would show the fairness conditional to be an analytic—and therefore, he worries—a trivial truth.

14. Consider a society that publicly affirms that citizens who lack the talent to fill these positions ipso facto do not have claims to primary goods that are ultima facie equal to the claims of the talented. I take it that such a society undermines the social bases of the self-respect of those who lack the relevant talents and that it in that way denigrates them. And I take it that Rawls would agree. The only question raised by my claim about Rawls in the text, then, is what grounds there are for thinking that he would regard this undermining or denigration as unjustifiable. While I cannot engage in the requisite exegesis here, I believe grounds can be found in passages in which Rawls says it tells in favor of the difference principle that it furnishes the bases of self-respect for the least advantaged. See Rawls, *Theory of Justice*, p. 156–57.

15. Scanlon, "Diversity of Objections," p. 208.

16. Of course, we will need to be told why those who participate to different extents, and why those whose efforts add different amounts of value to the product, get claims that are prima facie equal. Answering these questions may not be easy, but for present purposes I shall assume that it can be done.

17. The idea of participation in one's society is a central one in contemporary Catholic social thought, though the conditions have not been systematically laid out by those who rely on it. I have tried to lay down some conditions of participation in my *Religion and the Obligations of Citizenship* (Cambridge: Cambridge University Press, 2002), ch. 2. I am well aware of the inadequacies of the treatment there.

18. Admittedly a satisfaction unappreciated by those who spend their days surfing off Malibu.

19. As the text suggests, proponents of arguments from procedural fairness think prima facie equal claims to benefit are very easily acquired and extraordinarily difficult to defeat. That they think so might suggest that these philosophers think these propositions are trivially true and that the philosophers in question are really motivated by their commitment to a presumption in favor of equal distribution—hence really motivated by a fundamental (if defeasible) commitment to equality. I believe that this is a mistake, though I cannot pursue the matter here. It is a mistake of which I have been guilty in thinking earlier about arguments from procedural fairness; see my review of Scanlon's *The Difficulty of Toleration* in *Ethics* 114 (2004): 836–42.

20. At least, let's grant, this seems plausible if we add that the various roles in the scheme, the opportunities to fill those roles, and the incentives and education needed to fill them are all produced by the scheme itself.

21. An account that would have to be filled in by describing these interests in some detail and by distinguishing these interests from others that do not ground such claims.

22. It may be that considerations associated with shared citizenship or shared membership in a society whose basic institutions produce the benefits in question can serve as antecedent defeaters and/or consequent blockers, so that benefits need not be equally distributed across borders after all. Of course, anyone who wishes to maintain this will have to show why these relationships possess the force they are alleged to have.

23. Summing up his own discussion of the "diversity of objections to inequality," Scanlon writes:

> To conclude: relief of suffering, avoidance of stigmatizing differences in status, prevention of domination of some by others and the preservation of conditions of procedural fairness are basic and important moral values. *Within the framework of the principle of equal consideration* they provide strong reasons for the elimination of various inequalities. Taken together these values account for at least a large part of the importance that equality has in our political thinking. They may account for all of this importance, or there may be an important role to be played by a further moral idea of substantive equality. But it remains unclear exactly what that idea would be.
> —Scanlon, "Diversity of Objections," p. 218 (emphasis added)

I have stressed throughout that my aim is not to raise objections to Scanlon but to see whether egalitarianism can be defended without appeal to claims about human equality. I am prepared to grant Scanlon's claim that no such appeal is needed "within the framework of the principle of equal consideration." But it is important for my purposes to see why this claim seems so plausible and why granting it does not tell against the conclusions I have defended here.

The principle that citizens (or perhaps members) of a given society are entitled to equal consideration in the design of basic social institutions is deeply embedded in democratic culture. Indeed, it may be so deeply embedded as to need no further justification. For purposes of argument, I shall assume that this is so. I shall also assume that the principle says or implies that those who are entitled to equal consideration have claims to basic social benefits that are prima facie equal, on one of the interpretations of "prima facie equality of claims" canvassed above.

Given the second assumption, the principle says or implies that citizens (or members) of a given society have prima facie equal claims to basic social benefits. Given the first assumption—according to which we can take the principle of equal consideration as a starting point—that principle provides all the justification we need for citizens' (or perhaps members') prima facie equality of claims. So we need not look for some further support for the relevant instances of premise (2) in the argument for procedural fairness when the egalitarian conclusion to be supported is an egalitarian conclusion about distribution among citizens (or perhaps members) of a given society. Scanlon is therefore correct if he means—as I take him to mean—that we need not go outside "the framework of the principle of equal consideration" and appeal to "a further moral idea of substantive equality" in order to defend such a distribution.

But I see little evidence that Americans, at least, think that citizens of other societies are entitled to much by way of equal consideration. And so I would argue that the *only* version of the principle of equal consideration that is deeply enough embedded in American political culture to be taken as a starting point is one that requires the equal consideration *only* of others within one's own society. The only version of the principle of equal consideration that we can take as a starting point thus has what we might call a "domestic restriction." Because of the restriction, that version of the principle cannot support instances of premise (2) that range over members of more than one society. Instances of that premise therefore need some other justification. I have maintained that that further justification will involve appealing to an idea of human equality. In sum, it is international cases—and not the cases with which I have taken Scanlon to be concerned—that require us to go outside "the framework of equal consideration."

Seven

Torture, Justification, and Human Rights
Toward an Absolute Proscription

Sumner B. Twiss

I recently published an article entitled "History, Human Rights, and Globalization" that attempted to gauge changes since 1948—attributable in part to globalization processes—in the content of human rights, the major abusers and guarantors of human rights, and the justification of human rights.[1] It is the last measure—justification—that is revisited in this essay, prompted both by certain probative criticisms of a close colleague and human rights advocate, David Little, and by a recent reading of a 1996 essay by Philip Quinn, "Relativism about Torture: Religious and Secular Responses," which is dedicated to Amnesty International and its supporters.[2] Given the ongoing revelations about the mistreatment of prisoners in Afghanistan, Guantanamo Bay, and Iraq (not to mention the U.S. renditions of detainees to other torture-prone jurisdictions), the convergence of Quinn's topic and mine appears quite timely. In what follows I want to read his arguments about proscribing all torture in light of my typology of alternative forms of human rights justification and then highlight one United Nations approach to justifying in particular an absolute prohibition of torture (or alternatively the cogency of a nonderogative right not to be tortured) that both he and I overlooked or at least downplayed.[3]

Background

In my 2004 article, I argued that the Third Committee, which drafted and debated the Universal Declaration of Human Rights (UDHR) before sending it to the General Assembly for ratification in December 1948, reached a pragmatic consensus on a set of essential human rights norms protective of human dignity and welfare that was deemed sufficient unto itself without the use of contestable metaphysical or theoretical language or appeals. The article also pointed out that the view of Jacques Maritain about emphasizing these practical norms apart from justification and theory was explicitly cited during the Third Committee debate. This view was propounded by Maritain in his introduction to a concurrent 1948 UNESCO symposium on the philosophical bases of human rights: "[B]ecause . . . the goal . . . is a practical goal, agreement between minds can be reached spontaneously, not on the basis of common speculative ideas, but on common practical ideas, not on the affirmation of one and the same conception of the world, of man and of knowledge, but upon the affirmation of a single body of beliefs for guidance in action."[4]

The position apparently taken by the Third Committee, then, laid the groundwork for one common understanding in the international human rights community that the pragmatic consensus on human rights is a largely self-sufficient compact among nations that needs no further justification, philosophical or otherwise. Only the practical normative consensus and compact count; anything more is deemed superfluous. The Third Committee's position will be returned to (and revised) later in this essay.

The article went on to argue that globalization processes have so facilitated cross-cultural contact, awareness, and exchanges about worldviews, moral, political, and religious systems, and diverse patterns of reasoning and justification throughout the world that the human rights community has been compelled to acknowledge that human rights norms and their recognition are culturally embedded, interpreted, and justified in diverse ways. This acknowledgment, in turn, has led to the emergence of alternative efforts to justify human rights in the international arena, three of which appear particularly influential. The first is a continuation of the view that the pragmatic international consensus on human rights is largely self-sufficient (and now legally binding), needing no further justification but now buttressed by meta-reasons (for want of a better term) for accepting its self-sufficiency: for example, the invocation of skepticism about comprehensive schemes, frameworks, or doctrines of any sort that claim to provide grounds for human rights norms by appealing to essentialist understandings of human nature or human moral capacity. Such understandings are regarded as no more than quasi-mythical creations of outmoded currents of thought driven by unwarranted anxieties over the possible nihilistic and/or relativistic implications of the lack of absolute foundations for moral claims.[5]

The second approach also argues that human rights need no theoretical justification, but in this case it is because they identify claims that are logically prior to any theoretical justification and can be used to critique the very appropriateness of trying to provide such justification.[6] For this view, crucial human rights norms—or at least certain of them—are known to be true on an intuitive basis. This approach goes on to distinguish primary moral intuitions (such as the wrongness of torture and slavery) from other secondary human rights norms that are an outgrowth of them (e.g., norms of physical and civil security) because the latter are necessary to instantiate the former in a more complete protection system. In effect, this approach regards the pragmatic consensus as epistemically rather than metaphysically grounded and then further developed on a rational basis to preserve and expand the primary intuitions.

A third approach interprets the international consensus on human rights as a cross-cultural overlapping agreement on practical norms that is explicitly supported by diverse cultural, moral, and philosophical schemes. The development here—beyond the Third Committee, although possibly anticipated by it—involves viewing these schemes as alternative and complementary ways of justifying human rights norms, all of which are on a par, so to speak, because in our postmodern age we must recognize that no one cultural justification is likely to become dominant or succeed in convincing others outside a given culture that only it is reasonable and true. In effect, the consensus on human rights relies (and should rely) on many foundational arguments that converge in their support of human rights.[7] This approach is in principle open to the possibility that these diverse justificatory schemes might in fact share deeper reasons for accepting human rights norms. For example, certain general features of human nature or central elements of human functioning in the world command a broad cross-cultural consensus and constitute shared rationales for agreement on basic human rights norms.[8]

Before turning to Quinn's arguments about torture, it is worth noting that I attempted to identify certain weaknesses for each of the preceding approaches to human rights justification, if only for the reason that these will be revisited in addition to the typology itself. The article pointed out, for example, that while avoiding a possible indeterminable philosophical debate, the self-sufficient pragmatic consensus approach fails to engage the deepest beliefs of peoples, communities, and traditions, which, if engaged rather than dismissed, might result in greater social acceptance of a human rights ethos at the cultural level. It also indicated—in a much too dismissive way—that invocations of moral intuitions to ground human rights epistemically might well be unconvincing to those who suspect that such intuitions are no more than unsupported cultural biases. The argument further stated that the overlapping consensus approach fails to come to grips with the potential problem that cultural moral justifications might well embed intractable disagreements about the specification of norms and reasons, thereby resulting in worries about the contingency and fragility of the consensus itself.

Quinn's Position

Quinn begins his paper on torture and relativism by claiming that the shared morality of our society holds that torture is generally (or prima facie) wrong, that we would reject any ethical theory that told us otherwise, and that opposition to torture can be expressed in different moral vocabularies (i.e., duties or rights). At the same time, he also admits that there might be certain hard cases where some in our society might view torture as justifiable—for example, to find the location of the proverbial ticking bomb threatening a multitude of innocent people—so he does not think that the stronger claim that torture is always wrong is a part of our society's shared morality. Moreover, given the diversity of moral systems throughout the world and given what he takes to be the undeniable fact of epistemic relativism regarding moral justification—that such justification is always relative to epistemic contexts, which differ radically across the world—Quinn doubts that the stronger claim that torture is always wrong can be justified to members of any other societies. He also doubts that such a claim is part of a common morality of humanity as a whole—that is, a morality that applies to and can be justified to all persons as such.[9]

Quinn defends his skepticism in this regard by constructing valid arguments—one religious and one secular—for the claim that torture is always wrong, but he then points out that these arguments involve contestable premises that cannot themselves be justified to all rational persons. These premises involve, respectively, that human beings are made in God's image (a Western theistic claim) and that human autonomy is supremely important (a Kantian-like claim). In effect, Quinn appears to despair of our ever finding a justification for the absolute wrongness of torture that would convince all people, and he concludes that epistemic relativism with respect to this strong claim may be here to stay.[10]

To his great credit, Quinn is not content to end his essay on this negative note; instead, he goes on to propose two practical strategies for persuading increasing numbers of people that torture is always wrong. One such strategy involves making torture (all torture) look bad by redescribing it and by invoking vivid representations of torture in the arts as part of a campaign aimed at making the belief that torture is always wrong a part of the pretheoretical common morality of our society and eventually of all societies—on the model of the historic antislavery campaigns of the eighteenth and nineteenth centuries. A second strategy involves something like a "divide and conquer" approach combined with the possibility of attaining an overlapping consensus on the absolute wrongness of torture: that is, working with the idea that for every person there might be an argument that works, marshaling different sets of considerations for different people in an effort to achieve an overlapping consensus on this particular judgment. Quinn would count such an eventuality as moral progress.[11] Nonetheless, some questions are left that he overlooked or at least failed to address.

Before articulating these questions, it is important to observe that Quinn allies himself with the third approach of my typology—that of an overlapping consensus on human rights norms, although he does not take this as far as thinking that the consensus might extend to shared deeper reasons for accepting these norms. It is worth pointing out that in a 2003 essay on Christian ethics and human rights, Quinn discusses approvingly Louis Henkin's embrace of such an approach: "So we may, in effect, hope for what John Rawls describes as an overlapping consensus of various religions (each from the perspective of its own comprehensive doctrine) and of the human rights movement . . . a morality that includes a robust array of human rights."[12] Quinn is quite clear that from his point of view human rights constitute a "moral floor" of minimal standards for regulating human relationships and relationships between persons and their governments.

At the risk of some redundancy, certain features of Quinn's position on torture need to be highlighted and then questioned. First, he holds that the shared morality of our society generally proscribes torture, excepting some hard cases, and that we would reject any ethical theory that told us that torture is not generally wrong. Two questions need to be asked about this claim. First, on what ground does Quinn hold this view (on behalf of all of us)? Does he perhaps subscribe to the position that torture's prima facie wrongness can be known intuitively (e.g., a practical moral apprehension of the sort identified by W. D. Ross)?[13] Second, does Quinn hold the view that the moralities of other societies generally proscribe torture or regard it as prima facie wrong, and if so, on what basis?

The second feature of Quinn's position to which I want to draw attention is that, on the basis of accepting epistemic relativism, he doubts that the judgment that torture is always wrong is part of a common morality of humanity, a morality that applies to and can be justified to all persons as such, a universal audience of all humankind. Here his doubt is inductively derived: "Arguments and evidence sufficient to convince a universal audience that torture is always wrong seem not to be available in the historical record so far, and a pessimistic induction leads to the conclusion that they will not be forthcoming in the future."[14] After sketching his two arguments for torture's absolute wrongness involving the use of contestable premises, Quinn cites Robert Adams—"Nothing in the history of modern secular ethical theory gives reason to expect that general agreement on a single comprehensive ethical theory will ever be achieved"—and he concludes, "The best explanation is that there is no way to justify comprehensive theories . . . to human beings as such, . . . so I am convinced that chances are slim indeed that there is any secular argument that can be used to justify the judgment that torture is always wrong to all persons of good will."[15] Doubts arise about this claim. Putting aside the issue of a single comprehensive ethical theory, the question remains as to whether certain philosophers and human rights advocates have not offered promising arguments for an absolute proscription that are grounded in the grim realities of the nature, administration, and effects of torture and whether some of these might not be convincing to all persons of goodwill.

The third feature of Quinn's position to reiterate here is his proposed campaign to make the belief that torture is always wrong a part of the pretheoretical common morality of our society and of all human societies by describing torture and using vivid representations of torture in the arts to persuade people. While such a strategy is commendable and not unrealistic, one is inclined to wonder why exactly it might work. Are these redescriptions and vivid representations anything more than rhetorical devices in the process of moral (re)education, as Quinn seems to suggest? Or might they be more properly construed as a deepening and extension through reflection of an original intuition about the prima facie wrongness of torture? Or yet again, are they perhaps a combination of that intuition with some sort of consequentialist reasoning about the facts and effects of torture?

The fourth and final feature of Quinn's position that needs highlighting is his strategy for developing an overlapping consensus on the absolute wrongness of torture. Regarding this feature, I question whether Quinn is right to see this strategy restricted to a consensus on "some fairly specific moral judgements" as contrasted with a combination of those specific judgments *and* shared reasons for accepting them.[16] He appears to assume that there will be no consensus on how to argue the case regarding an absolute prohibition of torture; but why foreclose the possibility that there may be an argument (or set of arguments) for the judgment on which all moral systems can agree? As one might suspect, the articulation of these questions about Quinn's position serves as an introduction to another approach to the problem of torture by the international human rights community, and in describing that approach I must revisit and revise aspects of my initial typology of human rights justification, most particularly how I represented the Third Committee's position and how moral intuitions might be used to ground the absolute prohibition of torture.

Revisiting the Background

This section begins by returning to two significant moments in the Third Committee's debate—its discussion of Article 1 (pertaining to all human beings being born free and equal in dignity and rights) and Article 4 (which proscribes slavery, torture, and other cruel and inhuman treatment or punishment).[17] (The latter article was later split into two—one on slavery and the other on torture and inhuman treatment—but for convenience "Article 4" is used to describe the article's discussion of torture.) The debate over Article 4 was in fact replete with references to Nazi barbarities regarding slave labor, so-called medical experimentation, and other maltreatment in the concentration camps, and these barbarities were consistently characterized as "shocking the conscience of humanity." This latter theme of shock to the conscience was subsequently taken up in the UDHR preamble (which was debated last by the committee) as the principal reason for issuing the declaration: "Whereas recognition of the inherent dignity and of the equal and inalienable rights of the human family is the foundation of freedom, justice and peace in the world. . . . Whereas disregard and contempt for human rights have resulted in barbarous acts which have outraged the conscience of mankind." The question is what to make of these reiterations of recognition of rights and of outrage or shocks to the conscience of humanity. Are they merely rhetorical flourishes, or is something deeper going on?

The answer to this question is provided by the extensive debate over Article 1, which one might regard as the founding article of the declaration. It reads in full: "All human beings are born free and equal in dignity and rights. They are endowed with reason and conscience and should act towards one another in a spirit of brotherhood." In his book-length study of the Third Committee's discussion, Johannes Morsink argues quite persuasively that this article embeds both an inherence view of human rights—that they inhere in people as such simply by virtue of being human—and an epistemic claim—that reason and conscience are the means by which we come to know people's human rights.[18] Put another way, reason and conscience are the means by which we grasp the moral truths specified in the UDHR, and together with the various recitals of shock to the conscience regarding Nazi barbarities, these epistemic vehicles add up to a position of some sort of moral intuitionism. That is, according to Morsink's reconstruction, the Third Committee held the view that all normal human beings (of mature age, sufficient comprehension, and the like) would have the same reaction to the Nazi horrors because of their unaided access to basic moral truths. This reconstruction is strengthened by the little-known fact that the drafting committee was encouraged to insert "two-men-mindedness" (the Confucian idea of *jen*) into the article in addition to "reason" by the Chinese delegate P. C. Chang as, arguably, his way of drawing attention to the notion of the Mencian heart-mind, which within Mencius's thought functions intuitively.[19] Instead of the awkward "two-men-mindedness" (or even "heart-mind") the committee settled on the compromise term "conscience" in addition to reason, with the clear understanding that this was intended to capture the Mencian (or more broadly, Confucian) idea of intuitive moral knowing. Here Eastern and Western moral thought joined hands in a surprisingly unified manner.

Now I have already mentioned that approving reference was made in the Third Committee debate to Maritain's introduction to the UNESCO symposium on philosophy and human rights. In light of Morsink's (and now my own) reading of Article 1, it behooves us to review a bit more of Maritain's position than was explicitly referenced in the Third Committee discussion:

> Because . . . the goal of UNESCO is a practical goal, agreement between minds can be reached spontaneously . . . on common practical ideas . . . upon the affirmation of a single body of beliefs for guidance in action . . . [a] body of common practical convictions. . . . Is there anything surprising in systems antagonistic in theory converging in their practical conclusions? It is the usual picture which the history of moral philosophy presents us. The phenomenon proves simply that systems of moral philosophy are the products of reflection by the intellect on ethical concepts which precede and govern them, and which of themselves display, as it were, a highly complex geology of the mind where the natural operations of spontaneous reason, pre-scientific and pre-philosophic, is at every stage conditioned by the acquisitions, the constraints,

the structure and the evolution of the social group. Thus, if I may be allowed the metaphor, there is a kind of plant-like formation and growth of moral knowledge and feeling, in itself independent of philosophic systems and the rational justifications they propound. . . . Is it surprising, that, while these systems quarrel over the why and wherefore, yet in their practical conclusions they prescribe rules of behavior which are in the main and for all practical purposes identical?. . . . What is chiefly important for the moral progress of humanity is the apprehension by experience which occurs apart from systems and on a different logical basis—assisted by such systems when they awake the conscience to knowledge of itself, hampered by them when they dim the apperceptions of spontaneous reason. . . . [W]e have before us an entirely different picture, where no theoretical simplification is any more in question: then . . . not only is agreement possible between the members of opposing philosophic schools, but it must be said that the operative factors are . . . currents of thought . . . where the principal part has been played by the lessons of experience and history and by a kind of practical apprehension.[20]

While it is certainly possible to find in this statement support for a pragmatic consensus on human rights norms and perhaps a prescient gesture toward a proto-Rawlsian-like overlapping consensus, it is intriguing and important also to observe that a large part of Maritain's position involves his characterization of these norms as practical moral apprehensions, apperceptions, or convictions shared by people belonging to diverse, even somewhat antagonistic, moral traditions. Terms like *implicit recognition, natural operation of spontaneous reason, awakening of the conscience,* and *a kind of practical apprehension* (in addition to *the lessons and experience of history*) clearly point toward some operative notion of moral intuition. It takes no great leap to imagine (or hypothesize) that this aspect of Maritain's position was encapsulated within the Third Committee's rendition and discussion of Article 1.

Before returning to Article 4, we might ask whether anything more can be gleaned from the Third Committee's discussion of Article 1, and the answer, not unsurprisingly, is yes. What should we make of the claim that human rights inhere in human beings as such by virtue of their being human, that they are born free and equal in dignity and rights? Although the Third Committee explicitly eschewed appealing to Thomistic natural law as a way to ground human rights—because, for many, it connoted unacceptable connections with God's will and eternal and divine law—it seems that the inherence doctrine implies the claim that human beings share significant common characteristics in virtue of which some conditions and practices are bad for every human being and some other conditions and practices are good for every human being.[21] The whole point of the declaration is to identify those shared harms and goods and proclaim them to the world—in effect, reminding people and governments about those protections and conditions crucial to human well-being, ranging across physical and civil security, material necessities for life, and social and political empowerments. These project a minimal vision of the human good that amounts to a very spare natural-law position claiming that we share a common human nature that makes these protections and conditions good for us.[22] The Third Committee also advances, in addition to an epistemic moral intuitionism (or better, combined with it), a minimal natural-law view, shorn of religious implications.

How, then, does the preceding relate to Article 4 and, more specifically, its proscription of torture and cruel and inhuman treatment and punishment? The answer is quite simple and straightforward. The UDHR's proscription of torture is based on a primary moral intuition that such practices are prima facie wrong and work to the detriment of human well-being whenever and wherever they occur. I use the language—as does Quinn—of prima facie wrongness because the UDHR does not itself maintain the stronger position of an absolute prohibition of torture, leaving it open whether there might be cases of justifiable torture. It is important to observe, however, that the subsequent Articles 6 through 10 of the declaration identify a set of legal protections designed to minimize the likelihood that the legal systems of civilized nations could violate the proscription of torture as a matter of policy. Thus rights to recognition as a person before the law, to equal protection of the law, to effective remedy by a competent tribunal for violation of fundamental rights, to not being subject to arbitrary arrest, detention, or exile, and to a fair and public trial for criminal charges were designed to mitigate the possibility of ever again witnessing the kind of barbarities permitted under the Nazis' perverted legal system. Again, Nazi policies and actions were constantly referenced in the discussion of these articles. The development of these subsequent articles and their linkage by the Third Committee to Article 4 appear to exemplify—indeed, paradigmatically exemplify—what David Little describes as a position based on a primary moral intuition and then extended by means of reason into a more complete protection system that preserves that primary intuition.[23]

Toward an Absolute Proscription

The judgment that torture is prima facie wrong falls short of the judgment that such practices are always wrong or that the right not to be tortured is nonderogative. At this point, we need to turn to further subsequent developments on the proscription of torture by the international human rights community—in the form of the 1966 Covenant on Civil and Political Rights (which legally implemented pertinent articles of the UDHR), the 1975 Declaration on Torture and Other Cruel, Inhuman or Degrading Treatment, and the 1984 convention against such practices.[24] The 1966 convention expressly states that no derogation can be made from the article proscribing torture or cruel, inhuman, or degrading treatment or punishment, even for reasons of exigency in time of public emergency that threaten the life of a nation. The 1975 declaration avers that no state may permit or tolerate such practices and, further, that exceptional circumstances, such as a state of war or a threat of war, internal political instability, or any other public emergency, may not be invoked as a justification for such practices. The 1984 convention defines torture as

> any act by which severe pain or suffering, whether physical or mental, is intentionally inflicted on a person for such purposes as obtaining from him or a third person information or a confession, punishing him for an act he or a third person has committed or is suspected of having committed, or intimidating or coercing him or a third person, or for any reason based on discrimination of any kind, when such pain or suffering is inflicted by or at the instigation of or with the consent or acquiescence of a public official or other person acting in an official capacity.[25]

It also rules out any exceptional justifying circumstances whatsoever and adds that an order from a superior officer may not be invoked as a justification for torture. It seems that in adopting provisions such as these the international human rights community has moved far in the direction of an absolute proscription of torture, well beyond the prima facie prohibition in the UDHR.

What are the reasons accounting for this more stringent proscription? The record of comments of the UN Human Rights Committee and the reports of special rapporteurs to the UN Commission on Human Rights indicate roughly three sets of analytically distinguishable considerations, although these are often jumbled together in the actual record.[26] One set concerns the intrinsic nature of torture and its destructive effects on the victim. A second set concerns torture's effects on persons and communities other than the primary victim. The third set of considerations involves empirical hypotheses and evidence about the metastatic tendency or uncontrollability of the administration of torture.

With respect to torture's intrinsic nature and destructive effects for the primary victims, more is now known about what torture does to people than was known (or even suspected) in 1948. In the words of one rapporteur: "[Torture expresses] contempt for the personality of the other individual which has to be destroyed and annihilated. It is for that reason that torture is one of the most heinous violations of human rights as it is the very denial of . . . the recognition that each living being has a personality of his own which has to be respected . . . [making] the duty to eradicate torture . . . a primordial obligation."[27] These are strong words, and to explicate a bit, it is now known that the harm for the victim of torture, no matter the length of time it is administered, is both severe and permanent. The harms include not only permanent physical injury and disability (what we usually think of) but also chronic anxiety, inability to trust others, subsequent deliberate self-injury, violent behavior toward others, substance abuse, depression (often leading to suicide), paranoia, severe insomnia, uncontrollable nightmares and flashbacks, self-loathing, psychosomatic illness, shortened life span, permanent alterations of brain patterns, and so the list continues.[28] The empirical evidence is overwhelming that most survivors of torture experience the rest of their lives as a sort of living death. This knowledge sharpens, deepens, and extends the reach of the original primary intuition about the prima facie wrongness of torture and accounts for the rapporteur's language of destruction and annihilation, heinous violation, and primordial obligation of prevention. Informed reflection, to put it this way, so deepens and extends the primary moral intuition about torture that it converts it into an intuition that torture is always wrong.[29] These considerations could also be put to use in an alternative or ancillary consequentialist argument to the effect that the harmful consequences for the victims of torture (and in the aggregate they number in the hundreds of thousands) by far outweigh whatever benefits government elites may derive from the use of such practices to hang onto their positions of political power.

In regard to torture's effects on other than the primary victims, again a great deal more is known. Another special rapporteur gestures toward this by writing "Although in many cases the victims of such abuse are completely innocent, the inevitable effects of such practices is that mutual hatred increases and life becomes ever more violent. Torture breeds hatred and the increased hatred leads to more atrocities. . . . Governments should realize . . . that the vicious circle in which they seemingly find themselves may well have started with the abuses and the arrogant practices of the representatives of the official authorities."[30]

A statement such as this is just the tip of an iceberg involving well-documented case studies and empirical data that the torture of primary victims inflicts extreme hardship and trauma on the victims' relatives and does serious long-term damage to family relationships, in addition to imposing devastating effects on the wider community, not only fomenting hatred and spirals of violence but also resulting in a breakdown of civilian institutions that amounts to a kind of collective trauma for the entire community. Thus, in situations of systematic torture imposed by government agents, one invariably finds a set of deleterious effects on families and communities ranging from widespread substance abuse and domestic violence to violent crime, collective rage, and a stagnation of social and economic life.[31] Indeed, even beyond these specific effects, there is the additional phenomenon that the systematic use of torture in any society makes that society morally and historically dysfunctional.[32] The use of such torture is invariably accompanied by vigorous public government denial of its use, and the disconnection that evolves between what is officially stated and what is actually practiced leads to a false history that can be repaired only when public knowledge of the torture is later ratified through public acknowledgment—for example, in the form of prosecutions and truth commissions. Absent such efforts, the society loses its own sense of true history or identity, as if it too, like the primary victims, had been hooded and violated. Reflective awareness of all of these negative effects—in addition to the harms done to the primary victims—further strengthens the moral intuition that torture is always wrong, as well as constituting an even stronger ancillary consequentialist argument for why torture should be regarded as always wrong. One might even argue that these effects of torture on victims' families and communities themselves constitute violations of yet other human rights, for example, to the integrity of the family, to health and well-being, to the continuous improvement of living conditions, and to a social order in which all rights can be fully realized.

The final set of considerations regarding the practice of torture focuses on its tendency to become routinized and uncontrollable, which is certainly related to the previous sets of considerations, yet it introduces a distinctive line of reasoning that deserves separate attention. Again, in the words of a special rapporteur:

> Especially where civil strife has taken the form of guerrilla tactics . . . security personnel feel threatened and . . . gradually fall into the practice of physical abuse and torture to extract information about their opponents. Every person living within the guerilla area [is] seen as a potential enemy . . . and may, therefore be forced to disclose [information] by all available means. . . . It is used as a means not only to extract information but also to enforce behavior in conformity with the prevalent rules. . . . It is particularly disquieting that torture becomes so endemic in such a society that even a return to normalcy does not bring an end to the practice. . . . The Special Rapporteur was in particular alarmed by the fact that he received a number of allegations referring to the torture of children. . . . Torture is horrifying in all forms . . . but the idea of children, who are still in their formative stage, being tortured is mind-boggling indeed.[33]

Two related points are being made here. The first is that the practice of torture has a tendency to become routinized in a society, to become entrenched as an administrative practice or routine procedure for interrogation or governance. The second is that, once introduced, torture has a tendency to slide from being used for interrogation to being used to terrorize a whole population and to being used on vulnerable people either to intimidate third parties or (worst case) as a form of recreation. This slide is what I, following Henry Shue, would call torture's metastatic tendency or uncontrollability.[34]

Focusing first on the latter point, and again taking a cue from Shue, one might distinguish the following forms of torture according to "purpose": interrogational torture (to get information or a confession), punitive torture (as the form of punishment for a crime), terroristic torture (to control a population by instilling fear), and recreational torture (to inflict pain and inhumane treatment for fun).[35] Before discussing uncontrollability, I must say a few words about each of these types considered in itself. First, it is well known that interrogational torture is unreliable as a means of gaining accurate intelligence because the victim will say anything or confess to anything to stop the torture. Moreover, because the torturer himself has uncertainty about the reliability of information acquired under these circumstances, there is a natural tendency to overtorture in order to reconfirm the information received, but since the overtorture itself is unreliable, the whole process becomes a Catch-22, especially for innocent civilians who have no actionable information to begin with (most torture victims are innocent civilians). Second, punitive torture is often difficult to distinguish from terrorist torture, for the reason that torture as punishment is usually construed not only as retributive but also as a deterrent to others, in which case, though it may be self-limited (a certain number of whiplashes, the loss of a hand), the punishment is nonetheless intended to control others through terror. Additionally, those societies that do engage in punitive torture often exhibit tendencies toward governance through intimidation and violence.[36] Third, terroristic torture is manifestly not self-limiting—governance through terror is paranoiac and tends to rope in ever larger numbers of suspected dissenters to a regime on increasingly flimsy grounds. Finally, recreational torture is simply "useless violence," to adapt the words of Primo Levi, because it is paradigmatically done for no good reason even remotely comprehensible to the victim or others.[37]

There is considerable other evidence—for example, UN case reports, Amnesty International, and Human Rights Watch, not to mention social scientific literature—that interrogational torture has a tendency to slide into other types of torture: from interrogational into terroristic, from interrogational into recreational, from terroristic into recreational.[38] In brief, torture has a tendency to metastasize and spread into ever more horrific forms, even when there are supposed countervailing checks internal to a society and its subcultures. Moreover, and this returns us to the first point, practices of torture also tend to become routinized—to become routine administrative procedure—whatever their specific type. Much evidence for this proposition exists as well. Putting things in this way, of course, may reify torture as if it were an organic disease, whereas we well know that people intentionally engage in such behavior. This recognition points us toward another massive body of psychological and social scientific literature about the processes accounting for the emergence and training of torturers—involving socialization, dehumanization, moral disengagement, reshaping of identity, and the like.[39] Factors such as these lie behind the tendencies of torture to slide from one form into another and to become routinized. Indeed, some of these studies have even been cited in Appendix G ("Psychological Stresses") of the 2004 Schlesinger Report on Abu Ghraib—here referring to Philip Zimbardo's Stanford prison experiment, Robert Jay Lifton's studies of inhumane treatment during war, and Albert Bandura's research on the mechanisms of moral disengagement, among others.[40]

How does this final set of considerations about the routinization and the uncontrollability of practices of torture figure into arguments for the absolute prohibition of torture (or the nonderogative status of the right not to be tortured)? It does so in three ways. The first way is to mesh these findings with the previous sketched consequentialist argument, thereby further strengthening that argument by maintaining that the range of harms adduced are virtually unavoidable and that much more severe. The second way is to contend that these findings so enhance our comprehension of the intrinsic nature of torture that upon informed reflection we see or intuit that torture per se is absolutely wrong or that human beings have an absolute nonderogative right not to be tortured. The third way—which is actually a variation of the first and second combined—focuses on the fact that interrogational torture, terroristic torture, and perhaps punitive torture have an irreversible tendency to slide into or to "authorize" (if that is the right word) recreational torture. The thinking here is that recreational torture (just for fun) triggers the strong moral intuition that such a practice is clearly wrong, transparently wrong, if anything is, and further, that any series of actions leading to such a practice must a fortiori also be wrong. This line of thinking is prompted by various philosophers and human rights advocates. For example, Judith Thomson contends—plausibly—that the judgment that one ought not to torture babies to death for fun is a nontrivial necessary moral truth, the negation of which could not be accommodated by what would be recognizable as a moral code.[41] Her contention seems equally applicable to the modified specific judgment that one ought not to torture human beings (not just children) for fun, whether to death or otherwise. David Little, in part inspired by Thomson, similarly suggests that "the recreational or intimidational torture of children and other defenseless innocents" is "'transparently wrong'" and "an important part of what the concept 'moral wrongness' has to mean," but he goes a step further to link this intuition to the idea of condemning all forms of torture.[42] The point here is that this particular intuition is so strong and obvious that anything inevitably leading to its violation, especially on a routine basis, must itself be co-implicated as wrong. If this is so, then we have an intuitionally grounded case for an absolute prohibition of torture.

Conclusion

To recapitulate where we are at this point: I have identified a set of appeals and arguments that represent an important approach of the international human rights community to the prohibition of torture. It begins with the Third Committee's appeal to a moral intuition about the prima facie wrongness of torture, buttressed by a minimal natural-law position that a practice such as torture is bad for all human beings (as part of a minimal vision of the good for all humans). This approach continues by marshaling sets of considerations for prohibiting all torture and making the right not to be tortured nonderogative. One set of considerations reflectively deepens our comprehension of the nature of torture and its effects on the primary victims, sharpening and extending the original intuition about the wrongness of torture. A second set of considerations argues consequentially that torture's effects on other persons and communities constitutes such a grievous harm for them, as well as the primary victims, that it ought to be stringently prohibited for the benefit (or minimization of harm) for all. And the third set of considerations focuses on the tendency of torture to become routinized and metastasized such that it not only strengthens the consequentialist argument but also puts us in a position to realize or apprehend that all torture is wrong not only prima facie but absolutely.

Now the big question is whether this multiphased approach to an absolute prohibition of torture—or again, the derogative status of the right not to be tortured—survives Quinn's doubts about being able to ground that judgment, apart from prospective campaigns to persuade others and/or to develop an overlapping consensus. Put another way, does this approach involve essentially contestable premises that undermine its ability to be convincing *now* to all people of goodwill, whatever their social or cultural location? I am inclined to say no for four reasons. First, the reflectively deepened and extended intuition of torture's absolute wrongness is firmly grounded by full comprehension of the nature of torture as outlined above, as well as being buttressed by a comprehension of what is minimally good and bad for human beings. Second, if in some odd circumstance this grounding were to be denied (mistakenly) by someone, then the consequentialist line of argument would still stand, and frankly its conclusion for judging torture to be wrong in all circumstances is also compelling. Third, the facts about torture—its effects, its uncontrollability, and the like—whether conceived as reflectively deepening and extending our moral intuitions or informing a consequentialist argument, constitute empirically based unshakable premises; these facts are not going to be overturned by new studies, and they are not contestable like Quinn's appeals to being made in the divine image or the supreme value of human autonomy. Fourth, the convergence of the two lines of argument leads me to believe also that—contrary to Quinn's view—the absolute prohibition of torture is more firmly grounded than he may have thought.

Given that the world's moral systems all include prohibitions of assault on the innocent, defenseless, and vulnerable as a kind of moral primitive, as well as strands of moral intuitionism, natural law–like thinking, and consequentialism, it is not obvious to me that the considerations previously adduced are not already completely acceptable to and convincing within those systems.[43] In other words, we already have an overlapping consensus on the absolute proscription of torture, and we may also have an overlapping consensus on the grounds for accepting or justifying it. To really make good on these claims, of course, it would be incumbent on me to demonstrate their truth on a system-by-system basis, but that is a task for another day and another venue.

Short of such a demonstration on a system-by-system basis, perhaps a bit more can be said, reflecting on the fact that torture paradigmatically involves the infliction of pain so severe as to virtually unmake a person from the inside. That is, torture, though initiated by another, involves a kind of compelled self-betrayal in which the victim is forced to deconstruct himself and his world through his body and its natural responses as an active accomplice in his destruction as a person: this is debasement of the most extreme sort possible.[44] Now, I want to suggest that all of the moral and religious systems of which I am aware advance some notion of human dignity that condemns the torturous violation of that dignity in the manner just described. The dignity in question may be imaged and justified in a variety of ways—for example, being made in the image of God, being the expression of an underlying cosmic soul, or being a locus of intrinsic value unto itself. However, the claim is shared that every person qua person ought to be inviolable in the sense that he or she should not be intentionally compelled to commit a kind of suicide, destroyed in what is nothing short of a prolonged living death.

Epilogue

The question will arise as to whether this case for an absolute prohibition of torture is not undermined by variants of the ticking bomb scenario. The common elements in these variants are well summarized in Appendix H ("Ethical Issues") of the Schlesinger Report: impending loss of life on a large scale, a suspect who knows the location of the ticking bomb (and in most versions is responsible for its placement), and a third party who has no humane alternative other than torture to obtain the information in order to save lives.[45] The big question is, is it morally permissible for that third-party interrogator to use torture to obtain the information as expeditiously as possible, and if so, does this not show that the prohibition of torture is not and should not be absolute? The answer to both questions is no, for two reasons. The first focuses on the scenario itself and involves gaining some realism about it—in this I am assisted by both Jennifer Harbury and Henry Shue. The second focuses on the deleterious effects of allowing this scenario to govern our moral reflection and thinking about torture.

For his part, Shue, after suggesting that in philosophy artificial cases often make bad ethics, points out how unlike the usual circumstances of torture the scenario is.[46] It is assumed that the proposed victim actually planted the bomb and that the bomb is nondefective and will go off if not deactivated. It is further assumed that the torture will be conducted in the "cleanest" way possible by a trained interrogator (not a thug), with a doctor present, judicial authorities informed, and in a manner such that pain is administered only up to the point at which the information is divulged and then no longer—for example, the victim will not be raped or forced to eat excrement, and every effort will be made to avoid irreparable damage. For Shue, while such a case of carefully delimited torture is imaginable—and in a case just like this permissible—he is also equally clear that using this case to relax the legal prohibitions against torture, where these prohibitions amount to an absolute proscription, is unwarranted.[47] Why? Because "there is considerable evidence of all torture's metastatic tendency," and all that this implies about the grievous harms wrought by torture generally.[48] The lesson drawn from Shue's discussion of this scenario is deep suspicion about using extremely implausible and artificial cases to inform our moral intuitions about bedrock proscriptions.

For her part, Harbury challenges the realism of the scenario itself by pointing out that such a terrorist action is likely to be undertaken by a clandestine group of participants who are carefully selected and trained and who operate under strict "need to know" standards (compartmentalized knowledge of the operation).[49] This training will have likely involved preparing participants for the possibility of capture, including how to withstand torture for a given period of time and/or to give prima facie convincing but false information. Moreover, all participants will likely be carefully monitored—at least to the extent of following a check-in procedure—so that when an operative goes missing (e.g., is captured) the explosive device will be immediately moved. This is a real-world scenario, and Harbury is quite dismissive of the philosopher's artificial case. Notice how her scenario undercuts the very notion that useful, actionable intelligence could be gained through interrogational torture in this case. She further asks some hard questions, such as: How imminent must the threat of the explosion be? How big must the bomb be? Is it appropriate to torture the suspect's relatives to make him or her talk?—all suggesting an inevitable slippery slope of distinctions and permissions. She is also quite clear about the considerable data available showing that *interrogational torture does not work* because the information obtained is unreliable and that this unreliability leads to inevitable delays and confusion in taking subsequent correction action.[50] I frankly believe that linking the positions of Shue and Harbury utterly nullifies the moral power of the ticking bomb scenario.[51]

Allowing the ticking bomb scenario to govern our thinking is morally dangerous. First, rather than sharpening our moral intuitions about the wrongness of torture, it tends to dim or otherwise obscure them by injecting fear and anxiety into the equation. If we do consider Harbury's rendition of the scenario to be a realistic threat to our security, the answer does not lie in authorizing torture or regarding it as sometimes justifiable but rather in improving intelligence gathering, analysis, and coordination in an effort to prevent such a scenario from ever becoming actualized. Second, the ticking bomb scenario deflects our attention away from the well-known facts about the nature of torture, its tendency to slide into ever worse forms, and its tendency to grow. These facts warrant caution—indeed rejection—of any efforts to weaken an absolute proscription of torture.

Notes

I am indebted to the following colleagues for their critical comments: Terry Coonan, Sandy D'Alemberte, James Gustafson, John Kelsay, Hugh LaFollette, Paul Lauritzen, David Little, Bert Lockwood, Dan Maier-Katkin, and Michael Slater.

1. Sumner B. Twiss, "History, Human Rights, and Globalization," *Journal of Religious Ethics* 32 (2004): 56–65.

2. Philip L. Quinn, "Relativism about Torture: Religious and Secular Responses," in *Religion and Morality*, ed. D. Z. Phillips (New York: Palgrave Macmillan, 1996), pp. 151–70. This article was selected for some sustained attention because its arguments are the clearest and most provocative that I know on the subject.

3. The primary goal in this essay is to characterize and analyze a particular international moral approach to an absolute prohibition. Secondarily, however, it will be seen that I am inclined to endorse the wisdom of this approach.

4. Jacques Maritain, introduction to *Human Rights: Comments and Interpretations* (London: Wingate, 1950).

5. See, e.g., Richard Rorty, "Human Rights, Rationality and Sentimentality," in *On Human Rights: The Oxford Amnesty Lectures, 1993*, ed. Stephen Shute and Susan Hurley (New York: Basic Books, 1993), pp. 111–34; Richard Rorty, "The Priority of Democracy in Philosophy" and "Truth and Freedom: A Reply to Thomas McCarthy," both in *Prospects for a Common Morality*, ed. Gene

Outka and John P. Reeder Jr. (Princeton: Princeton University Press, 1992), pp. 254-78 and 279-90 respectively. I use the parenthetical phrase *now legally binding* because various legally binding conventions have been adopted; in addition, the UDHR has gained the status of customary international law.

6. See, e.g., David Little, "The Nature and Basis of Human Rights," in Outka and Reeder, *Prospects,* pp. 72-92.

7. See, e.g., Amy Gutmann, introduction to *Human Rights as Politics and Idolatry,* by Michael Ignatieff (Princeton: Princeton University Press, 2003), pp. vii–xxviii.

8. See, e.g., Martha C. Nussbaum, *Women and Human Development: The Capabilities Approach* (Cambridge: Cambridge University Press, 2001) and "Capabilities and Human Rights," *Fordham Law Review* 66 (1997): 273-300.

9. See Quinn, "Relativism about Torture." Indeed, one might argue that Quinn doubts the very existence of a common morality of humanity as a whole, beyond his skepticism that the claim about torture being always wrong is part of it—at least in his 1996 essay.

10. Ibid., p. 165.

11. Ibid., pp. 166-69.

12. Philip Quinn, "Christian Ethics and Human Rights," in *Human Rights and Responsibilities in World Religions,* ed. Joseph Runzo, Nancy M. Martin, and Arvind Sharma (Oxford: Oneworld Press, 2003), pp. 233ff.

13. W. D. Ross, *The Right and the Good,* ed. Philip Stratton-Lake (New York: Oxford University Press, 2003).

14. Quinn, "Relativism about Torture," p. 156.

15. Ibid., p. 165.

16. Ibid., p. 169.

17. UN General Assembly Official Records, 3rd Sess., 3rd Comm., Pt. I, *Humanitarian and Cultural Questions* (1948).

18. Johannes Morsink, *The Universal Declaration of Human Rights: Origins, Drafting and Intent* (State College: University of Pennsylvania Press, 2000), pp. 280-301.

19. See Sumner B. Twiss and P. C. Chang, "Freedom of Conscience and Religion, and the Universal Declaration of Human Rights," *Chinese Studies Forum* 3 (2002): 35-47.

20. Maritain, introduction, pp. 10-14.

21. See, e.g., Michael J. Perry, "Are Human Rights Universal? The Relativist Challenge and Related Matters," *Human Rights Quarterly* 19 (1997): 461ff. See also "The Natural Law Approach," in *International Human Rights: Law, Policy and Process,* 3rd ed., ed. David Weissbrodt, Joan Fitzpatrick, and Frank Newman (Cincinnati, OH: Anderson, 2001).

22. It has been suggested that this minimal vision counts as a comprehensive theory or scheme akin to a philosophical or religious system. I beg to

differ simply because identifying elemental constituents of what is good and bad for all humans does not in itself entail any particular worldview, concept of personhood, ideal political system, or the like. Rather, it sets constraints on the acceptability of the latter. A minimal vision of the human good is not a comprehensive vision. For another quite interesting minimal-law position, see, for example, H. L. A. Hart, *The Concept of Law* (Oxford: Oxford University Press, 1961), which represents a modified form of legal positivism.

23. Little, "Nature and Basis," pp. 6, 83–85.

24. These documents are available from many sources. See *Basic Documents on Human Rights*, 4th ed., ed. Ian Brownlie and Guy S. Goodwin-Gill (Oxford: Oxford University Press, 2002).

25. Ibid., p. 230. This essay refrains from the debate about where to draw the line between torture and cruel and inhuman treatment, as that subject would warrant an entire paper devoted just to it. For data on this issue, see *The Torture Papers: The Road to Abu Ghraib*, ed. Karen J. Greenberg and Joshua L. Dratel (Cambridge: Cambridge University Press, 2005).

26. These records are excerpted and reprinted in the entry "Torture," in Edward Lawson, *Encyclopedia of Human Rights*, 2nd ed. (New York: Taylor and Francis, 1996). All subsequent quotations from these records can be found in that entry.

27. Ibid., p. 1448.

28. These empirical findings are well summarized and documented in Jennifer K. Harbury, *Truth, Torture and the American Way: The History and Consequences of U.S. Involvement in Torture* (Boston: Beacon Press, 2005); John Conroy, *Unspeakable Acts, Ordinary People: The Dynamics of Torture* (Berkeley: University of California Press, 2000); Edward Peters, *Torture* (State College: University of Pennsylvania Press, 1985), pp. 141–87.

29. Here I acknowledge a debt to Robert Audi, "Intuitionism, Pluralism, and the Foundations of Ethics," in *Moral Knowledge and Ethical Character* (New York: Oxford University Press, 1997). I might elaborate that I accept Audi's characterization of an intuition as being a noninferential, moderately firm, and pretheoretical cognition formed in the light of adequate understanding of its object (i.e., what it is about). Moreover, I believe that adequate comprehension can be reflectively deepened by exposure to newly acquired information about that object: that is what I mean by "converting" or "extending" an intuition about the prima facie wrongness of torture into an intuition that torture is always wrong. Incidentally, I have nothing at stake in using the language of "intuition," as contrasted with, for example, "practical apprehension," "practical conviction," "self-evident truth," or "reflectively seeing what is the case." I point this out for those persons who are constitutionally uncomfortable with "intuition."

30. Lawson, *Encyclopedia of Human Rights*, p. 1447.

31. See Harbury, *Truth, Torture*, pp. 157–59; Amnesty International, *Torture Worldwide: An Affront to Human Dignity* (New York: Amnesty International, 2000).

32. This point has been eloquently argued by Terrence S. Coonan, "Rescuing History: Legal and Theological Reflections on the Task of Making Former Torturers Accountable," *Fordham International Law Journal* 20 (1996): 512.

33. Lawson, *Encyclopedia of Human Rights*, pp. 1447–48, 1451.

34. Henry Shue, "Torture," *Philosophy and Public Affairs* 7 (1978): 124–43, reprinted in *Torture: A Collection*, ed. Sanford Levinson (New York: Oxford University Press, 2004).

35. Actually, Shue develops only the first three categories and discusses at length only interrogational and terroristic torture. Recreational torture is, however, an extremely well-known phenomenon.

36. Amnesty International, *Torture Worldwide*, pp. 9–35.

37. Primo Levi, *The Drowned and the Saved* (London: Abacus, 1991), pp. 105–26.

38. The literature from these sources is voluminous and can be easily accessed online. See also Shue, "Torture"; Harbury, *Truth, Torture*; Conroy, *Unspeakable Acts*.

39. See, e.g., James Waller, *Becoming Evil: How Ordinary People Commit Genocide and Mass Killing* (New York: Oxford University Press, 2002); Conroy, *Unspeakable Acts*, pp. 88–122. Although I have not developed the point here, one should also note that torturers themselves are subject to considerable abuse in the form of radical dehumanization, with subsequent life-altering deleterious effects for themselves, their families, and their communities.

40. Department of Defense, *The Schlesinger Report: An Investigation of Abu Ghraib* (Arlington, VA: Department of Defense, 2004), reprinted in Mark Danner, *Torture and Truth: America, Abu Ghraib and the War on Terror* (New York: New York Review of Books, 2004): 329, 394. Particularly useful with regard to this research is Philip G. Zimbardo, "A Situationist Perspective on the Psychology of Evil: Understanding How Good People Are Transformed into Perpetrators," in *The Social Psychology of Good and Evil*, ed. Arthur G. Miller (New York: Guilford Press, 2004), pp. 21–50 (see also Zimbardo's bibliography at the end of his chapter).

41. Judith Jarvis Thomson, *The Realm of Rights* (Cambridge, MA: Harvard University Press, 1990), pp. 18–20.

42. Little, "Nature and Basis," p. 83.

43. This is an inductive conclusion drawn from my work in comparative ethics. For a bibliography of some of the relevant sources, see Sumner B. Twiss, "Comparison in Religious Ethics," in *The Blackwell Companion to Religious Ethics*, ed. William Schweiker (Malden, MA: Blackwell, 2005), p. 147, as well as the articles on specific moral traditions in Part II of that volume.

44. See David Sussman, "What's Wrong with Torture?" *Philosophy and Public Affairs* 33 (2005): 1-33. For religious and cultural views of prohibitions of (or at least constraints on) practices of torture, see, for example, Joyce S. Dubensky and Rachael Lavery, "Torture: An Interreligious Dialogue," in *The Torture Debate in America*, ed. Karen J. Greenberg (Cambridge: Cambridge University Press, 2005), pp. 162-80; Peters, *Torture*, pp. 92-97; Alison W. Conner, "Confucianism and Due Process," in *Confucianism and Human Rights*, ed. William Theodore de Bary and Tu Weiming (New York: Columbia University Press, 1998), pp. 179-92; Melissa Weintraub, ed., *A Rabbinic Resource on Jewish Values and the Issues of Torture*, www.rhr-na.org/torture/tortureresources.html.

45. Department of Defense, *Schlesinger Report*, p. 401.

46. Shue, "Torture," p. 141; in what follows I draw freely from pp. 142-43.

47. Ibid., pp. 142-43. It occurs to me to add that substituting *rape* for *torture* throughout this entire essay might help sharpen the intuitions of any diehard skeptics of the position being advanced and analyzed. Additionally, it is simply a fact that much actual torture of men, women, and children involves raping them in a literal sense. Is anyone inclined to deny the absolute moral wrongness of rape?

48. Ibid., p. 143.

49. Harbury, *Truth, Torture*, p. 166; in what follows I draw freely from pp. 161-69.

50. Ibid., pp. 161-69.

51. Some might not regard this case as finally convincing in every imaginable circumstance. For them, I would say this: if one came across a realistic case of so-called "necessary" torture (e.g., to save a massive number of lives), then although this necessity would be a mitigating factor—in terms of condemnation and punishment—the offender would still have committed a moral (and legal) crime and would have what political thinkers call "dirty hands."

Afterword

A Eulogy for Phil Quinn

Paul J. Weithman

Phil Quinn was a jewel. He was rare and valuable, a treasure whose loss we mourn.[1]

Phil had a powerful and supple mind of crystalline clarity. He was immensely knowledgeable in most areas of philosophy and contributed to many of them, writing more than 150 scholarly articles. He excelled as a commentator and interlocutor. Many of us are greatly indebted to Phil for his copious and insightful comments on our work—always delivered within a day, penciled in the margins of our papers in his textbook hand. But the lecture hall was the setting in which this jewel sparkled most brightly. Phil could listen to a paper on virtually any topic in philosophy—on virtually any topic in the humanities—and ask a question that cut to the heart of the matter. You always understood a paper better after Phil asked a question about it.

There are few rewards the philosophical world can offer that Phil did not receive. He was a chaired professor at an Ivy League university when he was little more than forty. He was elected president of the Central Division of the American Philosophical Association. Indeed, the association was a body to which he gave a great deal of his life, for it sustained the intellectual enterprise to which he was so deeply committed. It was through the APA that Phil formed many of the relationships that were most meaningful to him. He always looked forward to the meetings of the association, to the people he would see there, and to the dinners for which he would go out—especially the meals he had with his old friend Steffi Lewis.

But Phil did not just love philosophy. He loved the academy. Though his home was in the APA, his citizenship was in the republic of letters. He had a true patriot's affinity for his fellow citizens in that republic. The aging of his own generation of intellectuals occasionally made him nostalgic, as when he once noticed from a published photo that Susan Sontag had gone gray. Occasions that celebrated the life of the mind—like the Haskins Lecture by Clifford Geertz that Phil was privileged to hear some years ago in Philadelphia—brought him the greatest delight. The crowning glory of Phil's career was his election to the American Academy of Arts and Sciences in 2003. He savored every moment of his installation. The last piece Phil wrote was a contribution to the academy's journal *Daedalus*, which will appear in its next issue.

Phil looked forward to the next stage of his life. It would, he insisted, be lived in a better climate. Phil had a theory that one's tolerance for cold is irreversibly hard-wired during adolescence. He blamed—or credited—his teenage years in Texas for making him sensitive to the harshness of South Bend winters. When asked what he would do with his retirement, Phil was full of ideas and—it must be said—of dreams for second and third careers that are most charitably described as "Mitty-esque." He devoured mystery novels and planned to write one of his own.

Phil had an admirably, obstinately contrarian spirit. In the days when smokers were still permitted to indulge inside the Decio coffee shop, some tables had signs on them that prohibited smoking. If Phil was seated at a "No Smoking" table because the others were full, he would either turn the sign over when he was ready to smoke or move his sign elsewhere—sometimes impishly placing it at a table where someone he knew had already lit up a cigarette. Decio Commons remained one of Phi's haunts, and the primary source of his nutrition, even after smokers were banished to the outdoor tables. The place will not be the same without him.

Phil also had a tender conscience. He stood and fought for causes that engaged it. His readiness to pick up the cudgels for the liberal causes in which he believed, yoked with the power of his mind, could make him a very formidable presence in academic meetings. Yet his presence was also a welcome one that gave hope to many who shared his convictions. He was a gifted parliamentarian. No one could follow the ebb and flow of a meeting better, or intervene in a discussion more wisely and effectively, than Phil. Many of the decisions the Philosophy Department has made over the years are due to him.

Phil had a very large number of companions here at Notre Dame and across the philosophical world. He was not one to network his friends or to connect them with one another. However much time you spent with Phil, you were never sure whom else he knew. Eventually you assumed he knew everyone. One of the blessings of recent days has been finding out just how close to the truth that is. Another, of course, has been getting to know Phil's sisters, inviting them into Phil's world and learning something more about him.

Yet if Phil was a jewel we valued, he was also—like a jewel—impenetrable. He lived his life at some remove from us. The fences he put up to guard his inner core were high and kept us all at a distance. We caught glimpses of the inner Phil only on those rare occasions when he let down the guard that he usually maintained so jealously.

I caught one glimpse when Phil first began to discuss retirement some years ago. He said, with a tone of real humility and without a tinge of rancor, that he didn't think his retirement would matter. He didn't believe that he had ever had much influence in the department or that what he said and thought made any difference.

In that moment of his self-effacement, that moment in which Phil effaced himself from the recent history of a department to which he had given so much, I wondered whether he really *didn't* believe that he mattered. I have wondered ever since what vulnerabilities to hurt and rejection this man was protecting with the fences he built.

Perhaps it was Phil's own vulnerability that gave him such insight into the human condition. His work was at its best when he wrote about human vulnerability to the tragic and about its implications for human love. One of his most powerful and moving essays was on the novel *Silence*, by the Japanese author Shusako Endo. I know how hard Phil worked on that paper and how he thought about every nub of that book's subtle texture. In his essay Phil argued, in effect, that it is impossible for human beings always to love as we should. It's impossible because we can find ourselves trapped between the conflicting demands of the two great commandments, which enjoin love of God and love of neighbor. If Christianity forces us to choose between honoring God and alleviating the sufferings of our neighbors, what are we to do? I know that Phil, empathetic as he was, would have chosen his neighbors. But he would have wondered how God can be silent when we face so tragic a conflict. These were difficult existential questions that bothered Phil deeply but to which he had no answer.

But however tempting it may be to acquiesce when darkness and silence cloud our souls, God simply will not *allow* loneliness and isolation to have the final say. For however difficult it may be for us to love, God unconditionally loves the world and all of us who are in it. Where Phil is now, he knows beyond a shadow of a doubt that he is as completely and totally loved as a human soul can be.

Phil got some intimation of this love as his friends, his colleagues, and the staff and residents of Dujarie House rallied to support him in his illness. For in his last weeks and months, the stuff of life began to intrude on Phil in ways that could not be fenced out any longer. In those weeks and months, when he became increasingly dependent on others, I think Phil allowed his mind to go places he had not let it go before. He admitted to himself that people genuinely cared for him. Phil acknowledged that care with expressions of gratitude that had a depth not seen in the courtesies offered over the years when we gave him rides home or took him shopping. Phil's expressions of gratitude were never maudlin. They were heartfelt and were marked by a dignity and self-possession that became someone one of the brothers from Dujarie House described yesterday as "a gentleman twenty-four hours a day."

Last Thursday morning, Mary Lou Solomon and I went to see Phil at the hospital. When we were ready to go, we each gave him a hug. As we left Phil's room, he gave *us* a grin. It was not a cloying little smile. It was the kind of great big, open-mouthed, toothy grin that lights up a face and makes you feel like a million dollars.

That was the last time I saw Phil. He was anointed later that day, and he died as Friday gave way to Saturday. There may have been something sad about the solitary path trod by this impenetrable gem of a man. But thanks to those who walked the last mile with him, I think it ended in joy, for the last look I saw on Phil Quinn's face was the look of somebody who couldn't be happier.

Note

1. This eulogy was delivered at Phil Quinn's funeral. It is included here at the urging of Eleonore Stump, who not only is a contributor to this volume but also was a friend of Phil Quinn's. Her essay on personal presence and closeness was motivated by her interest in exploring what close friendship is. She was especially interested in exploring the difficulty of being close to someone like Phil, who was a person of high boundaries.

Contributors

Robert Audi
is professor of philosophy at the University of Notre Dame, where he also holds the Gallo Chair of Business Ethics.

Richard Foley
is professor of philosophy and the Anne and Joel Ehrenkranz Dean of the Faculty of Arts and Science at New York University.

Paul J. Griffiths
holds the Warren Chair of Catholic Thought at Duke University Divinity School.

Eleonore Stump
is the Robert J. Henle Professor of Philosophy at St. Louis University.

Sumner B. Twiss
is Distinguished Professor of Human Rights, Ethics, and Religion at Florida State University, where he holds a joint appointment in the university's Department of Religion and its Center for the Advancement of Human Rights. He is also professor emeritus of Religious Studies at Brown University.

Paul J. Weithman
is professor of philosophy at the University of Notre Dame.

Linda Zagzebski
is George Lynn Cross Research Professor of Philosophy and the Kingfisher College Chair in the Philosophy of Religion and Ethics at the University of Oklahoma.

Index

Abu Ghraib, 192
accurate and comprehensive beliefs, 47, 49–52, 54–55
Adams, Robert, 181
admirable, 5, 29–30, 35–39, 41–42
admiration, 5–6, 9, 30, 36–42
admired persons, 5–6, 8, 30, 36–40, 42
Afghanistan, 176
agreement in reasons, 126–27
    contrasted with agreement on reasons, 126
    regarding beneficence, 132
alternate selves, 39–41
Amnesty International, 176, 191
antecedent defeaters. *See* procedural fairness, the fairness conditional, antecedent defeaters
antislavery campaigns, 180
Apostle's Creed, 110
Aquinas, Thomas, 73, 82n.45, 95, 106, 113n.25, 115n.39
    and Augustine, 95, 98, 115n.39
    on divine conservation of the human soul, 97–100
    on incorruptibility of the human soul, 95–97
    on love, 59, 75, 81n.39
Aristotle, 95
Article 1. *See* Universal Declaration of Human Rights, Article 1
Article 4. *See* Universal Declaration of Human Rights, Article 4
Atonement, the, 3, 15
attentional engagement. *See* joint attention
Audi, Robert, 1, 18–20, 199n.29
Augustine, 84, 98, 106, 112n.14, 113n.21
    on divine presence, 60, 77n.4
    doctrine of sin, 89–92, 95, 99–100
    epigram about the Pelagians, 115n.39
    final state of human beings, 87–89, 92–94
    first death, 87–89, 93, 111n.3
    impossibility of self-annihilation, 94–95

210 Index

on the need for the person of
   God, 72–73
rational soul as image of God,
   89
second death, 88–89, 92–93,
   100, 115n.51
autism, 65–68
autonomy, 123, 134

Bandura, Albert, 192
basic institutions of society, 162, 163,
   169,
   as a cooperative venture, 161,
      171
   participation in, 161–63,
      166–68, 171
   —social conditions of, 163–65.
      See also presumption of
      equal distribution, of
      conditions of
      participation
   profound impact of, 167–71
basic social benefits, 146, 153, 159,
   161, 164–69
basic social institutions. See basic
   institutions of society
basic structure of society, 161. See also
   basic institutions of society
Benedict XII, 101
Benedictus Deus, 101
beneficence, 124–25, 127, 132, 136,
   140

Camus, Albert, 3, 10, 16–18
Catechism of the Catholic Church, 102
Catholic social thought, 173n.17
Catullus, 74
causal contact, direct and unmediated,
   10, 13, 62–63, 69
Chang, P. C., 184
citizenship, 164–70
civil disobedience, 143n.23

closeness, 11, 13–14, 60–62, 70–72,
   74–75
   of God, 76
   mutual, 10, 60, 62, 69–70,
      75–76
coherentists, 48
common morality of humanity, 21,
   180–82, 198n.9
Congregation for the Doctrine of the
   Faith, 103–4
conscience, 183–85
conscientious belief, 6, 27–29, 34,
   39–40
   two aspects of, 29
conscientiousness, 29–30, 33,
   40–41
consequent blockers. See procedural
   fairness, the fairness
   conditional, consequent
   blockers
contractarians, 125
convergence strategy, 124, 140

Daedalus, 203
Dante, 106
Declaration on Torture and Other
   Cruel, Inhuman, or
   Degrading Treatment, 187
democratic egalitarianism, 145–46
deontic egalitarianism, 149
Descartes, René
   necessary connection between
      justified belief and
      knowledge, 43–44
distributive justice, 147
   egalitarian principles of,
      145–47
doctrine of creation, 104
doctrine of sin, 104. See also
   Augustine, doctrine of sin
duties of manner, 124
duties of matter, 124

education, compulsory. *See* neutrality, liberal
El Capitan, 153
Endo, Shusako, 3, 10, 12–15, 205
England, 129
    English monarchy, 142n.14
Enlightenment egalitarianism. *See* epistemic egalitarianism
Enlightenment worry, 4, 29, 41
epistemic admiration. *See* admiration
epistemic egalitarianism, 4, 28, 32, 37–38
    rejected, 37–38, 41
epistemic egoism, 31–34, 38
epistemic egotism, 31–32, 34, 38
epistemic privilege, 28
epistemic rationality. *See* rationality, epistemic
epistemic relativism, 180–81
epistemic universalism, 31, 34, 38
equality, 147, 154, 156, 158, 170
    human. *See* equality, natural
    natural, 20, 145–46, 150, 162, 171
    political, 122, 128, 132–34, 138
    religious accounts of, 146, 170
    requires autonomy and political rights, 123
    symbolized in according one person one vote, 122
    value of, 20, 146, 147, 150, 156, 161–62, 164–68
establishment criteria, 125
exclusivist religion, 6, 9–10

fairness. *See* procedural fairness
Fall, The (Camus), 3, 16–17
fathers of the church, 90, 92, 102. *See also* Augustine
Fifth Lateran Council, 101–2
Foley, Richard, 1–2, 5, 7–10, 30–34, 35, 38–39
foundationalists, 48
Francis of Assisi, 61
freedom. *See* liberty
friendship. *See* love, between friends

Gaudium et spes, 102
Geertz, Clifford, 203
globalization, 176–77
Griffiths, Paul J., 15–17
Guantanamo Bay, 176

Harbury, Jennifer, 195–97
heart-mind, Mencian, 184
Henkin, Louis, 181
higher-order desires, 74–75
Homer, 62–63
Human Rights Watch, 191

icons, 11
ideal theorizing, 162
idealizing assumptions, 170–71
immortality, conditional, 84, 95, 102–4
    Arnobius of Sicca, first Christian defender of, 110n.1
impassibility, divine, 73
intellectual egalitarianism. *See* epistemic egalitarianism
Intellectual Trust in Oneself and Others (Foley), 30
intellectual virtues and vices, 37
internal division. *See* internal integration
internal integration, 11, 13, 14, 63–65, 73–76
International Covenant on Civil and Political Rights, 187
intuitionism, 184, 186, 194. *See also* Rossian principles
    and convergence strategy, 124
    religiously neutral, 128

intuitionists, 125, 134
Iraq, 176

jen. See two-men-mindedness
John Paul II, 115n.49
joint attention, 10, 14, 65–70, 75
   dyadic, 67–69
   in infants, 65–68, 70
   triadic, 66–8
justified belief, 7, 52
   and knowledge, supposed necessary connection between, 43–45
   varying stringency of intellectual standards for, 53–54

Kant, Immanuel, 122–23
Kantians, 125,
knowledge, 7, 43–45, 52, 55
Kretzmann, Norman, 62

Larkin, Philip, 17, 108
"Letter on Certain Questions Concerning Eschatology," 103–4
Levi, Primo, 191
Lewis, C. S., 116nn.60–61
liberal democracy, 121–44
   conceived of as *of, by,* and *for* the people, 123
   conditions of liberty, 134
   individualist, 123
   limitations on liberty, 128, 130–34
   moral grounding for, 18
   —distinguished from normative grounding for, 123
   —intuitionism, does not require general theory to provide, 127–28
   —Kantian ethics has resources of to provide, 123
   —utilitarianians, virtue ethicists, and natural law can frame argument for, 124
   non-liberal democracy, contrasted with, 123
   and political obligation. *See* political obligation
   religious ideals, may be inspired by but not subordinate to, 123
   religious neutrality of. *See* neutrality, liberal
   two constitutive ideals of, 132–35, 138. *See also* liberal democracy, two fundamental commitments of
   two fundamental commitments of, 122–23. *See also* liberal democracy, two constitutive ideals of
   value commitments of, 134
liberal faith, 2, 6, 8, 22
libertarianism, 130–31
liberty, 132–41. *See also* liberal democracy
   conditions of, 133
   duty to preserve, 137
   economic, 138
   equality, conflicts with, 138
   essential constituent of liberal democracy, 122, 132–33
   intuitionism and, 124–25, 128, 132
   liberal democracy promotes, 123, 130, 134
   Libertarian construal of, 130
   of movement, 127
   and religion, 139–40
   religious, 128

required for autonomy, 123
restrictions of, 132–33, 138,
of speech, 127
Lifton, Robert Jay, 192
Little, David, 176, 187, 193
Locke, John
   and epistemic egalitarianism, 4, 7, 28
   and intellectual egalitarianism. *See* Locke, John, and epistemic egalitarianism
   on justified belief and knowledge, 7, 43–44
   religious epistemic egoist, 33–34
love, 10, 12, 59, 62, 70, 75
   between friends, 10, 59–60, 75
   consisting in two desires, 59, 75

MacDonald, Scott, 77n.4
Magisterium, 100–104
Man Who Mistook His Wife for a Hat, The (Sacks), 77n.8
Maritain, Jacques, 177, 184–85
Mill, John Stuart, 124, 142n.17
moderate perfectionism, 134
Morsink, Johannes, 183–84
mutual closeness. *See* closeness, mutual

natural law, 124, 186, 193–94, 198n.22
Nazis, 183–84, 186
neutrality, liberal, 18, 121–22, 126, 130–35
   citizen's obligation of, 18, 139–41
   compatible with wide range of substantive value commitments, 135, 139
   and compulsory education, 128–31, 133, 135
   —and religious education, 128–29
   and liberty, conditions for, 134
   policy neutrality, 133
   preventing evils, 130
   religious, 128
   structural neutrality, 133
   toward comprehensive views of the good, 129, 130–35
   and value-neutrality, 130–31
Nussbaum, Martha, 147

omnipresence, 10, 11, 60, 76
open perfectionism, 143n.22
openness of mind. *See* self-revelation
operative agreement. *See* agreement in reasons
overlapping consensus, 179–82, 185, 194

Parfit, Derek, 149
Pascal, Blaise, 47, 50
Paul VI, 102
perfectionism, 134
performance criteria, 125
personal presence, 10, 11, 13, 14, 60, 62–63, 69
   of God, 60, 62, 65, 69, 76,
   minimal, 11, 60–63, 68–69, 75–76
   significant, 10, 11, 13, 14, 61–63, 68–70, 75–76
physical handicaps, 152–53, 160,
physicalism, 86
political obligation, 135–40
   conflicts between political obligations, 137–38
   —special place of liberty and equality in such, 138
   legitimate expectation of obedience, 135

when morally grounded, inalienable and ineliminable, 138
within non-liberal democratic societies, 135
pragmatic reasons for belief, 47, 49–51, 54
presumption of equal distribution, 147, 149–52, 154–57, 161, 162, 166, 169–70
of conditions of participation, 164–65
pride, 16–18
primary goods, 146, 152
principle of religious rationale, 140
principle of secular motivation, 19
principle of secular rationale, 19, 139–40
procedural fairness, 147–50, 154–56, 161–62, 166, 168
arguments from, 147–50, 152–54, 156, 161–62, 164–66, 169
and cooperative ventures, 165
the fairness conditional, 146–56, 164–65
—antecedent defeaters, 151, 154–55, 159, 165, 170
—consequent blockers, 151–56, 160, 165, 170
species of reasonability, 155–56
Prodigal Son, 91, 106
use of *ousia/substantia* in story of, 91
profundity of effect. *See* basic institutions of society, profound impact of
project of sin, the, 15–16, 105

psychic integration. *See* internal integration

Quinn, Philip, 1–4, 12–22, 173n.13, 202–6
on principle of secular motivation, 19
on principle of secular rationale, 19, 144n.30
on Rawls's principles of public reason, 19
on torture, 21, 176, 179–83, 186, 194, 198n.9

rational belief, 48–52
epistemic rationality, anchored by concept of. *See* rationality, epistemic
rationality, 7, 45–46, 48, 52, 54–55
epistemic, 47–55
general template of, 8–9, 45–46, 48, 52, 54–55
Rawls, John, 19–20, 129, 131, 152, 154, 160–61, 171, 172n.10, 173n.14, 181
account of rationality, 131
comprehensive doctrines of the good, 129
primary goods, 131
on public reason, 20–21
reasonableness, 46, 52, 55
standards of, 52
Redemptio missio (John Paul II), 115n.49
reliabilists, 48
Religion and the Obligations of Citizenship (Weithman), 173n.17

religious epistemic egoism, egotism, and universalism, 33-34. *See also* epistemic egoism; epistemic egotism; epistemic universalism
religious pluralism, 2
responsible believing, 52, 55
   beliefs, 54
   believers, 53, 55
Ross, W. D., 124, 132, 137, 181
Rossian principles, 124, 126
   common to all the best ethical theories, 137, 140
   possible Kantian justification for, 127
   reasonableness of, 137

Sacks, Oliver, 77n.8
Scanlon, T. M., 20, 148-50, 161-62, 172n.8, 174n.23
Schlesinger Report, 192, 195
second-order desires. *See* higher-order desires
second-person experience, 10, 14, 63, 68-69, 75
Second Vatican Council, 102
secular faith, 17
self-revelation, 71
self-trust, 5-6, 10, 28, 30-34
   conflicts within, 40-41
   in emotions, 34-38, 40-41
   extending to others, 35-36
   extending to traditions and historical institutions, 36, 39, 41
Sen, Amartya, 147
shared attention. *See* joint attention
Shklar, Judith, 17-18
Shue, Henry, 191, 195-97, 200n.35

significant personal presence. *See* personal presence, significant
Silence (Endo), 3, 12-15, 205,
social construction of beliefs, 32, 39, 41
Sollemnis professio fidei (Paul VI), 102
Sontag, Susan, 203
Stump, Eleonore, 10-15
sympathetic contact between peoples, 29-30

terrorism, 122, 137-38, 143n.25
Third Committee, 177, 178, 183-87, 193
Thomson, Judith Jarvis, 192-93
ticking bomb scenario, 22, 180, 195, 197
traditions and historical traditions. *See* self-trust
Twiss, Sumner B., 21-22
two-men-mindedness, 184. *See also* conscience

UN Commission on Human Rights, 188
UN Human Rights Committee, 188
UNESCO, 177, 184
union, 11, 13-15, 59-60, 62, 70, 73, 75
   desire for, 10, 14, 59, 62, 70, 75
United Nations, 177
United States, 162-63, 165-66, 176
Universal Declaration of Human Rights, 22, 177, 183, 184, 186-88, 197n.5. *See also* Third Committee; United Nations
   Article 1, 183-85
   Article 4, 183, 185-87

universalism, 105
utilitarianism, 124
utilitarians, 123, 125

virtue ethicists, 124
virtue ethics, 125
Von Balthasar, Hans Ur, 115n.49

Waldron, Jeremy, 146
welfare liberalism, 131
well-ordered society, 152, 154, 160, 172n.10

wholeheartedness. *See* internal integration

Yearley, Lee, 40
Yosemite National Park, 153, 160

Zagzebski, Linda, 4–10
Zeno's paradox of motion, 94
Zeus, 62–63
Zimbardo, Philip, 192